THE HIGHLANDERS – *warriors, musicians and bards.*
by
Maol Chaluim M'Domhnall.

I0165276

Dunstaffnage Castle, loch Etive, western highlands.

Defence by attack was the creed of the Highlander in the 12th century.
There was no challenge of "who goes there"
Too late for that, it was "go there if you dare."
Those were the days of live or die by the sword,/
to expect the warriors of an ambitious Lord
to roar down the Glen, targes up, dirks drawn
to burn, take life and cattle, leaving all forlorn.

COVERPIECE: Battle scene in the likeness of "The Charge at Killiecrankie, 1689" by Harrington Mann, the commencement of that Battle between the Jacobite Army and the Government troops.

ISBN: 978-0-9751966-5-6   Second Edition.

Malcolm C. McDonald, Esq.,OAM, FPA.   2017.
121/8 George Street, Caboolture, Qld. 4510.
Email: malmcdon@westnet.com.au

PROLOUGE.

THE HIGHLANDS of old evoke scenes of purple heather painted hills, a magnificent stag of twelve pointed antlers proudly claiming his place on a background of snow covered mountains with ice sheeted peaks – a place of solitude and granduer the home of the Highlander.

One imagines the skirl of the Pipes along the glen and feel the mystic past of incredable deeds, magical Druids, poetry and music.
The Highlands covered a wide region of Scotland from the Islands of the inner Hebrides to include Knoydart, Moidart, Ardgour, Kilmallie, Ardnamurchan and lands bordering the Great Glen up to Inverness and west to the Atlantic Ocean ruled by Clan Chiefs ever ready to send out the 'fiery cross' to rally their Highlanders to right a wrong.

This narrative is supported with historical references, photos and the Bards telling on these 'happenings'

The author's Crest includes a traditional symbol of his clan the sacred salmon of their folklore which relates to Somerled and even further back to the legendry Fionn mac Cumhaill in Killen.

We include an extract from the appropriate poem, "Song of Summer" by Alexander MacDonald.

"The swift slender salmon in the water is lively, leaping up-side down.
Brisk in the scaly white bellied shoals, finny, red-spotted, big tailed, silvery lights clothing it, with small freckles, glittering in colours; and with its crooked jaws all ready, it catches flies by stealth."

This edition is the sequel to "LOCHABER-land of history and laureate."

ACKNOWLEDGEMENTS:
Tearlach MacFarlane of Glenfinnan.
Fiona MacLean of Ardgour.
D.C. McWhannell, B.Sc. Hons.(1st.Class), Ph.D., C.Eng., F.I. Mech.E.
J. P. Maclean, PH. D., LMGSG. FSA.Scot.
K.N. Macdonald, 1900 –Oban Times.
The respected Historians who published in 1885 and 1900 on whose work contemporary research has so revised.
Prince of Wale's Own Regiment Yorkshire Museum, Curator.

INTRODUCTION.

The record of the history of the people of Scotland and the
Highlanders in particular has suffered because of their rural isolation
from the mainstream society.

This following of traditional values and cutural heritage enhanced their
lifestyle above others as told through the writings of outsiders:

James Boswell, the noted English Observer on writing of his tour
through the Highlands mid 1700 described how the people joined " the
pleasures of history and poetry to those of music, and the love of
classical learning to both ~~~ the harp, violin and bagpipe being the
musical instruments of the Scottish people ~~~ and all, even the
lowest in station, were sent to school in their youth."

In 1723 a Gentleman from the Border described a Chief and his
clansmen at a major cattle market:-

"The Highland Gentlemen were mightily civil, dressed in their
slashed short waistcoats, a Trousing [which is breeches and stockings
of one piece of striped stuff] with a plaid for a cloak held by a jewelled
broach and a blue bonnet.
They had a Ponyard, Knife and Fork in one sheath, hanging at one side
of their belt, their pistol at the other, and their snuff mill before, with a
great broad sword at their side.
Their attendants were very numerous."
It was a common practice to wear tartan trews if riding a horse.

The English strategy to divide the the folk of Scotland was a campaign
to denigrate the Gaelic language and the clan lifestyle as being
uneducated and barbaric. In reality poetry, folklore,the music of harp,
pipe and violin were a part of every Chief's household and of the
Ceilidh in every village.

Even so peace and tranquility could change to war and violence at the
whim of the ruling Lord or the covetous English Crown.
In the times from the 12th century this was common to all nations,
sudden death from disease, starvation or by the rope or sword was the
way of the life for all, be it cotter or aristocrat.

This narrative takes the reader on a journey through these hectic but
enlightening early centuries of Scotland.

DEDICATION.

This book is dedicated to my father Angus Alexander McDonald respectfully remembered as "a good man."
To our wide family with thanks to our ancestors, the folk of the Highlands who forged the traditions of the strong, ingenious scot, capable of heroic feats of arms and of withstanding severe winters and adverse conditions, but of a charitable and just nature, with a joyous and musical culture, who have influenced world cultural, medical, legal, financial and industrial affairs over the centuries.

In this we recognise the early historians and later scholarly researchers, who objectively recorded and correlated the history of our Highland Clans, maintaining the integrity of our birthright, and giving opportunity for us to study and learn of our heritage.

To ignore the past is to endanger the future.

Philosopher and novelist George Santayana said:-
"Those who cannot remember the past are condemned to repeat it."

Scotland in the 10th century was called ALBA.

CONTENTS:

ILLUSTRATIONS.

THE 10TH CENTURY - VIKINGS IN LOCHABER.

Alba or Albion was the name of northern Britain, there is no mention of another name save for 'Pictland' before AD 997[1]   ref:HASSH

In AD 900 the Highlands of Scotland were heavily forested with native Scots pine, a straight stemmed tree growing to 40 metres, this with areas of moorland of heather and gorse, fed by numerous streams and lochs, supported a great diversity of fauna.

The native fauna was cut off from Europe with the rising of seas during the end of the ice age which thereby isolated the Isles from certain animal species.   .

The highland forests and moorlands of Alba supported a large variety of animals, such as, wolf, brown bear, boar, badger and beaver, as well as Scotland's wildcat, red squirrel, pine martin, mountain goat, red deer, elk, with feral sheep, horse and cattle.

There were orsprey, ptarmigan, pheasant, capercaillie, puffins and guillemonts to name some birds, with seals, salmon, sardines and many fishes in the seas.

Alba was rich in these natural resources and in those early periods with a low and scattered population, all was looked upon as 'game' and hunted to sustain the populace.

For the common folk some 'game' was part of the Lairds reserve and was unlawful to trap or kill but poaching was an art and tradition – but could be costly if appredended by Gamekeepers.

Traditional 'wild' foods of the Highland people:
Fish such as salmon and sardines from lochs and esturies.
Fowl of pheasant, duck, swan, heron, pidgeon, any and all in season.
Fauna of hare, rabbit, squirril, goat, deer, horse.
Domestic: poultry, sheep, cattle, goat,

1 Ref.Historical Account of Settlements of Scottish Highlanders in America"
J.P.MacLean, PH.D, LM GSG - 1900

NAMES/IDENTITY - As with the 'Picts' of Alba, a group or tribe of people are given 'a name' by others as an identification.

Saxons were called: Sassenach in Scotland, Saesneg in Wales and Sowsnek in Cornwell. These primary invaders finally settled as farmers and traders.

Toward the end of the 9th century AD new, vicious raids from Scandinavia took place. This time the raiders are called: Danes by the Britains, Normans by the French, Ascomanni (ash men after the wood of the galleys) by the Germans and in eastern Europe, Rus, Rootsi, or Ruotsi meaning rowers. The use of the name Viking was their own, as they would go 'a Viking' ie, raiding. ref: JC.p.7: "The Vikings."

They followed their own gods and superstitutions. Thor and Odin were the Gods of war. In battle Odin was the Charging Rider, or the Spear Lord, the Author of Victory and patron of the front line fighter, the shield wall soldier, the esteemed warrior who wore the wolf pelt as a shirt and the head as a fearsome crest.

These warriors fought with such fury that others coined the name of 'Berserkir' to describe a person who fought with instinctive ferocity surpassing their training to superior proficiency in the arts of war.

They courted death in battle to be recalled in song as the ultimate accolade of a disciple of Odin or Thor and to go to Valhalla to the afterlife of fighting, feasting and fornicating.[2]

The sea was their environment , their movement was swift and their arrival dire.

We select one of these warriors whose early involvement in raids and minor invasions gained him wealth and power and whose family members were later to have an influence on the future of Lochaber. One being Olave or Anlaf Cuaran, "Anlaf of the Hebrides" or Olaf Sihtricson son of Sitriuc.

Our account commences in 839 with the raids by Dane Vikings on Irish ports and their wasting of Dublin and raiding into Alba in 839.

Relaliation came from Alba in 880 when Giric, son of Dungaile a strong fighter, took the mantle of Gregory the Great in the Pict succession.

---

2 "The Vikings" by Jonathan Clements, p.26

In the Registry of St.Andrews of 1251 he is said to have conquered Ireland and the greater part of Britain when he took Northumbria, under occupation by the Danes during the reign of Guthred the Dane.[3]

The incursions by the Danes against Ireland continued to increase in 917 and reached a climax when they attacked with two fleets.

One led by Sitriuc son of Ivar and the other led by his brother Ragnall/Regnwald against Niall Gludub and his Irish host. The ferocious attack by the Danes with war hammers and the short axe resounded in sure victory winning possession of Dublin and surrounds.

ref: Annals of Ulster.

Regnwald regrouped his warriors, sharpened their axes and set sail to invade Northumbria and conquer York.

From this warrior line of Ivar came Somerled, and from Somerled the mighty Clan Donald which in later years gave support and protection to the clans of the western Highlands against a heirarchy which threatened their culture and traditions.

For all their intertribal wars the Irish were no match for the ferocity and experience of the Danes and Sitriuc consolidated his position in Ireland by defeating Niall Glundub on every confrontation in 917.

The major victory for Sitriuc occurred in 919 when he repulsed an attack on Dublin led by the King of the O'Neill which resulted in the death of Niall and a number of Irish sub kings thereby securing his total control over those territories. Sitriuc placed his kinsman Godfred/Godfrey as the ruling king of Dublin.

The 'Pictish Chronicle' places the battle of 918AD at Tinemore or Tynemoor, near the mouth of the river Tyne in East Lothian.
"On this occasion Eldred, the ruler of Northumbria, was assisted by Constantine, (a Pict according to contemporary scholars), while Regnwald, King of Dublin Waterford and York, was supported by his brother Gothbrith (Godfred), the two Earls Ottir and Gracaban, and several young Lords.

The allied Scots and Northumbrians initiated the action by a fierce co-ordinated attack against three battalions of the Danes.

---

3 History of the Highlands & Gaelic Scotland. p.149 (HH&GS)

The massed charge over a wide front was powerful and vicious. The Danes faced the attack with a 'shield wall' but the charge by the Scots weilding two-handed swords and war axe hacked and slaughtered the Danes. Among the slain were the two Earls.

The Battle was not yet won for as the exalting allied forces were eagerly gathering the spoils of war, they were attacked in a rearguard action by a fourth battalion of Danes which Regnwald[4] had placed in ambush.
He led these Danes forward to kill many of the Scots and Northumbrian army but no important personage fell and night put an end to the strife, the battle drawn.

"Alban had proved their strength, for from this time they had welcome respite from Danish attacks for upwards of a century."

After the battle Regnwald took his army south and took possession of Northumbria.

Sitriuc was ambitious to expand his power and sailed with his fleet up the Mersey River which divided the kingdom of Mercia and the Viking Kingdom of York, held by Regnwald.
He invaded and took Mercia.

We find reference to this action by Sitriuc/Sihtric in the twelfth century chronicle of Symeon of Durham: "in AD 920 King Sihtric of Northumbria infregit (invaded) Davennport.
This suggests that Davenport had a strategic importance in the defence of Mercia from raiders across the Cheshire plain, deriving from its situation on the steep bank of the narrow valley through which the River Dane runs"[5]

Regnwald died in 921 AD. Sitriuc succeeded him in Northumbria, and according to the Egills Saga, they came from the race of Ragnar Lodbroc.

---

4 Alex Woolf, in his research of 'The Annals of Ulster' for 918 - here we come to a long entry describing the doings of the Gaill, in translation being:
"The Gaill of Loch dá Cháech, i.e. Ragnall, king of the Black Gaill and the two jarls, Oitir and Gragabai, forsook Ireland and proceeded against the men of Alba. The men of Alba, moreover, moved against them and they met on the bank of the Tyne in Northumbria. The heathens formed themselves into four battalions: a battalion with Gothfrith grandson of Ímar …"

5 Symeon of Durham, Opera Omnia ii,p.93&123

In 925 Sitriuc married the sister of King Aethelstan of England but died a year later and Aethelstan regained control of Northumbria.

The Danes invade Ireland from 839AD.
They take control of Dublin in 917AD and use this
as their base to invade Mann, Alba and Britain.

Sitriuc's brother Guthferth lead a warparty of Danes from Dublin in an attempt to wrest the kingdom from Aethelstan but was repulsed with losses.

Anlaf Cuaran, the eldest son of Sitriuc, sailed for Alba, where he established himself in favour to gain the daughter of King Constantine in marriage.

Fearing the probability of an invasion of Northumbria as the result of this alliance, Aethelstan in 933 anticipated events by invading Alban by sea and land, and harried the countryside.

The Pict Chronicles state that in 937AD a very large force mustered from Alba for an invasion to wrest Northumbria from the Wessex King.
Danes and Scots were together once more but against Danish relatives.

In this attempt, 'Anlaf of the Hebrides,' (the eldest son of Sitriuc) assisted by the Danes of Dublin, the Scots under Constantine (his father-in-law) and the Britons of Strathclyde who, with a body of Danes moved overland.
Later, Constantine in company with Anlaf and a large army, embarked by sea to enter the Humber.

Their tactics were no match for the army of Aethelstan with the descendants of Guthrum's Danes.
The Pictish Chronicle has the account of the battle at Brunnanburh or Dinbrunde resulting in the Army from Alban being defeated.
Geleachan King of the Isles and Cellach a Moarmor of Scotland were killed, leaving Constantine with his defeated men, to escape by sea.[6]

In 949, Olaf Sihtricson appears to have been accepted as King in York.

SUMMARY: Sitriuc married the sister of Aethelstan and Olave or Anlaf, his eldest son married the daughter of Constantine, with a further family connection to the Hebrides, ie, King of the Many Isles and later Godfrey mac Aralt, who bears the title of King of Innes Gall.

CONCLUSION: the DNA of the family of Sitriuc, Olave or Anlaf Cuaran his son, then Godfrey and Marcus his grandsons, of the 900s AD, would be the same. Therefore descendants of people of Davenport from Mercia with descendants of people from Kilmallie and of Sweden in the 21st Century with the same DNA signature with mutations of the 30 odd generations, would originate from these Vikings.

---

6 History of the Highlands & Gaelic Scotland p. 154-155 – HH&GS

VIKING BURIAL IN LOCHABER:

A Norseman or Viking of note would be buried with all honours as was due to a Warrior – the site would be excavated to allow his, or a replica galley to be placed into this pit.

The body of the Warrior in full battle dress would be laid on the floor boards with his shield, spear, axe and sword placed beside him as well as valuable items according to his status and wealth.
Stones would be placed in and over the galley and covered with earth.

Such a funeral site was excavated in Ardnamurchan as part of the Ardnamurchan Transition Project funded by the McDonald Institute for Archaeological Research and other respected societies and Universities
The Ardnamurchan Viking was found buried with an axe, a sword with a decorated hilt, a spear, a shield boss and a bronze ring pin.

About 200 rivets - the remains of the boat he was laid in - were also found.
Other finds in the 5m-long (16ft) grave in Ardnamurchan included a knife, what could be the tip of a bronze drinking horn, a whetstone from Norway, a ring pin from Ireland and Viking pottery.

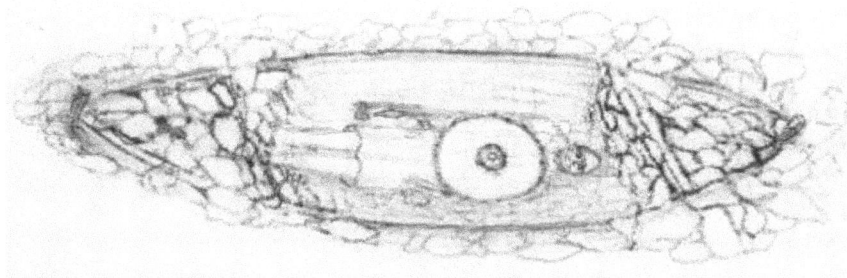

An artist's impression shows how the Viking would have been placed in the burial boat.

Viking specialist Dr Colleen Batey, from the University of Glasgow, has said the boat was likely to be from the 10th Century AD.

ARDGOUR PREHISTORY.

The early Lochaber district known as Ardgour was bounded to the north by Loch Eil, to the west by Loch Shiel and to the east by Loch Linnhe which protected it from incomers in general, as these blocked any arterial road through the region and to the interior, traditional access was by perimeter tracks fed from boats trading the locks.

Little is known of the region save for a few archaeological sites of prehistoric occupation[7] being a cairn at Duisky, a cist at Clovullin, a cairn at Corran and the fort at Loch nan Gobhar.

The isolation of the early settlers was interrupted when the Norse Vikings raided the Western Highlands and established strongholds where galleys could be repaired and crews rested.
Place names indicate some Norse occupation, such as 'Trislaig' and especially 'Inverscaddle' which could be 'Scat-Dail' or 'Rent Dale.'
'Eilean nan Gall' or 'Island of the Strangers' demonstrates that the Norse sailed the waterways and controlled the region, collecting 'rents or taxes' probably of produce, for some period of time.
Norse place names from Moidart are:-
(1) Moidart = Muydeort = mud flat. (2) Arisaig = Ari's Bay, (3) Acharacle = Ath Tharracail = Torquil's Ford, (4) Knoydart = Knut = Canute.

Over the centuries, from warring with the Romans and then the Danes and the Saxon lowland incursions, the people of Alba earned a reputation of being courageous, resilient and high spirited. This was forged on facing hardship from fierce weather, rough terrain and constant vigulance against sudden raid from feuding Clan or warring foreigner.

They were quick to stand against an injustice, steadfast in friendship, loyal to Chief and clan, upholders of the rights of all which they would defend to the last man.

The safety of the Clan and the protection of their property and boundaries were an ever constant concern, and to this end a specific emergency alarm system had been developed wherein great numbers of the clan could be alerted to gather quickly at a designated position – this by way of the 'Fiery Cross.'

---

7 Jennifer G. Robertson MA PhD Archaeological survey.

FINLAGGAN- THE HEADHOUSE OF CLAN DONALD.

Pagan religions and Cults followed after each other, the one taking the site of the previous religious group because the local people had already accepted that area as 'holy' so whosoever held rituals on this sacred site was accepted as a continuation of the previous Mediceneman/ herbalist/ Holyman who was looked upon as having the power of spells and curses.

Later Druid priests with the knowledge of the stars, prophesy, healing, literature, law and the netherworld followed and exercised their wisdom for centuries.

DRUIDS from Angelsey escaped the Romans to 'I' (Iona) and Islay.
Archaeologists have established that Druids had worshipped in Anglesey around 139BC from artifacts recovered from pools and rivers where they had been cast as ritual offerings.
Two centuries later in 61AD, after the Romans had conquered southern Britain, the Legate detailed a Roman Legion to make a concentrated attack on the Isle of Anglesey with the duty to exterminate the Druid residents and destroy their dwellings – some escaped by sea. ref: CJD. 'The Celts' by John Davies

A band of Druids fleeing the Romans sailed up the coast to reach Islay and then an island off the SW point of Mull where they sheltered.
They settled on this Isle and founded a library there, later named Iona.
Its earlier name 'Inis nar Druinach'[the Place of the Druids].
It's later name of 'I' was changed by Bede to 'Hy.'

It was later given the Latin name of Iova or Iona by Culdee Monks from Erie. ref:HSH&HR. v1, p37.

Thus too was Islay inhabited by prehistoric peoples who may have stayed awhile or been absorbed into stronger incomers, but it is certain from archaeological discoveries of artifacts dated from the stone to the iron age that Islay always had a resident population.

Any isle with a central loch as well as an isle in that loch, spoke of a sacred and holy place. This is confirmed by the standing stones and monuments symbolising early pagan rituals and religious ceremony.

Islay would have surly been a place of sanctury for Druids who fled up the coast from the Isle of Anglesey to settle and worship for a time as there is evidence of occupation of a normal society ranging from peasants to shepherds and farmers and also religious establishments.

Once more the religious ascetics searching for rightous denial of worldly goods and pursuits found the serenity of Islay and especially the seclusion of Eilean Morand Eilean na Comhairle as a sacred area.

This met the monks' every need and the establishment of a Culdee abbey there was given his name of Findlugan with the Loch later named Findlaggan.

NOTE: Findlugan or Fionn Lugainb is mentioned as a comtemporary of Columba and that his missionary work was in Scotland and the Isles.
It is accepted that 'the sacred Isle' was named after him.

The easily protected Isle with its safe harbours and the seclusion of Finlaggan with the infastructure of an independent settlement made it strategically ideal for the Head House of the Ruler of the territories of Gall-Gaehill.
The wide reputation of its ancient heritage of being a sacred place of Druid ceremony imposed a political mystique which enhanced its status.

Whether the ceremonies for the inauguration of Celtic kings and chiefs was ever enacted there previously, with the coming of Somerled came the dawning of the greatness of the Lords of the Isles and the establishment of a dynasty of just rule which would include Finlaggan.

Under the rule of Mhic Dhomnuill, the expansion of culture and the arts, support of the church and a court rivalling those of Europe followed.
By the 13th century the settlement was well set out with paved roads, numerous thached outbuildings for clanfolk, a chapel and a great Hall for meetings and celebrations with guest quarters for dignitries and guests.

Eilean na Comhairle was reached by a bridge to the mortared stone walled Council hall.

The Chiefs of Clans Donald cross the bridge at Finlaggan in 2001.

As the seat of the Lord of the Isles, Finlaggan sustained a population of some hundreds of warriors to maintain and man its fleet of galleys. Clan Donald dominated the seas with this fleet augmented by others from Clan Donald castles along the coast.

The ruins of the halls and dwellings of the original settlement.

2014 - The Toiseach of Finlaggan with Banner-bearer Lachlan MacDonald and Clansman Neil Macdonald Esq pays his respects with an obeisance to the spiritual home of the great Clan Donald.

THE 11th CENTURY: THE KING INTRODUCES FEUDALISM
– HE BANS GAELIC IN THE ROYAL COURT.

In 1058 Malcolm III, Malcolm Cann Mor, 'great Chief,' was king, but caused much rivalry between clans and antagonism between these clans and the crown. He married Margaret, sister of Edgar the Atheling, and introduced feudalism into Scotland and the English language into Court.
Margaret worked tirelessly to replace the ancient Celtic church with the establishment of the Roman Catholic religion.

Feudalism took the right of ownership of land from the Chief and clan and placed it under the will of the King to do with as he wished, thus gaining control over the landowners and increasing his revenues.

The continuance by successive kings to maintain feudalism and the English language divided the kingdom into the Celtic Highland and the Saxon Lowland, a rift which caused war and bloodshed for the next six centuries.

A third factor was the Vikings, the Scandinavian and Norse invaders who continued raiding at will, taking hostages, goods and produce from the inhabitants of the Western Isles and mainland. They are on record as invading Ireland in the early 800s AD and later being defeated by the Norse King of Dublin, which demonatrates the ruling influence of the Norse and Danes radiating out of Ireland and the Isle of Mann.

After a few generations there developed a group called the 'Gall-Gaedil' whose area of habitation was the Inner Hebridean area which encompassed Lochaber, Ardnamurchan, Argyll and Kintyre, with the Isles of Mull, Islay and Arran.

The western highlands and Isles of Alba have extensive archaeological evidence of ancient roundhouses, brochs, forts and duns, such as Dunadd which demonstrate settlement from centuries BC.

One definite example of settlement on the peninsula of Ardnamurchan is from the excavation of a Norse galley with the funereal accruements' of a Viking warrior dated 1100 AD.
Vikings roving the hebrides regularly raided the inhabitants of Lochaber, who had no leader to rally a force to oppose these incursions.

Tradition has it that a group of gaels living in the area led by McInnes, approached Somerled son of Gillebride, to lead them against these Norse invaders.

They found Somerled fishing, and put their proposal to him. He replied, "if I catch the salmon in this pool, I will be your Chief and lead you into battle, but if I do not catch the salmon then I will remain in Morven."
Somerled caught the salmon and the young hunter became a mighty warrior with an innate appreciation of the tactical situation of the battle and the ability to develop the strategy to win, even against a higher-numbered enemy force.

In 1103 Somerled Mac Gillebride, Ard Ri of Argyle, married Raghildis daughter of the Dane Olaf 'Morsel' King of Mann and The Isles, and he looked to expand his territory.
Islay which was well situated within this area with settlement over the centuries, an ideal location to be used for the Headhouse of an emerging ruler, and Somerled was that person.

In a number of battles from 1125 to 1135, Somerled secured the mainland by defeating the Norse invaders who held sway with a manned fleet of Dragon Longships driving them back to their base on the Isle of Mull. These galleys had a removable prow, which was changed to suit the voyage, whether it be in peace or in war, thus a 'Dragon headed prow' meant war.

Somerled continued with his plan to drive the Norseman from the land of the Scots by increasing his fleet of birlinn [galleys].
These ships were of an inventive design, they were the first clinker structured birlinns with fixed thwarts for added strength, and with the added improvement of a hinged stern rudder instead of the Norse steering oar. Shorter than the Norse Long ship, they were called Naibheag, pronounced Nyvaig, meaning 'little ship.'

Their style gave Somerled's galleys greater manoeuvrability for close combat in sea warfare, giving them a tighter turning circle. Some had a masthead basket for an archer to fire on enemy ships.
They were ideal for negotiating the island and inland waterways. With their mast lowered the galleys could be transported over land, from sea water loch to fresh water loch, on rollers.

They were also suited for long voyages, points along the west coast of

Alba and to the Isle of Mann were in easy reach in a galley, greater trading capacity, thus more wealth and power.

The main fleet was berthed in the safe harbour of Lagavulin Bay, protected by the fort of Caisteal Claidh/ Claig on the Fraoch Eilean, [Heather Isle], from whence comes the War cry of Clan Donald, "Froach Eilean."
The later Dunyvaig castle has evidence that it was built on an older fort. Might that be the original Dun Claidh?

"Dunyvaig Castle ruins, geograph.org.uk-115146" by Chris Heaton.

The original Fort and later Castle were essential to the defence of the Fleet of Somerled and later to that of The Lord of the Isles.
There was a sea gate for a galley to access the Castle.

One can imagine Somerled standing on the steering platform of his Galley when the lookout up the mast called, **"an seo`l, an seo`l, "** a sail! a sail!.
This followed by Somerled's direction and his shouted command of **"IONNSAIGH,"** ATTACK!

Then the acceleration of the fleet, water foaming white, as the oars bit deeper and the stroke increased until the Viking boats were in plain sight and the clan war cry roared from some hundreds of throats, "FROACH EILEAN ! FROACH EILEAN !"

Viking blood would chill on hearing that war-cry as Somerleds Naibheags suddenly appeared around a headland at racing speed, straight at them - then to expertly tack and turn to crash down one side of the Long-ships smashing viking oars and hurling the rowers every whichway. Bowman shooting from the wicker baskets at the masthead, the swish of grappling hooks in the air as they are thrown and the ropes made fast - then the short battle axes and two-handed swords flashing in the sunlight as the highlanders leap upon the Norsemen, to strike and slash and cut their way to victory.

The machinations to maintain power in the one family was replicated on the eastern seaboard when Earl Henry the heir to Scotland's throne died in Northumbria but the line from King David was assured with three grandsons inwaiting.

The eleven year old Malcolm being the eldest was immediately dispatched on a tour of Scotland under the tuterage of the Mormaer of Fife and a protective army to impress the populace. Mormaer Donnchad was in place to be Regent for Malcolm should King David die.

This was to be the situation for on the death of David in 1153 Malcolm was immediately inaugurated at Scone on 27th May 1153 as the king of Scotland. He was twelve years of age and had many rival contenders for the throne.

In June 1153 Olaf I, known as Olaf the Red, King of Mann and the Isles was assassinated, which provided the opportunity for his son Godfred to realise his ambition to rule and expand his new thiefdom.

The Gaels of The Isles soon found they had replaced one hard leader by an even more despotic one in Godfred II. His overbearing manner and covetous acts generated increasing anger among the local Kings and Chiefs of the Isles to the extent that they decided to gather a force to oppose him.

It is recorded that Thornfinn Ottarsson led a deputation of men to meet with Somerled, requesting him to lead them in a coup to replace Godfred II with Dugall Ottarsson.

Somerleds first course of action was to recruit and train a solid group of warriors to ambush the crews of lone Norse ships, overpower them and capture the Norse galley to gradually build up his fleet. This was augmented by setting boatbuilders to construct more of his "Little ships."

After gaining Somerleds agreement to lead the 'reformers,' Thornfinn and Dugall Ottarsson sailed through the Isles recruiting supporters to swear allegiance to their cause to depose the King – their plotting soon became known to Godfred II, who gathered his fleet of Galleys and sailed down the Inner Isles to attack and destroy.

The history of the western Highlands is of course as old as Alba, but in relation to events of the 12th century, the 'Battle of Epiphany' between the King of Mann and the Isles against Somerled Ard Ri of Argyle, might well be titled "the coming of Age of Lochaber."
It was this battle in January of 1156 that the future of Lochaber was decided.

Godfred gained no surprise on Somerled, for Signal fires flared skyward from headland to headland, giving Somerled prearranged warning, and when the fire flared on Islay, the warcry "Froach Eilean" rent the air, and every ablebodied islesman grasped sword or axe and targe and ran.

On reaching the beach, this organised chaos calmed to an ordered boarding of their respective galley.
The 80 strong fleet put to sea from Lagavulin Bay with Somerled on the steering platform of the leading galley urging the fleet forward to meet Godfred and his Dragon Longships.

The oarsmans back and shoulder muscles bulged and sweat dripped from wet faces as they strained to keep time with the increasing drum beat. This drove them on to gain the superior battle position north of Rubh` a` Mhaoil between Colonsay and Jura, on the night of January 5th or the 12th .

The sea boiled from thrashing oars and creaming bow waves. Sails were furled as the opposing ships sought to join battle with an individual opponent.

But Somerled raced for the the centre of Godfred's fleet, urging his crew to greater effort.

It seemed that he would self destruct, but at the precise moment he ordered "AN RA`MH" (loft oars), and his strengthened Naibheag crashed through, sheering the oars of the enemies ships, tearing the shafts from their oarsmans grasp and smashing them into faces and chests, tearing flesh and fracturing bones.

As fast as this transpired, his craft was through and "AN T-SREATH"(ROW) was ordered as Somerled used the manoeuvrability of the Naibheag to smartly tack and turn back to run down the other side of the stricken galley. Grappling hooks clawed the gunwals together - the Islesmen boarded her in a bloody frenzy of flashing axe and thudding mace, till the ship was theirs.

The sea battle raged for two days. Damaged and stricken galleys with slaughtered crews drifted toward Jura whilst depleted crews of warriors fought on, but this heavy toll to both sides could not be sustained.

The greater number of Somerled's fleet were the newly constructed Naibheag giving the islesmen greater manouverability over the fleet of Godfred II.
Sails and oars were used for the greater advantage by both Leaders, but it seems neither force could overcome the other. Possibly the size of Godfred's fleet against Somerled's manouverable Naibheags balanced out.

A point was reached wherein the oarsmen of both sides were near exhaustion.

A truce was declared allowing negotiations to proceed.

After discussions and agreement, Godfred II ceded the isles of Mull, Jura and Islay to Somerled, (thus adding to Moidart, Ardnamurchan and Argyle), with agreement that Godred II ruled over the Outer Hebrides and Skye.

It was the period when the Kings of the region were introducing major policy changes which would have a lasting effect on their subjects.
The marriage of King Malcolm III to Margaret, sister of Edgar the Atheling, heralded the commencement of the concerted effort to transform Celtic Scotland to an Anglo / Norman country.

Queen Margaret worked tirelessly to convert the populace to Roman Catholism and to remove the speaking of Gaelic from the Court. She assisted her cause by granting land and titles to the Norman followers of the Court.

David I, son of King MalcolmIII continued with these changes by i introducing the Feudal system into Scotland thereby creating divisions within the populace.

On the death of King David in 1153, his grandson became MalcolmIV of Scotland and supported Henry II in France causing unrest among Scottish nobles who raised an army against him to besiege Perth Castle.

With the aid of the Church he negotiated for peace. Evenso Malcolm should have seen that his subjects opposed any dealing with Henry II of England.

He certainly was not " a people's King" as he was known as "Malcolm the Maiden" due to his vow of chastity and he supported 'things English.'
He caused further unrest when he again stood for Henry at the siege of Toulouse in 1159.
On his return to Scotland Malcolm IV defended a major rebellion in Moray, and he was also aware of the separate political issue of the gathering strength of Somerled, King of the Isles with his stronghold in Argyll.
Malcolm IV recognised Somerled's territory by 'right of conquest' on his promise to serve Malcolm.

Somerled regarded himself as a ruler 'in his own right' as "Lord of the Isles," and local King of Argyll.
His strength was such that in 1164 he sailed up the Clyde with an estimated 160 armed Galleys of 15000 men to attack Glasgow and Renfrew.

This was too much for Malcolm, who sent his army to meet Somerled. Before any encounter was joined, Somerled was betrayed and assassinated.

His army dispersed without joining battle with Malcolm's forces.

On the death of Somerled the Lordship of The Isles was inherited by his grandson Donald.

Malcolm IV died the following year on December 9th.

The family of Somerled followed the precausion of the times by supporting religious orders to ensure forgivness of any sins.

It is recorded that 'Saddell Abby of the Cistercian order in Argyll was founded in 1164 by Raghnall mac Somhairle,' the year in which Somerled died.

Ranald had maintained the castle and donated to the building of the Abbey of Saddell for the monks of the Cistercian or Bernardine order.

The Cistercian Order was so named from the district in which their first monastery was built and Bernardines in honour of Bernard, a Burgundian,a who was later elected Abbot of Clairvaux and associated with the Knights Templar and the early Crusades.

The continuous state of war and conflict caused a spiritual devotion on the part of soldiers involved in all hostilities with the practice of being called to prayer for absolution before battle wherein all knelt to receive a blessing from the monk or abbot.

Knights and gentlemen grasped their unsheathed sword as a form of the 'cross' and kissed the hilt.

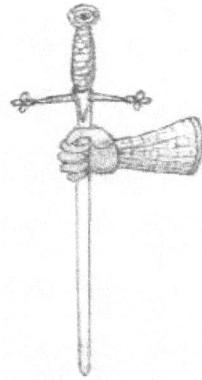

On the death of MalcolmIV in 1165 William the Lion took the throne of Scotland but had a shaky career.

In 1174 he was captured by the English and held to ransom, forced to do homage to the king of England.

In 1189 RichardI annulled this servitude in return for William to agree to the Army of Scotland assisting England in the Crusades.

The oath was sworn on their sword before any Battle commenced

Kings and leaders of various countries had a high respect of the power of the Church in Rome with its constant threat of excommunication to ensure support for its projects and control of followers.

The naval power of the 'Hieland galeyis' should be reiterated, as the ruler relied on his fleet for security and defence.

Their size being defined as a vessel with 16 to 24 oars, and a birlinn[8] as having twelve to sixteen oars.

In 'battle' mode the vessel was manned with 3 men to each oar; some war galleys had 26 oars = 78 oarsmen plus bowmen and commanders.

---

8 'birlinn' or west highland galley, is of the Norse 'byrdingr.

In attack mode the rower's time was by the increasing beat of a drum.

The Piper was part of the 'crew' and on a peaceful voyage he played to keep the rower's time when crossing the Minch, or the rowers sang an Iorram (a rowing song.)

The emblem of the black Galley, or 'Little Ship' was the badge or seal of Islay and their Clan.
This was a continuation of the Royal line of the "Peace Kings of Uppsala" whose use of the 'black galley'originated from the male incarnation of the goddess spirit 'Nerthus.'

Heraldic design tells the history of the family where the black galley denotes their ancestry and shows the sovereignty of the Lords of the Isles over the Western seas.
It flew on a gold background as the banner of Angus Og at Bannockburn.

Even with the variations to some Macdonald arms over the ages this emblem stands out prominently as belonging to the Family of Isla.
Other western clans have the Galley on their armorial bearings, but save for MacDugall, these have borrowed the emblem from the House of Islay.[9]
This through marriage to a daughter, to which in previous ages they were but feudatories and vassals.   ref: TCD p.439

The three sons of Somerled and Ragnhild - Dougall, Ranald and Angus, continued his line.
Dugall was given Argyll and his son Duncan was recorded as Ergadia of Lorn, his son Ewin was King Ewin of Argyll which established the Lords of Lorn.

Ranald or Reginald was King of the South Isles, and had two sons :-
(a) Donald, who carried forward the title Somerled had won, that of " Lord of the Isles," and established the mighty Clan Donald and its branches.
(b) Rauri / Ranald who became Lord of Garmoran and established the

---

[9] The Clan Donald, p 439. The 'galley' on the Campbell arms was gained when they married into the House of Lorne - the name Cambel is only recorded after 1222, and an Archibald (Gillespie) Campbell, of Anglo-Norman lineage, married the daughter & heiress of the Lord of Lochow about 1263. Record of Parliament of Robert Bruce of 1320, has the then head of the family entered as Sir Nigel de Campo Bello.   ref:HSH&HR

great western Lordship of the MacRauris of Garmoran, whose 'head house' was Caisteal Elan Tirrim in Lochaber.

His son Allan Mac Rauri became one of the most powerful Chiefs having his lands of Knoydart, Moydart, Arisaig, Morar and North Kintyre confirmed by Alexander III of Scotland, who added lands of Barra, Uist, Harris, and the lesser islands of Eigg and Rum.

Allan MacRauri made his daughter Christina heiress to his lands even though he had three sons, Roderick, Allan and Lachlan.

Why this was done is still not clear, for in time Roderick succeeded and Christina ceded the lands to him.

Later on Robert the Bruce granted Roderick the MacRauri lands by Charter.

Christina Macrauri married Duncan son of the Earl of Mar and her sister-in-law Isobel married Robert Bruce King of Scotland.

Princess Marjory married Walter Stewart the 6th Steward, whose son John became Robert II of Scotland. Robert II's daughter, Princess Margaret, married John of Isla of Clan Donald, the Lord of the Isles establishing this as of the royal line of Scotland.

Somerled's third son Angus, was made Lord of Bute and Arran, and this line joins with the Stewarts and the future Kings of Scotland and the Stuart Royal line of Scotland and England.

Somerled's daughter married Malcolm MacEth, Earl of Ross.

The Clan Donald line originates from Donald the grandson of Somerled King of Argyll and of the South Isles.

Donald Lord of the Foreigner's Isles, to Angus 'Mor'[10] Lord of Islay, to Alistair Og [the eldest son of Angus Mor], who was present with his father at the meeting at Turnberry in 1286 to favour Bruce the elder against the Maid of Norway.

Alistair Og acted for Angus Mor, Lord of the Isles, in 1291 with the oath of allegiance to Edward 1st.

This later alienated him from Robert the Bruce and he lost the Lordship.

---

[10] 1284 Alexander III invited the 3 nobles of Argyll - Angus Mor; Alex'MacDugall of Lorn; Macruari of Garmoran, to the Convention of Estates to settle the succession to the Throne.
    'The Clan Donald'(TCD) vI p82

The Lordship of the Isles and leadership of Clan Donald was then inherited from Angus 'Mor', by his second son Angus 'Og'.

Angus Og, Lord of the Isles, from his position of power, offered Bruce his friendship as an equal in the earliest days of RobertI claim. Angus Og gave Bruce his protection and Galleys to carry him to Arran, under the command of his brother-in-law Roderick Macrauri. ref:TCD,v.II,p.18

Kintyre was part of the territory of The Lord of the Isles and its importance in the defence of the Island kingdom is demonstrated by the castles of Largie and Saddell and another at the south eastern tip. Caisteal Dunaverty stood on a high rocky headland at the south east corner of Kintyre, a stronghold protected by the sea on three sides and by a drawbridge and fosse on the other.

With clear view of the sea lanes it commanded the approachs to Scotland where the sea between it and Ireland is the narrowest.

Few ships escaped the demand to pay 'toll' to the Macrauris for passage past Dunaverty.

The seal of Angus Og featuring the galley of that line.

The Lordship passed from Angus Og to Eoin 'the Good' , to Donald Lord of the Isles who died in 1423, until we come to his son Alasdair.

Alasdair (Alexander) Lord of the Isles was granted the Earldom of Ross through his mother as the heiress, in 1435 earning the right to add the red eagle of Ross surmounted against the mast of the black galley to the Macdonald arms.

Macdonald grave slabs Kilmory Chapel – note the 'Galley' engraved.
photo M.McDonald 1969

HISTORY OF THE WESTERN HIGHLANDS,
the 12th century AD

Lochaber was part of the territories of the Lordship of Garmoran, then of the Lordship of the Isles and finally Clanranald land with a share to the MacLeans, so was active in the history of the western highlands, rich in national leaders, military strategists, bards, musicians, courageous clansfolk and a cultured proud people.

One of the most powerful dynasties was that of the "Lord of the Isles" which was initiated by the sea power of Somerled in the early 12th century, continued by his grandson Donald, and consolidated by John in the 14th century AD. This was a cultural and colourful period when the Lord of the Isles ruled over half of Scotland.

He kept a European style Court with Heralds and Puisavants; appointed a Council of Finlaggan to advise on the business of The Lordship; formalised Charters in Latin witnessed with their seal.
He gave grants to the church and Iona in especial, supported church parishes and encouraged all forms of the arts and the culture of the Highlands.

Under the authority of the Lord of the Isles, the Chiefs of Clan Donald held a number of caisteal strongholds along the Atlantic coast and inland, whilst his Headhouse was built at Finlaggan on a loch in the

Isle of Islay.

These being, Na Caisteal Dunaverty, Duntulm, Strome, Dunscaith, Dunavaig, Mingarry, Kenblane, Invergarry, Brove, Tioram, Aros, Ardtornish, Dunluce, and Beagram.

Hugh Macdonald, Sennachie of Sleat records the particulars of the Council and some of Macdonald's Officers:

As Ruler of the Isles, Mhic Dhomnuill presided over The Council of Finlaggan, [the independent Parliament of the Isles], at Island Finlaggan, in Isla.

This to the number of 16, viz: four Thanes, four Armins, that is to say Lords or Sub-Thanes, four Bastards, *i.e.* Squires, or men of competent estates, who could not come up with Armins or Thanes, that is freeholders or men who had their lands in factory (in virtue of some office), as MacGee of the Rinds of Isla, MacNicol in Portree in Skye, and MacEachern, MacKay, and MacGillivray in Mull.

MacLean of Ardgour was his treasurer; Munro of Fowlis was his Chamberlain; Cawdor was his armour-bearer; MacLean of Duart, MacNeil of Barra and MacDonald of Largie held offices in his Court; Macfinnon was obliged to see weights and measures adjusted; Macduffie or Macphie of Colonsay kept the records of the Isles; there was a table of stone where this Council sat in the Isle of Finlaggan.

They met on Eilean Mor on which there was a feasting Hall, Chapel, burial ground and numerous houses. This was connected by a causeway to Eilean 'a Chomhairle and Mhic Dhomnuill's Head house[11]   ref. Hugh MacDonald & TCD.v.I,p.399.

Moreover there was a judge in every isle hearing all complaints, making judgement and ruling on misdemeanours; these were provided with land and received one eleventh of the value of decisions and fines levied. Clansfolk retained the right of appeal to the Council of the Isles.

In 1545 Donald Dubh assembled the Council of Finlaggan to appoint Commissioners to treat with Henry VIII, these being:-

Chief of Clanranald, MacIain of Ardnamurchan, Macdonald of Kintyre, Alasdair Carrach of Lochaber (the Macdonalds of Keppoch), and MacLean of Duart, MacLean of Loch Buie, MacLeod of Harris, and MacLeod of Lewis, with MacKinnon, MacNeil of Barra, MacNeil of Gigha, MacDonald of Largie.

---

11 ref. Hugh MacDonald & TCD.1,p.399.

The Council was also attended by the Abbot of Iona and the Bishop of the Isles."
Heralds ensured every man 'had his due recognition.'

Mhic Dhomnuill had his own Officer-of-arms, Islay Herald and Kintyre Pursuivant; as Earl of Ross, he had other officers-of-arms, Ross Herald and Dingwall Pursuivant, as his northern capital was at Dingwall where the local assembly or Tingwald had been held since Norse times.

The Lord of the Isles had his Bard and Piper. The bard to record all important deeds and events, he attended births, marriages and deaths and the succession of the heir, he was the keeper of records.
The bard was there where the battle raged, albeit in a position to keep the 'oral records' of victory or defeat safe.
The bard addressed the warriors before battle, recalling the valient deeds of their forebares and extolling the courage and powess of the Chief, enthusing them to perform great deeds for the honour of the Clan.
The hereditary Physicians of the Lords of the Isles were the family of Beaton/Beatie. These continued into the future with William Beatty the Surgeon on HMS Victory at the time of the Battle of Trafalgar.

Thenceforth many mainland clans, such as Mackintosh and Cameron, Mackenzie and Matherson, Ross and Munro, acknowledged Macdonald's authority.

How could such a wide and rugged territory be ruled.

On examination of a map of the Lordship of the Isles two things become obvious, the extensive coast line and the Great Glen running from Mull to Moray Firth. These were the Highways of the Highlands, by sea and by land, "Per Mare Per Terras."

There was nowhere on the coast that was exempt from the easy attention of Isla's Galleys, and the Great Glen was the pathway used by Columba in late 500AD in his travels from Iona into Pictland to visit Bridie of the Picts, "quelling a monster which he encountered in Loch Ness," and used again by the warriors of the great Clan Donald.

From early history our kinfolk walked this bridlepath and sailed these lochs for trade, forays and feuding.

Many a time wolf, bear and deer slid into the forest bordering Loch Lochy, Oinch or Ness, as Islesmen loped past on the way to firmly rebuke a wayward chieftain or to recoup cattle and horses in a raid.

Often was heard the movement of thousands of warriors on their way up the Great Glen into Glenmoriston and on to Castle Urquhart.
These were the times when the Highland Clans were fighting to hold their traditional lands and culture as the King and rival Clans worked to establish the feudal system.

After 1493 with the forfeiture of the Lordship of The Isles the Heraldic appointments to the Council of the Isles ceased.

In 2005 the High Council of Clan Donald reconstituted the position of Finlaggan Pursuivant with the Installation of the Hon. Adam Bruce Esq.
Photo right centre: The newly installed Finlaggan Pursuivant with the author after the ceremony at Glencoe.

The Hon. Adam Bruce, WS was later installed as Marchmont Herald of Arms to the Lyon Court.

The High Council appointed Thomas Miers Esq. as Finlaggan Pursuivant in 2009.

2014:Thomas Miers Esq appointed in 2009 as Finlaggan Pursuivant with Malcolm McDonald Esq Toiseach of Finlaggan Council, leading the March to The Arasaig Games.

Territories fromSomerled in 1156 to the Lords of the Isles from 1249 to the forfeiture in 1493.

The territories from Somerled in 1156 to
The Lord of The Isles – 1493.

Somerled after 1156: . . . .
Ard Ri of Argyle, and king of the south Isles.
Territory 1249 – 1438: ————————
Donald, Lord of the Foreigners Isles, 1249
Territory 1438 – 1493: - - - - - - - - - - - - - -
Lord of The Isles

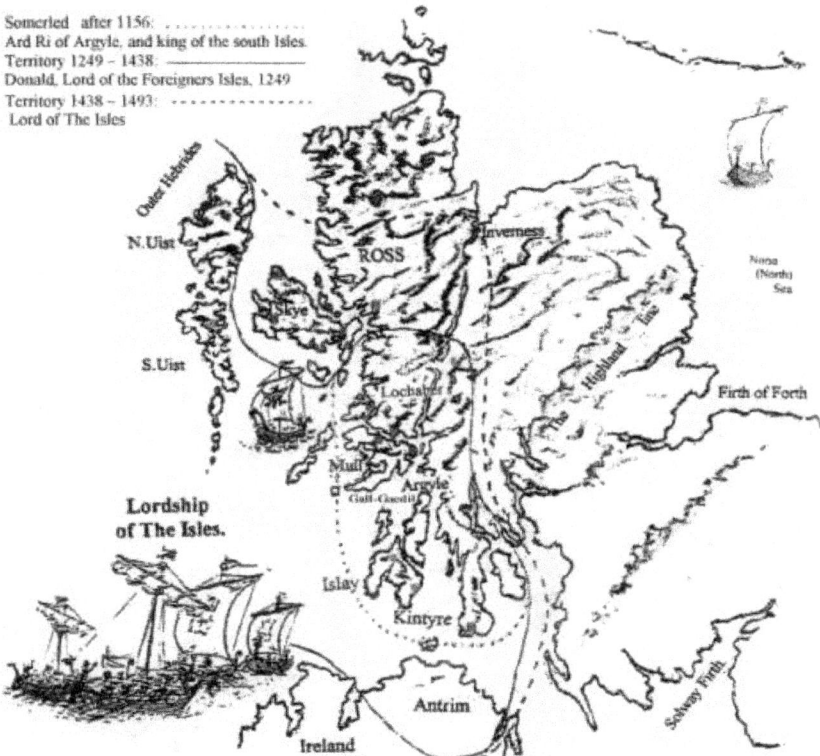

References: The Clan Donald vol.I, Smyth 1984:156-57-59, the Orkneyinga Saga

References:(1) Smyth 1984:156-57-59;(2) the Orkneyinga Saga;(3) The Clan Donald V.I.

The activity was feverish when the Lord of the Isles called a meeting of the 'Comhairle nan Eilean' sending out word for all to attend.

At the 'call,' sixteen and twenty-six oared galleys all around the Isles would be readied for sea.

Only the swiftest war galley sailed crewed by the ablest warriors, (Dougall curses his slashed arm, wounded in the last sea raid, so he couldn't go), each armed with targe, dirk, short axe or sword. One never knew when a rogue chief would be sailing the Sound to relieve others of their loose 'siller.'

MacLeod of Lewis was under full sail with bow wave creaming, gliding down the Little Minch and then into the Atlantic Ocean, MacLeod of Harris had joined him off Renish Point.

MacIan from Ardnamurchan used oars until he rounded Mull and saw MacLean of Duart under full sail on his port bow.
The Finlaggan Council was gathering from all points of the Isles.

What a sight it was when MacLean and Clanranald arrived together off Rudha a`Mha`il leading into the Sound of Islay as they raced for the shore.

Every oarsman straining - 26 oars flashed and smacked the water as one to surge the galleys forward, the steersman increased the oar rating as the shore came closer and bow waves foamed white. At the last second the call to "loft oars" and the galleys slid up the shelving shingle to come to a sudden stop - calls of "FEAR-BUANACHADH" (winner) echoed from both crews.

Then the splashes of bright tartan, the sparkle from sword hilt, jewels and badges as the Clan Chiefs were assisted down by their Gille casflue.
What a scene.

The Lord of the Isles maintained a period of calm through fair rule, justice for all, and the encouragement of celtic culture. This was oft times difficult in balancing the perimeter defences of his realm. He allowed attacks on any English ship which ventured into the waters of the Lordship of the Isles.

The Fleet of The Lord of the Isles calls at Tioram 13th century.

Oft times the Lord of the Isles and AlexanderIII king of Scotland suffered some disagreement, but to the subjects of Alexander east of the Highland line he was a wise King and his unfortunate and early death spelled a disasterous time in Scotlands rule.

The populace held grave concerns as to the future of Scotland on the death of Alexander in 1286 , as told by the Bard.

'Ode to Alexander III'

When Alexandyr our king was dede
      That Scotland led in lowe and le,
Away our sons of ale and bede
      Of wyne and wax, of gamyn and gle.
Oure gold is changed into lede –
      Christ born into virgynyte
Succour Scotland and remede
      That stodt is in perplexyte.   Ref: by Wyntoun. TCD vI,p.80

CATTLE AND SHEEP WERE AN ASSET FROM 1250 :

Those who bred cattle and sheep in Scotland did very well in the late 13th and 14th centuries according to national records for hides, skins and wool exported.

Landowner and crofter alike pastured stock in the summer shielings where they were fattened and any increase husbanded. Cheese and butter made from excess milk was to be kept over the next months.

Any surplus stock was sold from June to September.

With the coming of autum all stock was brought down to the farms and crofts to be mustered for sale or holding. Unimproved stock might be slaughtered before winter set in and salted down. Only the breeding stock would be kept in byres and feed through the severe winter months.

Of frugal necessity when isolated by winter storms, these cattle would be bled and this mixed with meal and cooked for the famed black pudding.

In the western highlands the drovers started from Skye generally swimming the cattle across the sound of Sleat with a tether to their jaw or in small boats to Glenelg. They then picked up cattle as they followed the droving routes to local markets at Corpach and Fort William. Here they might be met by drovers bringing herds down from Inverness and northern districts.

They drove these ever increasing herds to the main Fairs at Crieff where they either purchased more or onsold to others. By 1723, 20000 were sold there annually. The sale of black cattle between 1740 and 1790 rose in price by 300% - these main Fairs had peddlers, play-actors, stalls, beggars and traders.

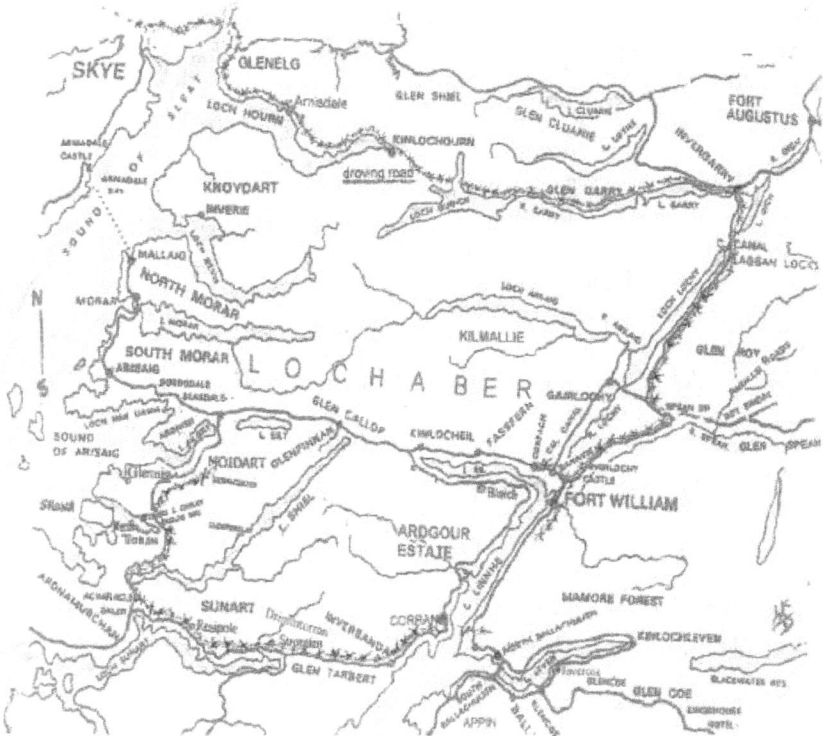

Lochaber region showing droving routes -x-x-x-x-x- from Skye to the Corpach markets outside Ft. William, and from Moidart to the south.

TRADITIONAL SYSTEM OF ALARM AND COMMUNICATION:

In times of sudden emergency or attack, the clan could be alerted by their traditional resource of "The Fiery Cross."

This ritualistic 'call to arms' required the Chief to quickly sacrifice a goat, whilst others made a cross of light wood which was charred with fire at its ends - the Chief then doused this with the blood from the goat.   ref: HASSHA

A chosen swift runner was informed of the rendezous, given the 'fiery cross'and instructed to race to the first hamlet and deliver the message to the Leading man of that village.

The recipient then dispatched the cross and message to the next village with the utmost speed, and this continued through the territory of the Chief until the whole Clan had been alerted. If it was a common enemy, then the alarm was sent to all Clans in the region.

Every able bodied male of age sixteen to sixty immediately gathered their arms, a package of meal, a spare plaid and answered the call to muster.

The Fiery Cross had a secondary name as 'the Cross of Shame' because if a clansman disobeyed the call he was branded with infamy, (as a vile coward,) and suffered the penalty of 'fire and sword.'

Almost as a contradiction to this fierce portrayal, the people of the Highlands were musical, poetical and artistic, with great imagination and a belief in the netherworld of dreams and visions – there were certain members of the clan who were 'fey,' that is they had the gift of 'second sight.'

Their lives were steeped in the 'happenings' of fairies, kelpies, urisks and witches and the utterances of seers or prophets, but this in no way interferred in their stand against injustice nor an enemy host, in fact, it may well have made them more steadfast and courageous, to strive and overcome great odds.

FEUDS, FORAYS and the CREACH.

WHAT'S YOURS IS MINE – one thing that would be a given is that the genetic footprint of the black cattle of the highlands would have a definite common DNA fingerprint no matter where it was taken for the simple explanation that cattle had been 'lifted' from one district to another, sold and bought and been lifted again to a far off district since day one.

There is much written by outside 'observers' of feuds and warfare between Clans when some (to the highlander) were but a FORAY to either replace stock after sales at markets, or to retrieve cattle previously taken – it was a way of life, a testing of manhood, a day out.

Now a CREACH was somewhat different.

A CREACH was as a result from some previous insult or injury suffered by the Chief or Clan where there had been no overtures of reconciliation made by the offending party to right the grievance.

Finally retribution was planned by the Chief and his advisers with the approval of the whole clan, the action to be effected on an auspicious date.

Such raids were serious affairs supported by just cause to right a wrong and great care was taken to ensure no friendly neighbour or clan suffered any consequence from this action, so participation was offered to neighbours if they wished. It being understood that all warriors involved shared in the plunder as a prize of war, and all were welcomed to the celebration feast and entertainment on their return.

The Chief was expected to provide a feast after any successful 'raid' at which 100 or so of whole deer and cattle were roasted over pits of hot coals then laid out on temporary tables.
This was augmented by a plenteous supply of spirituous liquors accompanied with the music of Pipers and dancing.
"Author and historian J.P. Maclean, PH.D. provides an illustration of the view in which the FEUD was held, the case of Donald Cameron may be taken, who was tried in 1752, for cattle stealing, and executed at Kinloch Rannoch.   At his execution he dwelt with surprise and indignation on his fate.
"He had never committed murder, nor robbed man or house, nor taken anything but cattle, and only then when on the grass, from one with whom he was at feud ; why then should he be punished for doing that which was a common prey to all ?"   ref: HASSH

A FEVER FOR INDEPENDENCE.

The victory at the Battle of Stirling Bridge in 1297 for Scotland might not be large as battles go but in its influence in the politics of Scotland it would rank amongst the greatest.

To expand this observation further, the victory over England at the battle of "BANNOCKBURN" way well be accepted as the turning point for Independence for Scotland.
This event might never have taken place were it not for the preceding fervour of a relatively small band of Highlanders dedicated to winning Independence for Scotland, who lived a life of isolation and deprivation of any small luxury, on constant guard of attack.

They fought and won many a skirmish during the English campaigns to subjugate the people of Scotland to accept the rule of England.

Internally they battled against privation and the opinion of Scottish aristocrats whose main concern was their title and lands, they maintained their opposition to English rule and thereby supported the general wish of the populace for self- government and Scottish Independence.

The earliest escapade of the group led by William Wallace was in 1297 for the execution of Willian de Heselrig high Sheriff of Lanark the rapacious English overlord whose subjugation of the people was tyrannical.

This earned him respect among other rebels such as the Lord of Douglas whom he joined for the ambitious raid on Scone. They operated out of the uninviting terrain and dense growth of Ettrick Forrest,travelling through the night to attack English positions then retreating back into the Forrest's impenetrable depths.

William Wallace, [Uilleam Uallas], Knight and Guardian of Scotland with Andrew Moray from the north lead a small army of Highlanders in 1297 to hinder the advance of the English army which was marching through the highlands to Caisteal Stirling in an exercise to quell rebel activities supporting the growing cause for Independence for Scotland.

A number of offences by Rebel groups led by Scottish nobles occurred across Scotland but came to an inglorious end when these "offenders' surrendered to English intervention at Irvine. It was some relief that neither Wallace nor Moray were named.
This resulted in the combination of the groups of Wallace and Moray into an experienced force.

Edward I, the Hammer of Scotland sent an army of around 3000 cavalry and 8000 infantry into Scotland to eradicate the rebellious groups from operating in the Highlands, specifically those of Wallace and Moray.
The English army finally reached the River Forth within closing distance of their objective of Caisteal Stirling.
They had only to cross the River to reach their first objective.

What the arrogant English Generals did not appreciate was that Wallace had initiated an alternative into the strategy and tactics of warfare whereas they were enmeshed in the accepted strategy of the chess game of war wherein the two sides lined up, (too bad if the opposition only numbered half the English contingent) and the Generals moved the troops on command by signal of banner, horns or drum. If the battle went against them, they safely retreated, surrounded by their personal body guard.

Wallace and Moray did not have the benefit of such opulence, they perforce introduced the sudden thrust of attack by a smaller mobile force who struck with precision and planning then withdrew to retreat to safety – these tactics threw the Generals into confusion and they defended their losses with calls of "foul play." Of course warfare was but a game to the aristocracy played by the supposed 'rules of chivalry' which was in reality but a pathway to riches for the winner.

On receiving word from sympathetic supporters that the English contingent was on the move and marching toward Caisteal Stirling, Wallace discussed the situation and developed tactics particular to the terrain and the disposition of the English army.

The army of about 3000 cavalry and 8000 troops under the command of John de Warenne, Earl of Surrey marched onward to the only bridge crossing the River Forth.
This was a narrow structure only wide enough to allow troops three abreast to pass across.

Wallace had made a reconnaissance of the area and devised a strategy to 'divide, contain and conquer.'

He allowed something of one third of the English army of infantry and heavy cavalry to cross the bridge and then attacked, decimating the leading ranks and then forming schiltrons of outward pikes and lances to combat and unhorse the cavalry whilst protecting the Scottish archers and swordsmen within, who fired into the English or who dashed between pikemen to dispatch unhorsed Knights.

The Scots then led a charge forcing the remaining English to retreat back onto the bridge causing a bottleneck by the retreating troops and the continuing momentum of the English army onto the bridge.

Finally the bridge collapsed from excessive weight spilling the English into the river to drown.

On 11 September 1297 the remaining English force retreated in ignoble defeat from a much smaller Scottish contingent leaving their dead and wounded on the field, one being Hugh Cressingham the Treasurer of Scotland for the English Parliament.

This victory gave heart to the Scottish patriots fighting for the cause of an Independent Scotland.

This success lead to the Scots invading the north of England as far as Cumberland later in November, but with differing results.

By September 1298, Wallace had decided to resign as Guardian of Scotland in favour of Robert the Bruce, Earl of Carrick and future king, and John Comyn of Badenoch, King John Balliol's nephew.

The fever for an Independent Nation continued to grow and gain solid public support and a steady increase of Nobles accepting the inevitable opinion of a national uprising.

This set the scene for Robert the Bruce to move to claim the empty throne of Scotland.

THE 14TH CENTURY – THE BRUCE IN SCOTLAND.

The 14th century was a period when Scotland was subjected to the external forces of the English King Edward I, as he wove his covetous web to enmesh Scotland with political intrigue and war.
He was aptly named "the Hammer of Scotland."

When Robert the Bruce made his bold move against Edward I to gain the throne of Scotland, he suffered losses and after the Battle of Methven and the capture of his wife and family by EdwardI, he was forced to retreat.

It was with some little relief that he saw the fleet of black hulls and white sails of Clan Donald galleys creaming the seas as they raced to lift him and his band off the Scottish mainland.
Christina Macrauri of Garmoran had received word of his plight and set out immediately to rescue her relative in his hour of need.

Angus Og MacDonald Lord of the Isles sheltered Bruce at Saddell, then in Caisteal Dunaverty at the toe of Kintyre, and finally at Rathlin Island, giving Bruce protection and great support by blockading the Isles from King Edward's ships of the Line.

1306 and according to the Bard, Angus Og Lord of Kintyre gives succour to 'Bruce' on this occasion by assisting him to escape Edward I troops by lifting Bruce and his men off Galloway and sailing to Caisteal Dunaverty.

" Angus Og gives succour to Bruce"
'and Angus of Ile that tyne was Syr
And lord and leader of Kyntyr
The King rycht weill resawyt he
And undertook his man to be
And he and his on mony wyes
He abandowynt to his service
And for mair sekyrness gaiff him syne
His castle of Donaverdyne.'

Ref: Barbour, poetic biographer of The Bruce.
TCD.v.1,p.92.

Lookouts on Clan Donald Castles along the mainland and the Hebrides kept watch and, using signal beacons, directed the war galleys to any 'misguided' English ships which sailed past.

Finally the ailing Edward I, the 'Hammer of Scotland' weakened and passed his last wish to his son Edward II, that he was to harass Scotland and reduce 'The Bruce' to a vassal of England.

This "passing of the guard" gave Bruce a breathing space - with the knowledge that he had the support of Angus Og and the Highlanders of Lochaber, it allowed him to continue recruiting an army as he waged a war of guerrilla fighting and open skirmishes against Edward.

The Bruce met up with Jamie Douglas, squire to Bishop Lamberton, early in 1306 with their trust and friendship being quickly tested in the defeats at Methven and shortly after at Dalrigh from John of Lorne.

This experience strengthened their confidence from the battle strategies and tactics so learned which they put into effect after the winter of 1307 in guerrilla warfare harassing English outposts and armies with devastating success.

'Jamie' was known as 'The Black Douglas' feared by the English for his fierce and ruthless attacks upon the English garrisons on Scotland's soil.

After years of steadily gaining recruits and the diplomatic wooing of Scottish magnates, Robert the Bruce was ready to challenge the English in 1307 at Loudoun Hill and win.

In 1308 he defeated the MacDougalls at the Pass of Bander.

Robert the Bruce.

BUT THE GREATEST TRIUMUPH WAS YET TO COME.

BANNOCKBURN – THE WORD THAT STIRS A NATION.

In 1313 Edward Earl of Carrick led troops to besiege Caisteal Stirling, but after a time he grew bored with the inaction and accepted the negotiations from it's Commander, Sir Philip Mowbray.

Caisteal Stirling: drawn and etched by J. MacWhither, A.R.A. 1888.

Edward Bruce was as impetuous as his brother was deliberate and he caused 'The Brus' many a problem just as he did when he came to an agreement with Sir Philip Mowbray to lift the siege of Caisteal Stirling on the proviso that if the garrison was not relieved by the English by midsummer of 1314 then Mowbray would surrender.

This in reality gave the English time to revitalise their forces and ready an army to attack Scotland, and the political excuse to do so.
This was something Bruce could well do without.

There are a number of accounts of "The Battle of Bannockburn" written some time after the event. Some using information from the once terrified survivors of the battle who only saw the three schiltrons they faced and not the Rearguard schiltron of King Robert with Angus Og at New Park.

Respected accounts of 'Historiana Anglicana' by the English chronicler Thomas Walsingham and of 'BANNOCKBURN' by the Historian Peter Reese and most importantly 'The Bruce,' the writings and verse of John Barbour, who was the only one of those times.

Historian Peter Reese is acknowledged as one who has carried out very extensive research on all available resource material of historical accounts, military lore, art and archaeology and has presented these in his "BANNOCKBURN" which is accepted "as aught be."

Bruce was well aware of the implications of another invasion so set about assembling a force to oppose an English attack by June of 1314. He called in every Scots Nobleman to assemble his obligated retainers and to meet outside Stirling. Most highland clans were represented.

He set his Commanders and recruits training to follow direction and signals especially in the formation of the defensive schiltrons. Each was a six ranked rectangle or square of Foot soldiers armed with 10/12 foot long pikes or lances which could withstand an attack by cavalry but could also open ranks to allow their own soldiers to enter the square or move out to attack. Bruce was the first to train his men to advance or change direction whilst maintaining the structure of the schiltron, he changed the purpose of the schiltrons from defence to attack on command.

Robert the Bruce's force of seven to nine thousand men-at-arms, archers and light cavalry mustered from all parts of the Kingdom to support the cause.
These were retainers, tradesmen, farmers, Lairds and Nobles.

They were required to supply their own arms which was no impediment for them as they had 'acquired' weaponry over decades from the salvage of wars.
The basic equipment for infantry was arms of: helmet, a toughened leather or padded jacket from neck to knee or a mail shirt, plated gauntlets, a spear or lance, a targe and the personal sgian dubh.

Bruce had one further proviso that each man had to be willing to give his life for the cause, if not, he was 'free to go.'

The tactics of battle and the strategies employed had been learnt by Bruce over the years and some as recent as the Battle of Falkirk and the Battle of Loudon Hill.

Almost to the last minute, he was prepared to withdraw, but as an experienced general he was familiar with the geography of the district and had reconnoitred the obvious route Edward II would have to take leading to Caisteal Stirling and one place stood out as ideal for consideration.

Robert the Bruce appreciated the strategic position of the Bannock Burn with an area of open ground of the reserve, the heavy woods of New Park, the sometimes dry Carse to the right crossed by streams from the Burn with grassy hummocks between.

He decided that this was the place to make a stand to confront the English and impede their cavalry.

One might well be confused with the terminology of the times as division, battle and schiltron are all but synonymous in their usage.

Due to what can only be the estimated size of Bruce's army his four schiltrons were three each of 1250 men, and one of 2000 men as the rearguard, making a total of four divisions/battles, plus a light cavalry unit of 500 horse.

The English army was of a total strength of 2400 cavalry, 16000 infantry including 500 bowmen in the formation of the Vanguard, a Main body and a Rearguard, BUT, there is some discussion on the number of battles/divisions under command.

The accepted opinion is that ten 'battles' would be the most probable formation as more would be too unwieldy.

Even a total of 10 'battles' would also cause the problem of a cohesive command structure for the English.

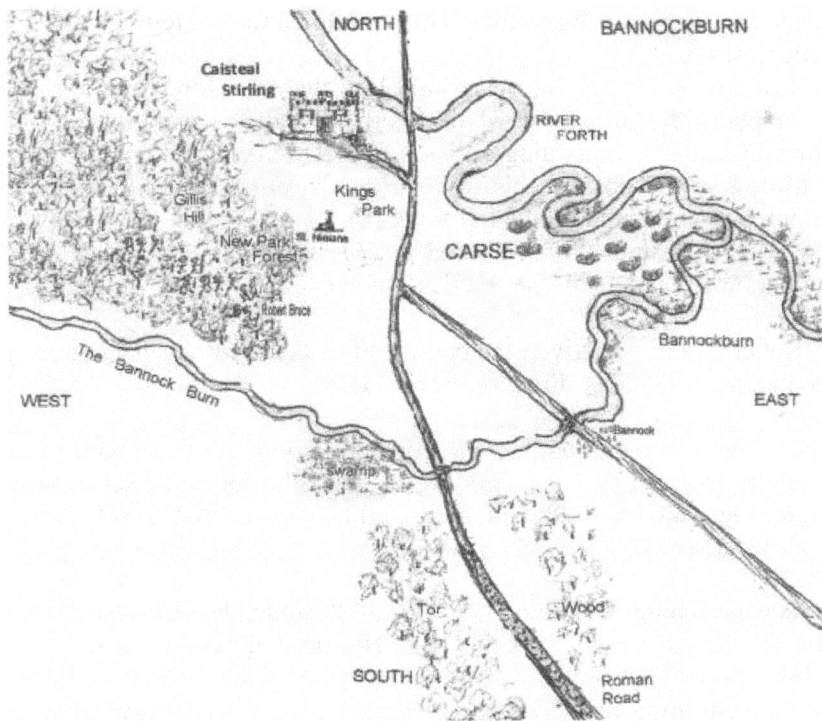

An illustration of the site south of Caisteal Stirling – not to scale.

THE BATTLEGROUND CHOSEN BY 'THE BRUCE.'

Having mustered his forces into 4 'battles' plus a cavalry unit, he marched and countermarched them in schiltron formations and familiarised them to signals of command and the proposed battleground tactics of defence and attack.

Bruce now prepared the ground to force the English army to advance in a narrow front along his chosen path by directing pits and trenches to be dug each side of the old Roman Road to trap cavalry.
These were disguised with grass over branches.
Caltrops were scattered between these to injure man and beast and disrupt any charge.

IF King Edward followed this route, then once the English crossed the Bannock Burn and reached open ground they would be contained within a wide loop of the brook to north and east, behind then to the south, with a patch of swampy ground to the west.

This was a natural encirclement strategically chosen by Bruce.

Before the proposed engagement Bruce outlined the strategy for the battle positions.

Edward Bruce, Earl of Carrick would lead the main force on the right (1). Walter FitzAlan Steward of Scotland and the experienced Sir James Douglas commanding division (2). Thomas Randolph, 1st Earl of Moray would position his division to the north near St. Ninian's Church below Stirling on the left flank (3).

The Earl of Lennox, Sir Gilbert Hay, Sir Neil Campbell with their retainers would augment the 'battles' numbers.

Sir Robert Keith was given the command of the light cavalry unit as a moving division under direction from Bruce.

Bruce himself would command the operation with the Rearguard from the slope in front of New Park wood, with the men of Carrick and Angus Og and his Islesmen and Highlanders as the 2000 strong reserve.   ref: TCD v1. p.96

There was a camp 'following' of some 3000 souls, the small folk, who were directed to remain back on Coxet Hill until all was decided.

The English army lead by King Edward II of England marched with full equipment, their movement encumbered with support wagons of food for man and beast, equipment and stores of armour, spears and arrows; gold service for King Edward and the Nobles; all the needs of an army of 2,000 horse and 16,000 foot.

There were not only English/Norman nobles in Edward's train, but also the discontented Scottish nobles who wished to rule in Bruce's stead. Ingram de Umfraville, a former Guardian of Scotland and his kinsman Robert de Umfraville the Earl of Angus, as well as others of the MacDougalls, MacCanns and Sir John Comyn of Badenoch.

They crossed the border, on to Edinburgh, then to Falkirk by 22nd June just short of Caisteal Stirling.

Bruce's forward Scouts warned him that Edward had reached Falkirk. He immediately moved his force from the open ground of Tor Wood into the north end of the heavily wooded area of New Park where they were concealed and protected from any Cavalry charge by the English and had a 'back door' if needed for a withdrawal.

WHAT IS IT?

First they noticed a dust haze in the distance, then a murmur in the air, next the ting and rattle of harness and chains and finally the combined sounds of men and horses, the chrunch and squeal of wagon wheels, and all this grinding and rattling stretching snakelike for miles.

It was the might of the English army on the move and headed for Stirling.

Edward II's Vanguard was led by nobles in fine gleaming armour and colourful emblazoned surcoats, on spirited warhorses prancing along the well used old Roman road.

Sunday 23rd June 1314 would be the first day of contact for the events which would stir a nation.

It was a time for the English to approach slowly, to reconnoitre and decide tactics for the coming battle, if there was to be one!
Unintentionally, Edward already had a spy in the local camp. Sir Phillip Mowbray had left Caisteal Stirling early in the morning, circled widely round to meet Edward II to warn him of the placement of Bruce's force and of the preparations he had witnessed to the approaches to New Park.

Edward only half listened, He and his nobles were seasoned campaigners of the Scottish Wars and were confident of winning any contest.
In fact they expected King Robert de Bruce to retreat on viewing the size of the opposing English Army.

This underestimation of the capability of the Scottish force was but one of his failings. He was not a strong General and had already lost leadership of the very large army he had assembled.

Edward II had allowed a split command of the vanguard of his army.
When the Earls of Hereford and Gloucester had argued as to who should lead the vanguard, Edward could not make the strong decision but weakly gave joint command to both.

This resulted in two arrogant armoured knights in surcoats of striking colours depicting their personal Arms and their separate retinue prancing up the old Roman Road on spirited war horses, eager to be the first in combat to teach the Scots a lesson.

The English Vanguard marching a little behind.

Along the road through the forest of Tor Wood they came, splashing over the ford of the flowing Bannock Burn.
There was swampy ground to their left, the flat ground of the Carse was to their right and Stirling Castle was visible to the north.

In the middle distance of the open space of New Park reserve were some of the King of Scotland's troops near the forest opening, and a lone horseman some distance between.

Fate lends a hand:
Robert the Bruce had ridden out on his palfrey onto the reserve to observe the movement of Edward's troops to gain fair warning of their formation for the coming battle.

One the English Knights ever eager to win glory was Henry de Bohun. He was riding ahead of his uncle the Earl of Hereford when his attention was alerted by the sparkle of sunlight reflected off the golden circlet crowning The Bruce.
Henry instantly recognised the King's rich red and gold surcoat.

The young knight lowered his helmet visor, put spurs to his heavy Destrier, couched his lance and thundered toward the lone horseman to win fame and 'glory.'

The Scottish leaders called out in alarm! and formed ranks.
To flee in front of the armies was out of the question, it was not his style.
'The Bruce' steadied his agile palfrey unencumbered with heavy armour, unfastened his short war axe from the saddle hook, his eyes steady on the fast approaching lance point with a couple of hundredweight of man, armour and horse driving it toward his breast.
De Bohun sighted the lance tip for the strike, totally committed.

At the last instant, the experienced Bruce jigged his horse to the left and stood upright in the stirrups and as the impetuous Henry came level Bruce swung the axe down onto the helmet splitting all to the shoulder – the now riderless warhorse galloped aimlessly away.

Roars of triumph from the Scots and of dispair from the English rent the air.

Bruce wheeled his mount and galloped back to the New Park forest to pass through the hastily formed, excited and cheering ranks of the Scots division.

He complained that he had broken the handle of his war axe, but was quickly fitted with helmet, armour, sword and a new axe by his squires.   ref: p.131 'BANNOCKBURN' by P. Reese.

This sudden and unexpected bloody death of de Bohun outraged his brothers-in-arms who reacted with shouts of rage, viciously spurring their armoured destriers into an undisciplined charge of the English vanguard.

This was led by Gloucester and Hereford galloping forward to avenge the death of their kinsman.

Superior force does not equate to superior strategy:

This charge was met by the first division of elated Scots who advanced down the slight slope in schiltron formation to meet the English cavalry vanguard.

The English found themselves facing this closed rectangle of pikes and lances forming an impregnable wall which harried man and beast.

The cavalry charges were thunderous and massive, the fighting fierce and bloody.

The pikes of the Highlanders targeted the warhorse's heart, the point touched the shoulder as it turned and the forward charge punched it through to puncture and rupture the heart and lungs with massive blood loss and collapse, unseating the Knight exposing him to being trampled to death.

As each of their assaults failed and bodies of horse and man lay where they fell, the English became disorganised.

The Earl of Gloucester crashed to the ground when his horse was lanced and fell.

His fellow Knights grasped him from each side and with Hereford and party they galloped in retreat across the front of the English Vanguard which would have caused them to wheel right and retreat onto the Carse.

Bruce commanded his men to stop their attack and for his forces to reform and take up defensive schiltron formations along the Roman road.

In this first engagement between the two opposing groups, Sir Thomas Gray along with a number of English was captured.

This unexpected commencement of hostilities, the wheel to the right by the English vanguard and the defensive schiltron formation of Bruce's men on the west of the Roman road, caused a major disruption on the advancing main body of the English army.

This forced them to move right after crossing the Bannock burn and to establish a defensive formation on the Carse of their Infantry, Archers, Cavalry and the Rearguard with the baggage train.

General Stewart in his *Sketches of the highlanders* writes that twenty-one bodies of men from within the Highland line responded to the summons.

Their chiefs were: Stewart, Mac Donald, MacKay, MacIntosh, MacPherson, Cameron, Sinclair, Drummond, Campbell, Menzies,MacLean, Sutherland, Robertson, Grant,Fraser, MacFarlane, Ross, MacGregor, Munro, MacKenzie, MacQuarrie . MacRuari was also there. ref:HH&GS.p.303

Extract from Barlours Bruce lists the fourth 'battle' as under Bruce the king:

"The ferd bataile - 'The fourth battle'

"The ferd [fourth] bataile the noble king
Tuk till his awne gouernyng:
And had in till his cumpany
The men of Carrick halely;
And off Arghile, and off Kentyr,
And off the Ilis, quharoff wes Syr
Anguss of Ile an But, all tha.
He of the plane land had alsua
Off armyt men a mekill rout:
His bataill stalwart wes and stout."

c/ref p.50 with p.303 of the "HISTORY OF THE HIGHLANDS & GAELIC SCOTLAND," by Dugald Mitchell, MD

Illustration of the site of the 'Battle of Bannockburn"– day 1 and 2.

The map diagram illustrates the dispositions of the Scots and English. From the first engagement between the Vanguard of both armies on day one resulting in the English Vanguard retreating across the path of the advancing English army. This forced the main body to divert to their right onto the Carse. It demonstrates the positions of those 10 divisions (battles) of the English army at the close of day one and the start of day two.   ref: BANNOCKBURN by P.Reese, p. 140-141

So due to the undisciplined charge by the English Vanguard, the army of Scotland now had their schiltron divisions in a strong and threatening position west of the Roman Road preventing any flanking move on their right.
This forced the English Army to take up defensive positions on the Carse with the encircling Bannock Burn to their south, east and north.

The English were left with no other choice.
This was a crisis for the English camp.
An advance guard of cavalry with Henry de Beaumont and Robert Clifford attempted to skirt the Scottish left flank to run for Stirling.

Bruce ordered the schiltron under Moray to block them and turn them back.

Day ONE ends with the army of Scotland lead by their King, Robert the Bruce, formed along the Roman road blockading King Edward II and the English army on the Bannockburn Carse.

Night fell with no change. English sentry outposts were set with some armoured cavalry held in a state of readiness, the flare of fires to illuminate the perimeter and for cooking.
English troops not on guard spread back on the Carse to recuperate for the oncoming Battle in the morning – tussock islands their only resting place.

Bruce stood his army down to a state of readiness and called a meeting of his officers to outline the tactics for the morning.
There was an uneasy unofficial truce.

The Bruce had two important Clergy supporting his action, Abbot Maurice of Inchaffray who held the embossed silver reliquary of St.Fillan and Abbot Bernard of Arbroath with the Repository of St.Columba with which they blessed the army of Scotland and held a mass at first light of the second day.

At daybreak on the second day of contact with the forces of Edward II King of England, Bruce gave the signal for Scotland's army to form attack schiltrons under their respective commanders. Edward Bruce, Earl of Carrick leading the right flank. Walter FitzAlan Steward of Scotland with the experienced Sir James Douglas Lord of Douglas to hold the centre with Malcolm Earl of Lennox, Sir Gilbert Hay and others. Thomas Randolph, first Earl of Moray to command the schiltron holding the left flank.

The fourth 'battle' reserve manned by Angus Og Mac Donald with his Islesmen and the Highlanders and the Carrick retainers, all commanded by 'The Bruce' in the rearguard position behind the three schiltrons along the Roman Road spanning the Carse. c/ref:Barlour'The ferd ataile'p.51. & TCD.p.967

Sir Robert Keith Marshall of Scotland, in command of the light cavalry unit was at the ready direction of The Bruce.

The banners of Earls and all Knights to be held high the morning breeze holding then unfurled in rich colours.

This to maintain morale but more importantly for Bruce to view the positions of each Scottish section of his army from his elevated Command Post at the rear.

The Scottish army knelt in prayer to absolve their sins and commit their souls to the Lord, this to the amusement of King Edward and to the relief of the English army who were struggling into their armour and grabbing for weapons.

Their Squires scrambling to control skittish warhorses.

In trained schiltron formation the Scottish army advanced and crossed the Roman Road holding the English within the confines of the Bannock Burn.

This was the first time in warfare that a defensive schiltron formation was used to advance, keeping their unassailable formation.

Archers were able to fire from the centre of each rectangle under the protection of their comrades with their 10 to 12 foot lances.

The quick action by Bruce in advancing on the English 'battles' caused consternation among the English leaders at the audacity of infantry challenging heavy armoured cavalry.

This was *unheard of.*

The Earl of Gloucester towering over all in full armour and mounted on his 17 hand warhorse led the cavalry attack against the Scots.

Against schiltrons bristling with three levels of lances, the first rank kneeling with their lances butted in the ground and against the soldiers' boot. The second rank with lance at waist height under their shoulder and braced by straight right arms, the third rank with lance at shoulder-height of the man in the second rank. All held firm.

Gloucester with many others died in the first disorganised charge. The earth trembled when the English cavalry charged again and again suffering heavy casualties as Scots pikes and lances penetrated the horses bringing them down with bloody nostrils.

Scots darted from within the schiltron to dispatch fallen horsemen with a slash of the sword or a swing of a battleaxe until the now decimated cavalry force retired to the rear.

The schiltrons advanced.

The English infantry now engaged only to perish on their first short charge against the lances of the schiltrons.

Then it was targe to shield, man to man, stabbing with dirk and short sword, slashing with broadsword, cleaving with axe. It was bloody dismembering and beheading of bodies. Men fought like demons for survival.

A group of English horse broke for Stirling Castle but under Bruce's direction, Sir Robert Keith raced with his light cavalry to cut them off and to engage to kill. Knights were captured and held as hostages, to be ransomed.

King Edward ordered his archers to fire but the combatants were so close that they would have shot their own English soldiers.

Edward Bruce, Earl of Carrick was crushing the left flank of the English toward their own centre or into the mud and water of the Burn to flounder and drown or be killed with a sword thrust.

The war cry of each Scots leader echoed forth as a rallying call for greater effort as the crush and the exhaustive body heat with the stink of sweat and blood started to take its toll.

The adversaries were now standing on the bodies of the fallen, but supported by the living mass of struggling fighters.

The welsh archers were the few who were free of the seething bloody mass, and they moved to the right flank and fired into the Scots but Bruce directed Keith with his 500 horse to charge amongst them with sabres slashing to cause their retreat.

Angus Og MacDonald Lord of the Isles was there beside The Bruce at the command position, informing on the dispositions of the armies.

The warrior host from Lochaber and the Isles was eager to enter the fray and was stamping with impatience, but Bruce held them in reserve until the heaving mass of the two armies were neither advancing nor losing ground.

IT WAS NOW TIME TO COMMIT ALL.
With an exhortation of "FORWARD - MY HOPE IS CONSTANT IN THEE," Bruce gave the highlanders entry to the battle.   ref:TCD.I.97

The gold banner with the black galley was held aloft, and their warcry of "**FROACH EILEAN**" roared forth.

The Highlanders surged forward into the mass of bloody humanity, reinforcing the divisions under Edward Bruce and Douglas, allowing the near exhausted men to ease back through their ranks.

They pushed forward to engage the embattled English.

The Highlander's now bloody claymores slashed, dirks stabbed and Lochaber axes swung, all to horrendous and deadly effect, as they forged onward carving into the English host.

This fresh strength tipped the battle, the English started to give ground; they were pushed back into the swampy waters of the Bannock Burn which was already contaminated with the bodies of horses and of their soldiers-at-arms.

The Scots shouted "Dh'eigh na h-Albannaich! Gabhaibh dhaibh! Gabhaibh dhaibh! Tha iad gu bhi ullamh!"
"For Scotland"   " lay on"   "lay on"   "they are failing"
                                                   ref: ml & pr

King Edward's Guard surrounded him as he fled the field to escape to Caisteal Dunbar.
The English right wing turned to flee, only to slide into the waters of the Burn to become easy victims.

The fleeing archers roused the exhausted infantry to escape.

The step by step advance from the mass of Bruce's men turned the retreat of the main body of the English into a rout.

A large number of English troops were trampled underfoot and into the mud of the Bannock Burn as they fled.
English Knights took to horse and some escaped over the Burn.

The camp followers, 'the small folk' seeing the start of the English retreat rushed down the hill making a great noise and waving makeshift flags in jubilation.

They wanted to be on the scene at the end to make "easy pickings" from the belongings of the fallen soldiers.

Sir Walter Scott writes later of the battle.

" Bannockburn 1314 " by Scott.

"One effort more and Scotland's free!
Lord of the Isles, my trust in thee
is firm as Ailsa rock;
Rush in with Highland sword and targe,
I wish my Carrick spearmen charge;
Now forward to the shock!
At once the spears were forward thrown,
Against the sun the broadswords shone;
The Pibroch lent its maddening tone,
And loud King Robert's voice was known –
Carrick, press on, brave sons of Innisgail,
The foe is fainting fast!" [12]   ref: TCD. p.97.v.I. & K.N. Macdonald,

The highlander's contribution to victory earned great respect from Robert the Bruce, and as a mark of favour he granted Angus Og the lands of Mull, Coll, Tiree, Morvern, (Moidart), Ardnamurchan, Duror, part of Lochaber and the lands of Glencoe.   ml & pr

Angus Og is succeeded by his son John as Lord of the Isles and of Lochaber, being confirmed in the lands of Mull, Coll, Tiree, Morvern, (Moidart), Ardnamurchan, Duror, part of Lochaber and the lands of Glencoe ceded to his father.

In uniting Scotland with the victory over the English at "Bannockburn," Bruce still had the political battle to win, that of defeating England's political line that Scotland was essentially a vassal state of England.

---

12 ref: ref: p.97.v.1.TCD; ref: K.N. Macdonald, 1900 –Oban Times

THE DOCUMENT – THE DECLARATION OF ARBROATH – 1320.

England had solicited the assistance of the Pope whose full support was evidenced when His Holiness Pope excommunicated 'The Bruce' and proclaimed Scotland under English subjugation.
The fear of excommunication with eternal damnation reduced the support of some subjects, but Bruce countered this by appointing Bishops to maintain the religious welfare of the Scottish nation.
Bruce and his advisors, both political and sectarian, wrestled with this problem by sending emissaries to the Pope, and to world leaders.

It was decided that a Document stating the ideals for Nationhood of the people of Scotland, their origins, their aspirations, their hard won independence, their long established government, be developed by Abbot Bernard of Arbroath. After many discussions and amendments as to the perceived beliefs of the people and the requirement to recognise the traditional history of Alba, the document was completed.

This Declaration is applauded as the most important and complete legal paper of the times. The Declaration of Arbroath of April 1320, by omission, divorces Ireland from the Scots and recognises Scotlands ancient connection to Scythia without stating that it was the Celts of Scythia who migrated through Europe to reach Scotland.
This notwithstanding, Bruce had perforce to defend his claimed undisputed right by perceived Celtic line to the Kingship of Scotland.

[NOTE: Robert de Bruis of Chateau d'Adam in Normandy accompanied William the Conqueror to England. His son Robert le Meschin received Annandale from David I. The fifth Lord of Annandale married a descendent of King David I. The sixth Lord became Regent and guardian of King Alexander II. The death of the Maid of Norway gave this Bruce a claim to the throne.]

Robert the Bruce decided that this Petition to the Pope was so important to his success that he called the leaders of Scotland together to be involved in the support of the Declaration as prepared by the Chancellor of Scotland, Abbot Bernard of Arbroath.

THE DECLARATION OF SCOTTISH INDEPENDENCE.

'The Declaration of Arbroath' spoke for all the people of Scotland and declared their origins:

" This nation having come from Scythia the Greater, through the Tuscan sea, and the Hercules Pillars, and having for many years taken its residence in Spain in the midst of a most fierce people, could never be brought in subjection by any people how barbarous soever; and having removed from these parts, above 1200 years after the coming of the Israelites out of Egypt, did by many victories and much toil obtain these parts in the West which they still possess, having expelled the British and entirely rooted out the Picts, notwithstanding the frequent assaults and invasions they met with from the Norwegians, Danes, and English; and these parts and possessions they have always retained free from all manner of servitude and subjection, as ancient Histories do witness.

This Kingdom hath been governed by an uninterrupted succession of 113 Kings, all of our own native and Royal stock, without the intervening of any stranger." etc.

ref: extract: the declaration of Scottish Independence, "The Declaration of Arbroath" 1320

This document was signed by the various Earls, Lords, Leaders and Gentry of Scotland and "the rest of the Barons" of the Kingdom of Scotland.

1320 AND SCOTLAND IS AN INDEPENDENT NATION.

But it seems the 'new' Scotland endowed from 'Robert the Bruce' has awakened ambitions in John who in 1342 is given an incredible dispensation direct from Rome to allow him to marry his cousin, Ami Macrauri of Garmoran. They have sons John, Godfrey, and Ranald. Ranald being the only son to sire offspring to be the Chiefs of Clans Ranald and Glengarry.

Some 15 years later, John is once again successful in gaining the indulgence of Rome by a second dispensation, to now divorce Ami and to marry Margaret Stewart daughter of Robert, High Steward of Scotland, later Robert II of Scotland.

In one stroke John takes the lands of the Lordship of Garmoran from Ami and cements his line with that of the Kings of Scotland. A political feat envied by many but to be paid for later in stone and mortar.

The last decade of the 14th century witnesses major changes to the two ruling figures of Scotland.

In 1380, John the Good, Lord of the Isles is succeeded by his son Donald of Isla and Robert II is succeeded by Robert III in 1390.

These events change the dynamics of Scotland.

Where Donald of Isla had been on friendly terms with his grandfather Robert II, his relationship with his uncle the feeble Robert III soon deteriorates due to the actions of the King's ambitious and unscrupulous brother the Duke of Albany.

Albany immediately takes steps to remove any opposition to himself gaining the throne. He quickly removes one threat by murdering his nephew the Duke of Rothesay and then he neatly betrayed Prince James into English hands.

The stress was too much for his brother Robert III who died shortly after in 1406.

Though the 15th century saw Scotland win through for Independence, the 17th century enacted the first change which set the conditions for the final 'ACT' whereby Scotland joined with England as one nation and therein forfeited her Independence.

THE UNION OF THE CROWNS - Aonadh nan Crùintean.
When Queen ElizabethI of England died the next in line was James VI, King of Scots, who acceded to the thrones of England and Ireland. This united the three realms under James and the official "Union of Crowns" was officially promalgated on March 25th 1603.

THE ACTS OF UNION:

1702 Queen Anne succeeded to the throne and continued working with Her ministers to bring to fruition the joining of the crowns of Scotland and England.

These negotiations between parliaments, between religious bodies, between commercial interests, between the people of the two nations finally came to agreement.

First with the 'Union with Scotland Act 1706' passed by the Parliament of England, and the 'Union with England Act 1707' passed by the Parliament of Scotland.

These Acts joined the Kingdoms of Scotland and England into the United Kingdom of Great Britain.

2014 saw a further attempt for Independence by Scotland with a Referendum on the 19th September to vote for Scotland to separate from England and the United Kingdom.
The vote was lost and the United Kingdom remained intact but Scotland won new powers on tax, spending and welfare.

THE BRUCE INTO IRELAND.

The folk of Lochaber were not rested when Scotland turned its attention to Ireland in 1315, when Edward Stewart brother of 'The Bruce,' sent word to the Chiefs and Lords to gather their warriors and obligated crofters into their forces to support his forays in Ireland.

They left their farms to the younger sons to tend and to defend.

His initial successes encouraged the Irish Gentry to join with him, (one should be on the winning side), but then he suffered defeat followed by discontent due to being over ambitious.

So to the Scots in Ulster:

Edward Bruce, brother to the king of Scotland was a man of action and went warring into Ireland in 1315 defeating Edmund Butler the Royal Governor, south of Dublin.   He then turned to the Castles of Carrickfergus and Greencastle.

He put Carrickfergus under siege and successfully attacked Greencastle putting the garrison to the sword.

Sir Thomas de Mandeville attacked the besieging Scottish force but was himself defeated and Carrickfergus was also taken by the Scots.
Edward Bruce's zeal continued and after negotiations with the local Irish kings in 1316, he was proclaimed 'High King of all Ireland' at his coronation service in Dundalk on the 1st May,1316.

The coronation of his impetuous brother caused quite a problem for Robert Bruce, King of Scotland as there were now two Bruce Kings and Edward was ever vying for the senior role.

The situation swiftly changed as Edward lost control of the Irish factions from internal feuds and men deserted to return to farms and family.
With depleted forces, he was wont to call on his brother King Robert the Bruce to bring troops to bolster his weakened position   forcing Bruce into an unwinnable War.

THE 15TH and 16TH CENTURY - the populace constantly alert.

The folk of the western highlands lead an active mobile lifestyle, in hunting and fishing for provisions, or in raiding of cattle from rival Clans to replace domestic stock or to trade, they travelled great distances by foot, horse or boat.

Dwellings were essentially for rest and recreation and winter shelter, as most domestic activities were done outside the dwelling to make use of the natural light.

There was a stone seating shelf built into the external wall of dwellings where folk sat and worked. Men would mend leather and harness equipment, fletch arrows, weave wattle creels for the pack horses, whilst the women might spin, weave, sew and tend gardens.

In season the men would cut and stack peats, gather kelp, harvest crops, dry grain and distil whisky.

In summer, families moved with the stock to the 'shieling,' (the summer pastures) and made butter and cheese to last the year.

Folk initially were small farmers scattered through an area under the protection of a local Leader. Later they generally lived as crofters or tenant farmers more or less as permanent residents within a district.

In the later Clan system the Chiefs closer relatives held 'tacks' for a lease period.

These would fall due on a Whitsunday of a specific year and could be given to others in the next generation.

So folk would move in accord with a change in tenure, improved circumstance, or due to prolonged adverse seasonal conditions.

The other main influence was from political action when aspiring Leaders led bodies of troops, gathered from farms under their patronage, through districts and parishes attacking a political or baroncy rival, foraging for provisions, then ravaging and burning the farms in their passing.

If the Leader believed "a serious lesson was to be learned" a number of the village men were hanged.

Those early centuries were basic and violent times and folk lived with the sgian dubh close to hand, only trusting in blood relationships.

This meant that those left on the farm had to either flee from armed forces, driving their stock before them into the forests to later return to burnt out farms, or moving to neighbouring or distant parts and starting afresh.

Times were hard but they were a hardy people.

Some major disruptions of the populace and influences for movement:-

Battles along the Great Glen with disruptions to the populace 1400 to 1700s.

1156 – Battle of Epipheny.
1306 – Battle of Bannockburn.
The second wars for Scotland's Independence:-
[1332 - Battle of Dupplin Moor
[1332 - Battle of Annan
[1333 - Battle of Halidon Hill
[1335 - Battle of Culblean (Kilblain)
[1346 - Battle of Neville's Cross
[1357 - King David was released on a ransom of 100,000 merks.
[1380 - Battle of Benrig (sometimes called Horse Rigg)
1411 – Lord of the Isles leads army from Morvern through Ross to Harlow.
1427 – James1 leads an Army of retribution to Inverness.
1429 – Battle of Lochaber – James I.
1464 – Celestine Sheriff of Inverness.
1491 – Alexander harrassed Badenoch and Gordon lands.
1513 – Macleans gain Ardgour and Ardnamurchan
1516 – Clan Donald takes Caisteal Urquhart and lands.
1554 – Huntly leads troops against Moidart.
1645 – Argyll and Montrose waste farms through the Great Glen.
1689 – Battle of Killecrankie.
1692 – Massacre of Glencoe.
1715 – Rising – Battle of Sheriffmuir.
1745 – "The '45" and Culloden.

Other factors were famine, plague, stock or crop failure from disease or pest, excessive local taxes and religious persecution – times were hard but they were a hardy people.

THE WARS FOR SCOTLAND'S INDEPENDENCE –
fought again from 1332 to 1357.

The death of King Robert I without an heir re-enacted the instability of
Rule by a Guardian. King David II was but four years of age and his
Guardian Thomas Randolph, 1st Earl of Moray who was on the field at
Bannockburn when he died suddenly which left the infant King at the
mercy of the principal rival in Edward Balliol who claimed the throne.
He was backed by Edward III of England.
The Battle of Dupplin Moor was fought on 12th August 1332 when the
Earl of Mar as Regent of Scotland faced the English backed army of
Balliol and was defeated due to his own dallying but mainly from the
attack by the English bowman whose withering fire fatally wounded
Lord Robert Bruce and the Earl of Mar.

In 1332 the ruling power struggle was reversed when the Scots lead a
victorious surprise attack on the army of Balliol at the Battle of Annan
on 17th December 1332 chasing them back into England.
1333 sees Edward Balliol gaining the assistance of Edward III of
England who replied by invading Scotland with a siege of Berwick-
upon-Tweed .

On 19th July at The Battle of Halidon Hill Sir Archibald Douglas lead
the Scots against the English but again the power of the English
archers with the massed fire of their longbows won the day.

1335 the division between the families of Bruce and Balliol continues
with The Battle of Culblean on 30th November. So once again Scotland
is ruled by joint Guardians of the 3rd Earl of Moray and Robert the
High Steward of Scotland. King David of ten years with Queen Joan
sails for France under the protection of Philip VI.

1346 - Having received protection from France the now twenty-two
year old David II answers the plea from France for support by sending
an invasion force into England to reach Durham. The English army
engaged them on the 17th October 1346 at The Battle of Neville's
Cross.
Finally in 1357 there is some reconciliation between Scotland and
England with the signing of a Treaty at Berwick-upon Tweed which
released King David on a ransom of some 100,000 merks.
David II died in 1371 without an heir.
He was succeeded by his relative Robert II and Scotland has an
independent King once again.

WHEN REGENTS RULE.

It is 1406 and the Duke of Albany is now Regent of Scotland and the throne is for his taking. Bar for the hostage Prince James, now King James of Scotland, who was a prisoner of the Court of Henry IV of England.

It is only the might of the Lord of the Isles and his highland warriors who maintain the balance of justice in Scotland, he is the only force strong enough to challenge the machinations of the Duke of Albury.

The young King James was a full cousin of the Lord of the Isles and the recorded visits of Donald to the Court of Henry IV were undoubtedly missions to keep James informed of events and to formulate strategies to gain his freedom or at least to thwart Albany's devious plans.

Albany schemed to gain the Earldom of Ross by influencing Euphemia Lesley heiress of Alexander Lesley [Earl of Ross], to relinquish the title and enter a convent. Her heritage of Ross was extensive, her lands were from the districts of Ross and Cromarty to Argyle; from Glenelg to Lochbroom; extending easterly inland to Urquhart, including the parish of Kilmorack.

Donald immediately reacted with a counterclaim. He said that as Euphemia had retired to a convent, she had given up her heritage of the Earldom of Ross, and that this then should be held by the next in line.

This was Lady Margaret, the wife of Donald, Lord of the Isles.

To force Albany to declare himself, and as a stratagem to draw Albany's forces away from the border and give JamesI a chance to escape to Scotland, Donald declared that if Lady Margaret did not receive her heritage he would march upon the city of Aberdeen.

From Ardtornish in Morvern, Donald unfurled his banner and sent the Fiery Cross from glen to glen, calling his clansmen warriors to his side. Macdonalds, Mackinnons, Camerons, MacLeans, McLeods, Mackintosh and of Chattan gathered to the cause.

The Macdonald host sailed and assembled at Strome then marched through Wester Ross on Dingwall, to be met by Angus Dubh Mackay with 2500 fighting clansmen. The battle was fierce and resolute but the Mackay army was defeated and Donald took possession of Dingwall Caisteal.

He then marched via Beauly and gave the Laird of Lovat and his

Frasers at Caisteal Downie a lesson in good manners, then on to Inverness.

He raised his standard and called the men of Ross to join him.
In the last days of June 1411 Donald led his army of 10,000 men towards Harlaw. News went before him that Aberdeen was to be put to the flame.
Still the Regent did not march against him, instead Albany sent the Earl of Mar with a well equipped army of Lowland chivalry and the gentry of Aberdeenshire with their armed retainers to do battle.

Each side in The Battle of Harlaw fought with the tactics of their race. Donald forming his army in the Pict wedge formation, or Roman Phalanx, his men armed with reinforced wood and leather targe and dirk, as well as broadsword or Locharber axe, with archer support.

The Earl of Mar formed up with front ranks of armed retainers supported by mounted, armoured Knights and Esquires, in the Norman fashion.

The Highland force charged, shouting their clan war cry and pipes playing; they were met with disciplined armoured force, but the highlanders were too many and too strong. By nightfall the Lowland army of Mar was annihilated.

The Lowland historians recorded the Battle as a victory for Mar and the Norman/Saxon nobles, but those they left on the stricken field belied their propaganda.

They were, Sir James Scrymgeour, Sir Alexander Ogilivy (Sheriff of Angus), and his son Sir Thomas Murray, Sir Robert Maule of Panmure, Sir Alexander Irving of Drum, Sir William Abernethy of Saltourn, Sir Alexander Straiton of Lauriston, Sir Robert Davidson (Provost of Aberdeen), Lesley of Balquhain and six of his sons, James Lovel and Alexander Stirling.

Further losses were the principal gentry of Buchan and the greater part of the burgesses of Aberdeen, all honourably dead on the field of Battle.

It is difficult to understand how the Earl of Mar was able to call the result, "a great Lowland victory" as Donald only lost two Chiefs of MacLean and MacIntosh on the field, and Dugald of Sunart died from the Battle, but both armies suffered heavy losses of men, roughly 500 to 600 on each side.

Some lines from the Bard Lachlainn Mo`r Mac Mhuirch,(Lachlan Mor MacVurich) evokes the grief and the scale of payment from the aftermath of the "Battle of Harlaw":
"There was not sin' King Kenneth's days,
Sic strange, intestine, cruel strife
In Scotlande seen, as ilka man says---
Where monie likelie lost their life;
Whilk made divorce 'tween man and wife,
And monie children fatherless.
And monie a ane will mourn for aye,
The brime battle of the Harlaw."   TCD. vol.I, p.161.

JamesI of Scotland had been under the "care" of King HenryV since 1406 wherein he received an education and training in sport and arms as befitted a King.
His full cousin, Donald, Lord of the Isles made many visits to the Royal Court to keep James informed of affairs in Scotland.

Even so, James came under the influence and intrigue of the English Court and during the French Wars he was asked by HenryV to command the Scottish Forces assisting France to desist and retire, but was ignored by the Scot leaders.
This humiliated James and he did not forget it.

HenryV died in 1422 and the nine month old HenryVI of England reigned under the direction of Regents who continued with the arrangements for the marriage of JamesI to Joan Beaufort, a cousin to Henry VI, thus ensuring the continuance of English influence.

Clan Donald had to stand strong to hold their territories during this turbulent era of the 'Rule of Regents'and to maintain control over Chiefs of lesser clans who had recently grown in wealth and power whilst under the banner and security of the Lord of the Isles.

JAMES THE FIRST RETURNS:

On his release from the English and on his return to Scotland in 1424, JamesI moved quickly to establish his support base by rewarding those who had sworn to provide men for the Kings army.
He granted land and position to Norman knights from England and promoted lowland landowners to Barons of districts. This generated a strong following loyal to him for their new wealth and position.

James then sets about to secure his position and invites Alexander of Islay to be present at an auspicious occasion. The trial and execution of the Duke of Albany and his sons, and the Duke of Lennox,[all royal Stewarts and competitors to the throne], there was no doubt as to the guilt of the parties. James then confirmed the Earldom of Ross on Alexander.

In 1426 Argyle continues with his covert activities to unseat the Lordship of the Isles. Firstly a John MacArthur Campbell uses forged documents to lodge a claim on lands on the North Isle and on the mainland.
Then John Mor Tanaister is murdered by a James Campbell. It is not coincidental that at this point in time Argyle accepted appointment as hereditary 'Tale-Bearer in Chief' to the King.

JamesI was induced to believe the 'tale' that the Lord of the Isles was no longer able to maintain law and order in his lands.
Alexander and others were imprisoned and some executed without trial, including James Campbell to keep his mouth shut. Alexander was later released as there was no substance in any of these charges against him.

Probably as a 'sup' for his unjust imprisonment, Alexander is referred to as Lord of the Isles and Master of Ross in 1426.

It was into the third year of his return in 1427 when the fickle James decided that he should act to curb the arrogant and aggressive attitude of his nobles and settle old scores.
Maybe his "Tale-Bearer in Chief" had been successful with his tale-telling after all.
He set his plan in action by calling a Parliament at Inverness Castle and travelled through Lochaber and up the Great Glen with a retinue of Lowland Barons and a large army.

With outward cordiality he called on all of his vassals to attend.

Mackay, Mackenzie, Ross, Leslie, Moravia (Earl of Sutherland),as well as Macarthur, Campbell and Chiefs of Clan Donald, of Alexander Lord of the Isles and Alex' Macrauri of Garmoran, answered and attended the Convention.

When the Highland host were assembled, JamesI entered into deeds which besmirched his character and laid the base for the future acts of retaliation by Clan Donald to reclaim their honour from the treachery that James had enacted.

John Mor Lord of Dunnyveg was attacked and slain. Clan Donald members were imprisoned with Alex' Macrauri and others executed. Mackintosh and Camerons deserted their long time patron.

Alexander Lord of the Isles and his mother the Heiress of Ross were imprisoned and held at the King's pleasure. These unjustified and treacherous actions did cause a few Chiefs to defect from the Lord of the Isles over to James, but it was to cause James and his Lowland Barons much grief in the future.

JamesI appears to have given token agreement to each party competing for his patronage as his tactic of 'control by division' for within a couple of months he releases Alexander (now named as Lord of the Isles and Master of Ross) but keeps his mother the Heiresss of Ross as hostage.

Jame's treacherous action and unjustified imprisonment left Alexander seething with wrath for this casual disrespect of his position and he quickly gathered men of Clan Donald and Clans who owed allegiance to the Lord of The Isles "to right the wrong."

He demonstrated his strength by marching up the Great Glen to lay waste to Inverness town and beseige na Caisteal.

The logistics of supply to maintain an army of this size in the field caused Alexander to disengage from the seige of the Castle and return to friendlier climes. This was not to be the case, for James had gathered an army of Royalists and set forth to do battle with Alexander.

THE BATTLE OF LOCHABER 1429:

Alexander Lord of the Isles and his Clans had reached a district of Fort William in Lochaber and were crossing the moor when they were confronted with JamesI and his army. This show of force by the King immediately identified the 'turncoats' in Alexander's army as the

Mackintoshes and the MacMartin Camerons who immediately deserted Alexander and joined the King's forces. This resulted in King James not only holding the superior position for battle but also now having the superior numbers.

Alexander was defeated and he and his army disbursed in retreat.
This "Battle of Lochaber" took place on either the 23 or 26 June of 1429.

It is also named the "Battle of Split Allegiances" by the Camerons of Lochiel as they stood firm with Alexander whilst the MacMartin Camerons defected.

'Behind the scene' negotiations followed between the parties of the King and the Lord of the Isles and finally Alexander presented himself before the King in an attitude of debasement and humility dressed only in a simple shirt to beg clemency – his life was spared but he was imprisoned in the remote Tantalum Castle. Also imprisoned were: Lachlan McGillane (MacLean), Torkell McNell, Tarlan MacArchir & Duncan Persoun. ref: HH&GS,p.327.
The army of the King led by the Earl of Mar and the Earl of Caithness, tasked by the Crown with 'the keeping of the peace' within the territories of the Clans Donald, wrecked havic on Lochaber lands and property to finally establish their forces at Inverlochy.
Mar believed he had a superior army and that Clan Donald was a spent force.

This action gave Clan Donald righteous motivation to take to the field in a cause of retribution for injustices perpetrated against them by the King and jealous Barons.

Donald Balloch, Lord of Dunnyveg, sent off 'the fiery cross' to call the Clan together and moved to avenge their honour and the injustices perpetrated by the Crown and its assassins.

In 1431 the 'FIERY CROSS' went from glen to glen calling Clan Donald to gather as espoused by Walter Scott in his writings, the "Piobroch of Donald Dhu."

"Piobroch of Donald Dhu,
Piobroch of Do'nuil,
Wake thy wild voice anew,
Summon Clan Conuil.

Come away, come away,
Hark to the summons!
Come in your war array,
Gentles and commons.

Come from deep glen
And from mountains so rocky,
The war pipe and pennon
Are at Inverlochy.

Come every hill plaid and
True heart that wears one,
Come every steel blade and
Strong hand that bears one."

ref: K.N. Macdonald, 1900 –Oban Times.

Mar was unaware that Alexander, Lord of the Isles, had been in communication with his Chiefs for some time and had sent his final message of exhortation for his clansmen to be strong in spirit, brave of heart and fierce in battle.

MacIain, MacAllan, Ranald Bane and their men gathered, whilst Macleans, Macduffies and MacGees landed in their galleys at Inverskippnish - Alastair Carrach brought 220 archers to support Donald Balloch and positioned them above Inverlochy.

The Earl of Mar realised that he had a major situation on his hands and positioned his troops to meet the advance of the Ilesmen, but had learned little from 'Harlow.'

The Highland charge again smashed his troops as claymore, Lochaber axe and dirk cut them down and the bowmen of Alastair Carrach rained death from the sky.

The Earl of Caithness with his bodyguard, a number of Lowland Knights and Barons with hundreds of their troops died on the field, the Earl of Mar was wounded.

After the battle of Inverlochy, (1431), the arrogant Earl fled the field and wandered in the hills lost and hungry. He came upon some women tending cattle, who gave them some barley meal from their meagre provisions.

For want of utensils, The Earl mixed this with water in his shoe:

"The Earl of Mar and his shoe."
"S maith an co`caire `n t-acras
`S mairg a ni tailceas air a` blaidh
Fuarag eorn a sail mo bhroige
Baidh a b` fhearr a fhuair mi riamh."

" the pangs of hunger are a skilful cook,
Woe to the man who scorns the humblest brew,
The sweetest fare of which I ere partook
Was barley meal and water in my shoe."

        ref: p.186 v.1 TCD.; K.N. Macdonald, 1900 –Oban Times.

Donald Balloch then marched into Lochaber and put the lands of the alien Camerons and Mackintoshes to ruin for their past desertion of the Lord of the Isles.

The Islesmen retired with their booty and dispersed into the hills and Donald Balloch sailed for the Glens in Antrim, inherited from his mother Marjory Bisset.
James reacted swiftly by increasing a tax "for the resistance of the King's rebels of the north" from 2 pennies to 10 pennies, which financed his expedition into the western highlands to restore order, but mainly to take Balloch in irons to prison.

Balloch was safe for the moment but he knew that James would not rest until he was captured. He then employed a wily stratagem - Hugh Buy O'Neill sent James the 'head' of Donald Balloch thus establishing his death, but it was the 'head' of another, so Donald could move freely once again.

Events now move quickly and JamesI realises that he must halt the discontent and stabilise politics within the realm.
An heir born to the throne in October 1431 was a reason for rejoicing and gave the excuse for reconciliation, so James declared amnesty for a number of political prisoners.

Now was the politic chance to release Alexander Lord of the Isles, allowing him to retain his lands and position and hopefully calm the situation, for James needed a respite to give time for his next strategy for power to germinate.

JamesI now initiated a campaign to separate the western highlands from the ruling class of Scotland by driving a wedge between east and west through the language of the realm. He openly supported the Norman barons and changed the language of his Court from Gaelic to Lowland Scots and publicly stated that Gaelic was 'Irish' and anyone speaking Gaelic was Irish.

England saw the benefit in supporting this division as it weakened the Scots as a co-ordinated nation - they encouraged English writers to take up this labelling of the Highlanders as barbaric Irish – this is still parrotted today.

The folk of Lochaber across the highlands were sore affected by the Kings action, but they had a champion in Alasdair, Lord of the Isles.

The Lords of the Isles had always been patrons of music, the arts and culture of the west and it was an anathema to them that the King should be changing the tradition of the land in this and introducing feudalism through the Norman and English incomers.

Finally in 1435, Alasdair (Alexander) Macdonald, Lord of the Isles is granted the Earldom of Ross through his heiress mother, making him the overlord of Skye and Lewis.
Thus he acquired Ross which included The Black Isle a peninsula within Ross and Cromarty and much of modern Inverness-shire.

He is now one of the most powerful Earls in the Kingdom, as Justiciar, or High Sheriff of the region north of the Forth.

He appointed the Bishop of Ross his delegate to the Council of Regency.   ref:The Clan Donald,vol.I, p.194.

Alexander justly rewards the earlier duplicity of the Camerons by reducing the lands of Lochaber from Donald Dubh and exiling him to Ireland, he then grants these lands in Lochaber to Iain Garbh, son of Lachlan Maclean and grandson of Lachlan Lubanach 5th of Duart.

In 1436 JamesI marched on the Douglas Caisteal at Roxburgh with his army and cannon, his pride was a great bombard, the "Lion" which had been manufactured in Flanders as a present for the king.

On the 1st August the "Lion roared" but to little effect as James had to withdraw when an English force moved across the border against him.

JamesI had shown favour to Saxon and Norman on the one hand and meted out a harsh 'justice' to the Highlanders on the other, so it was no surprise for those times that he was assassinated on 21st February 1437.

Once again Scotland is ruled by Regents on behalf of the six year old King James II.
On the death of Alexander, his son John succeeded as Earl of Ross and Lord of the Isles and was heavily involved in the affairs of state and politics and was included within the King's court. At the Kings encouragement, (and promise of a grant of land), he married the daughter of Sir James Livingstone.

As 'Monachs by Divine Right' do, the king reneged on his promise of the land grant to the Earl of Ross and this so disappointed John that he not only lost his trust in the King but became involved in adverse actions politic – of supporting the new Earl of Douglas and providing him with shelter in 1455.

John launched the strategy to divert the King's attention from Douglas, by a diversionary tactic lead by Donald Balloch of Islay to invade the Ayrshire coast. This being a fleet of one hundred galleys with a force of five thousand men.
When word spread of the intended 'exercise,' Chiefs of Macdonalds, Mackinnons, Camerons, MacLeans, McLeods, Mackintosh and of Chattan gathered with their warriors to be part of the 'action' to share in the spoils, and spoils there were.
The Highlanders burnt mansions in Inverskip, put Arran to flight, took Brodrick Caisteal then destroyed the buildings. They wasted the Islands Cumrays.[13]
This with little injury to the populace as the highlanders were issued orders to preserve life where possible.
The reported victims of these raids were, 15 men; 2 or 3 women; 3 or 4 children.

The plunder was well worth the effort as they took 5 to 600 horses, 10000 oxen and kine, more than 1000 sheep and goats and levied 'tribute' on Bute of one hundred marks of silver as well as butter and cheeses.

---

13 .This action was reported in the "Auchinleck Chronicle" – ref: p.333 "History of the Highlands and Gaelic Scotland" published 1900.

Days of entertainment and feasting celebrated the creach.

The Truce between Scotland and England ended in 1460 and King JamesII immediately opened a campaign in July to rid Scotland of English troops starting with the town of Ruxburgh which he lays bare but na caisteal garrisoned by the English defied every attack.

HISTORY REPEATS ITSELF:

In 1436 JamesI marched on Caisteal Roxburgh with his army and cannon, his pride was a great bombard, the "Lion," manufactured in Flanders. On the 1st August the "Lion" roared but to little effect as James had to withdraw when an English force moved against him.

In July of 1460 the scenario is repeated, but it is James II and his army who now lay siege to the (ex) Douglas Roxburgh Caisteal. The Earl of Ross demonstrates his political loyalty by attending with 3000 highlanders from Lochaber and the Isles.

 The army is reported as "all armed in the Highland fashion, with halbershownes (coats of mail), bows and axes." They would also have the usual arms of sword and dirk.
The siege is difficult to bring to a conclusion as the English hold fast in the thick walled caisteal girded by a deep moat, confident there is nothing which can broach it's walls.

JamesII was interested in the development of artillery and encouraged the manufacture of the largest cannon of that time, it was constructed of iron bars welded together and bound with metal rings to form the great barrel of the gun which was loaded through the breech.

This massive cannon was presented to James by Phillippe the Good of Burgundy, and named "Mons Meg."
James called for this 'destructive beast' to be brought to the scene to blast a hole in the castle walls.

Tradition differs as to the actual detail of the happening, but it appears that in the train of cannon in place with "Mons Meg" was also the "Lion" of JamesI.

The scene was one of military pageantry, for James II enjoyed a royal display.
The cannon were loaded and James demanded that he have the pleasure of firing a 'salvo' and invited Huntly and some of the Courtiers to witness the power of this artillery piece.

None envisaged the explosive result.

"Mons Meg" at Edinburgh Caisteal Caisteal – courtesy A.Marr

James II took the ' slow match' and held the smouldering tip to light the quickmatch fuse to the gunpowder charge, there was a hiss of burning fuse, there was a massive explosion and the great cannon disintegrated at the breech.

Metal shrapnel hissed as it cut through the air. When the smoke cleared the king lay bloody and mortally wounded – the Earl of Angus and others lay injured and bleeding, but John of Islay was unhurt.

There has been some discussion over the years as to which of the King's cannon was destroyed at Roxburgh.

This being as it may, it seems the breech could be recast as there are records of a "Mons Meg," a giant muzzle loader capable of hurling a 300 lb stone ball, 18 inches in diameter for 2 miles used by James IV in 1497, which was in use in 1681 when it too burst on firing.

Later cannon were constructed of brass or bronze and then iron cast, these were muzzle loaded so as to remove the danger of detonation through the breech.

The castle was finally captured after negotiation with the occupants who were granted amnesty.

The empty castle was then razed to the ground..

James II –
ref: 'The British Army, a concise history.' Pub.1972, p.22

" The Siege of Roxburgh" a border ballad collected by John Leyden about 1802.

"Roxburgh! How fallen, since first in Gothic pride
Thy frowing battlements the war defied;
Called the bold chief to grace thy blazon'd halls,
And bade the rivers gird thy solid walls.
Fallen are thy towers, and, where the palace stood,
In gloomy grandeur waves your hanging wood;
Crush'd are thy halls, save where the peasant sees
One moss-clad ruin rise between the trees –
The still green trees, whose mournful branches wave
In solemn cadence o'er the hapless brave."

The infant James III was proclaimed King of Scotland.

Thus the wheel of fortune turns once more to bring a few wayward clans back into the fold.
Thenceforward many mainland clans, such as Mackintosh and Cameron, Mackenzie and Matherson, Ross and Munro, acknowledged the authority of the Lord of the Isles.

Twenty-eight years later Scotland was once more without a strong King.
In 1488 after the Battle of Sauchie, James III was injured on being thrown from his horse and taken to the Millers house to recover only to be stabbed by an assassin. The Earls of Huntley and Atholl grasped the opportunity.

John, Lord of the Isles now delegated much of the leadership of the Clan to Alexander of Lochalsh, whose estates were part of the previous holdings of the Earl of Ross.

In 1491 Alexander sent out the 'firey cross' for allied Chiefs to join him in regaining lost territory, much spoil and to put 'Huntley' in his place.

The men of Lochaber were once more to the fore when the Clanranald of Lochaber and the Clanranald of Garmoran answered the call, and when Alexander raised his banner and marched through Badenoch, the Clans Cameron, Chattan and Hugh Rose the younger of Kilravock joined him with intent of putting the lands of Huntley to waste.

This army of rightous rebels marched for Inverness where the castle was stormed and won by Farqubar MacIntosh.
The main body continued into Cromarty to ravish Sir Alexander Urquhart lands.
The booty taken was estimated to be of 600 cows and oxen, 80 horses, 1000 sheep, 200 swine and 500 bolls victual.   ref: HH&GS p. 342-343

The Crown was not impressed by this wanton act lead by Alexander, nephew of John Lord of the Isles, and it set in train decisive plans for the Crown to take action to curtail that mighty dynasty once and for all.
In 1494 the King acted.

Even after the earldom was forfeited to the Scottish crown, clans remained loyal to Macdonald, and this continued after the annexation of the Lordship of the Isles by the Stewart kings of Scots, [James IV], in 1494.

In 1509 James divided the West between Huntley [a Gordon] and Argyll [a Campbell].

This action removed the stabilising strength of the Lord of the Isles and plunged the Highlands and Lochaber into turbulent times.

After the decimation of Macdonald's kingdom, the great Chieftains of the MacDonald royal stock became Chiefs of separate clans.

The other clans chiefs went their own way, feuding amongst themselves over complaints and supposed wrongs oft engineered by Huntley or Argyll.

The Battle of Flodden field in 1513 was but to support 'the auld alliance'with France by causing a diversion to engage some of England's troops from the war in France.

It was ill conceived, Scotland lost with James IV and many of Scotland's gentry slain, and thousands of the army killed.

WESTERN HIGHLANDS – division of lands.

It was in that year that John, the Lord of the Isles, gave over the lands of Ardgour to Hector MacLean with the MacDonalds who worked their land within that district – these are neighbouring lands to Moidart in Lochaber.

Dougall succeeded as VI Clanranald but inter family/clan power feuding surfaced with his assassination in 1520.

Allan MacRory married a second time to Isabella daughter of Thomas, Lord Fraser of Lovat. They had a son Ranald/Ronald and resided in the district of Beauly at the top of the Great Glen. By 1498 his son Ranald Bane had taken on the duties of Chief of Clanranald.

Ranald Gallda the youngest son of Allan MacRory, spent most of his life in Fraser country around Beauly under the favour of the family of Lovat. Thus the addition of 'Gallda' meaning 'Stranger.'
One needed powerful patrons in those boisterous times and in 1540 the old adversaries of Clan Donald, Fraser of Lovat and Gordon of Huntley obtained for Ranald Gallda a Crown Charter for land in Moidart and Arisaig whilst John of Moidart was in prison.

At the start of 1541, as the direct descendent he was ensconced in Caisteal Tioram as Chief of ClanRanald, but he quickly came into disfavour with his clansfolk from his mean attitude in his supply of poor provisions and lack of generosity. He provided fowl at feasts in place of meat and reduced other items of the menu as traditionally expected of the host.

The battle of Solway Marsh of 1542 was a sorry affair from the start, as it resulted from Henry VIII's breakaway from the Roman Catholic Church and in JamesV of Scotland refusing Henry's invitation to do likewise.

JamesV died shortly after at thirty years of age, leaving Scotland with an infant heir to the throne in Mary Queen of Scots and Scotland in the hands of Regents once again.

John Moidartach, (of Moidart), was released from imprisonment after 1542 and immediately raised an army of loyal clansfolk and attacked Casteal Tioram to unseat Ranald Gallda, the usurper.

There was more relief than resistance from the permanent staff of the fortress and the unpopular Ranald Gallda was forced to flee under the protection of Lord Fraser of Lovat and his cohort.

John gathered his clansmen and pursued the Frasers and Ranald Gallda and caught up with them.
Shouting their slogan and throwing off their plaids to fight in their shirts for greater freedom of movement, they immediately joined in a ferocious battle - there was no lack of courage on either side, swords slashed and blood stained dirks stabbed, an axe swung with fatal effect, the carnage was terrible.
It is said only twelve men were left standing on each side.

A reassuring comment was made: "fortunately most woman of the clans were with child."

Ranald Gallda fought bravely and well, but along with the leaders of the House of Lovat he was killed on the field in this Battle of Blar Leine (Battle of the Shirts) in 1544.
He and Fraser Chieftains were later buried at Beauly Priory.

John of Moidart returned to Caisteal Tioram and continued to lead his clan and to maintain their independence in spite of efforts by the MacKenzies, who strove to discredit him with complaints of unlawful acts to the new Queen, Mary of Guise.

The Queen tried to entice John out of his territory, but having been betrayed by her once, he mistrusted her and with the clan supporting him as chief, no one could overcome them.

1545 and the Battle of the Shirts was to be avenged as a CREACH against the Grants wherein retribution was sought from the previous insult and lack of reconciliation over past years and the recent injury suffered by the Clan in the death on the field of chieftains and clansmen in that battle of 1544 – Urquhart castle was to be attacked by the men of Clan Donald.

The history of this castle grew from 1288 when Alexander II crushed an uprising by the Men of Moray and promoted Sir Thomas Durward to Lord of Urquhart.

The first defensive Dun was attributed to Alan Durward who had this erected on high ground with Loch Ness as a natural defence

augmented by cutting a ditch through rock on the mainland. This afforded a view along the Loch and to any approach from the glen.

The Castle reverted to the crown in 1275 when the family line ended and John Comyn was the recipient of the King's favour of the estate.

Urquhart castle continued its chequered history with the invasion by Edward I and the capture of the Castle in 1296 only to be regained on the Scottish victory over the English at the Battle of Stirling Bridge in 1297.
Politics are a fickle master or rather followers of Politics are fickle and arrivous for in 1303 we find Sir Alexander Comyn fighting for king Edward I and being rewarded with the castle Urquhart.

The machanations enjoyed by Edward I over the power of Scotland between the families of Bruce and Comyn culminated with The Bruce winning the throne of Scotland defeating the English and banishing the family of Comyn.

Castle Urquhart was again held by the crown but in an unruly period where Clans fought for their rights and Castle Urquhart came within this sphere of Clan Donald's interest who raided whenever an opportunity arose.

In 1479 the King brought in Sir Duncan Grant to try to establish some stability to the area.
He, and his grandson, John, had some success and as a reward the Lordship of Urquhart was granted to them in 1509.
Part of the King's charter stipulated that they repair the castle and build a tower.
However they were still not at peace with the MacDonalds and construction at the castle had to wait until after the last MacDonald raid in 1545.

In 1545 the Macdonalds declared a 'creash' against the Grants of Urquhart Castle. A Macdonald led force stormed Urquhart to totally overcome the defenders to take control of the casteal and surrounds.

This was the catistrophic finale for the Grants initiated from their joining with the Frasers at the Blar na Le`i`ne (the battle of the shirts) and from the years of frustraion on the part of Clan Donald from never having held the Castle very long in 'right of conquest' being forced to relinquish it each time by Royal command.

Now came the last and complete action of the traditional creash.

Over a short period they stripped the castle of its fittings and valued contents and those of the surrounding dwellings in Glen Urquhart.

The requisioned horse drawn wagons were loaded with:-

12 feather beds with all bed linen, bolsters and blankets.

Kitchen ware of 5 pots, 6 pans,2 brewing vats, 1 basin and 6 roasting spits.

Furnishings of doors with locks; tables; chairs; benches; beds and iron gates.

Grain of: 1,700 sacks of oats and 750 sacks of barley.

Loch transport of 3 great boats.

Poultry and liveshock of: 64 gese; 122 pigs; 2,204 goats; 3,377 sheep; 2,355 cattle; 2 oxen and 371 horses.

The tower that the Grant family built is the best preserved part of the castle and a climb to the top offers spectacular views across the Loch. During the 17th century the castle went into decline.

In 1644 it was attacked by a group of Covenanters who robbed the building of most of its contents. The castle had its last lease of life in 1689 when it was garrisoned by three companies of Grant Highlanders. In 1690 they managed to withstand a siege by a Jacobite force of more than twice their number.

When the last soldiers left in 1692 they blew up parts of the castle to prevent any further use.

The Queen tried to entice John out of his territory, but having been betrayed by her once, he mistrusted her and with the clan supporting him as chief, no one could overcome them.

In 1554 the Queen sent the ambitious Huntly through Lochaber to attack John Moidartach from the mainland and dispatched the covetous Earl of Argyll with a Man o' War to attack Caisteal Tioram from the sea as a strategy to cause Clanranald to divide his forces.

This strategy was listed for failure from the start as the Earl of Huntley experienced 'disturbance within the ranks' and gave up on reaching the 'rough bounds' when his cavalry found the country unsuitable for 'the charge.'

The conscripted soldiers from the Lowlands started to show their fear

of meeting the waiting Highland warriors of Clanranald.
Huntley turned back to face the anger of the Queen for his failure.[14]

The Earl of Argyll anchored to the east of Tioram and had the French troops provided by the Queen set up a battery near the Dolin Cliffs to the south of the caisteal.
Argyll gave the order to "open fire."
With a roar of thunder the defenders on the ramparts saw flame and smoke belch from the cannon on the ship and from the cannon near the Dolin cliffs, but the first shots fell short.

The cannon fire continued with some better directed shots striking the wall of the caisteal.
Clanranald defenders replied with musket fire and possibly some light cannon fire, as 'The Clan Donald' volume II records, "the castle was well fortified."

1554 - Argyll bombards Tioram from a Man-o-war and a cannon below the Dolin cliffs, *by M. McDonald.*

The thick curtain walls of Tioram withstood the crash of direct cannon balls smashing into the stone and the Highlanders of Clan Ranald remained courageous under the continued bombardment from the Man-o-war and the battery on the shore.
Argyll called on them to parley but the Highlanders would not surrender, undoubtedly replying with shouts of derision from the castle ramparts, supported by unkind gestures.
The news of the attack reached John who was waiting for the Earl of

---

14 Reference The Clan Donald, vol.II, p. 280-282

Huntley's forces to appear in northeast Moidart.
John of Moidart quickly returned and took the shore battery.

Argyll gave up and sailed[15] back to Edinburgh to face the wrath of Queen Mary for his failure to contain John of Moidart and to take the castle.
MaryI Queen of Scots, or 'Bloody Mary', or 'Mary of Guise' depending on your nationalism, politics or religion, re-introduced Roman Catholicism to England with her husband PhillipII of Spain.
MaryI was executed in 1558 and ElizabethI succeeded as Queen.

Mary Queen of Scots, from "The Art Journal"
of London: J.S.Virtue & Co. Limtd. 1889, p.16.

Phillip and the grandees of Spain viewed ElizabethI of Scotland and England as a heritic and illegitimate Sovereign and with the blessing of Pope Sixtus V declared a Crusade to free England of heresy.

THE SPANISH ARMADA.
Phillip used heavy taxes over a number of years to raise an Armada to invade England.

The Armada sailed for England under the command of Don Alonso Per`ez de Guzma`n, Duke of Medina Sidonia - the majestic Galleons sailing in 'line astern' formation for England, protecting the large Merchant vessels laden with marines, soldiers, weapons and

---

15 James IV Scotland established shipyards in Scotland to build the 1st warships in Britain – the 'Margaret' of 1 cannon and 6 smaller Falcons of 5 to 600 tons was launched in June 1506 and in 1511 the 'Great Michael' of 1000 tons armed with 12 bronze cannons each side and 3 massive Basilisks'.
Henry VIII launched his 'Mary Rose' in 1509 and his 'Great Harry' in 1512 to counter Scotland's 'Great Michael.'
This shows that James IV of Scotland was in fact the "father" of the Navy in the British Isles.

equipment of war.

The heavily armed Galleons carried the necessary 'bullion' to support such an enterprise and to pay the troops.

On reaching the approach to English waters the Armada redeployed to combat formation with the larger Galleons in tight formation at the head of a massive crescent of hundreds of ships, the wings in the direction of the approaching English fleet.

What a magnificent sight when viewed from the heights of Dover, the 1000 ton Spanish ships of the line, proud coats of arms on the mainsails.

The sun sparkling off the gold embossed fore and stern castles commanding the scene. Colourful pennons floating from masthead and bright banners from the stern. They sailed on, ready to do battle.

The English fleet under the Lord High Admiral Charles Howard, Earl of Nottingham, had been waiting for days and at last they had their chance but against a massive opposition.

The battle was opened with the declaration of one cannon shot, and the English man-o-wars sailed into the fray in line astern before engaging with their bow chaser cannon, then tacking to blast a broadside into the enemy hulls as they passed.

The sea battle was ferocious, thunderous broadsides from the "74s" of the English Fleet roared and cannon balls smashed into the Spanish hulls and into gun ports leaving a mutilated, bloody trail. The return fire from the Galleons blasting along the English decks, smashing down men and splintering masts. Gunsmoke obscured the scene and the roar of cannon numbed the senses.

Ships of both nations suffered extensive damage, some on fire, others limping away.

The sea battle went back and forth for days with neither side gaining a major victory. All were low on cannon balls and powder, as well as victuals for the crews. Then a sudden change in wind direction alerted there was bad weather to follow.

Angry seas smashed across the decks and into any open gun port, storm winds shrieked through the rigging ripping sails, creating havic in the steerage for all ships.

The Spanish Captains took evasive action and set course to escape around the coast of Scotland where some were taken off track by the Gulf stream currents to be wrecked along the unknown coast.

One such Galleon was the ' Florida' which sank in Tobermory Bay, Isle of Mull in 1588.

Years later much gold bullion was salvaged from the sunken hull.
Thus, even in death Mary Stuart still influenced the politics of Scotland and England.

These international "goings on" interferred little with the activities of Clan Ranald in Lochaber and their connections with Inverness.
The Clan Ranald still carried on business as usual in the north at the end of the Great Glen as recorded in the 'The Clan Donald' volumes:-
"on the 3rd. of July 1556, Donald McConquhe Cheyr, a Clanranald, with Johne Mc Inteyr,[McIntyres were pipers for the Macdonald Chiefs], had their horses taken from them in the town of Inverness."

Allan MacRanald was designated 'of Easter Leys' as his property was near Inverness, and he also received a gift of the non entry duties of Moydart and Arisaig in 1562.
In the same year he married Margaret the daughter of Hugh, Lord Fraser of Lovat. They had three sons recorded and others referred to: John, Angus, Alex', and others.
This left Angus to succeed his father Allan and he was recorded as Angus MacRanald of Moidart. He was now the recognised heir of Ranald Gallda.

There was at least one more son, for in 1610 John MacAllan MacRanald, a descendent of Ranald Gallda, came to the notice of the Privy Council for continuing the feud with Donald XI of Clanranald in support of his brother Angus MacRanald.
It is obvious that John MacAllan was young, tempestuous and 'active' in many respects.
He is described in the colourful language of the Privy Council as, "murderer, common thief and masterful oppressor," and the Chiefs were asked to apprehend him.
From this we can interpret that John MacAllan MacRanald was: *'young, a good horseman, a skilled swordsman and intelligent; he also had friends.'*   :TCD. v II, p.313.

Oh what a turbulent time was enjoyed by the warriors of Clans bordering the Atlantic in the early 1600s. Clanranald and MacIain of Ardnamurchan were having a great time with the passing ships in the island seas, which their unfriends called piracy, but which the crown ignored, as well as having a wee spat between themselves in the quiet times.

The Chiefs enjoyed, (one might opine), an opulent lifestyle which the Government of the day made moves to control in 1617.

The Bard Neil Mor MacVuirich sang of the festivities at Dunvegan Castle which lasted for six days of feasting, drinking and entertainment of Harp and dancing. He remarks that there were numerous drunken guests.

Donald Gorm Og of Duntulm Castle entertained on the grand scale, the indoor amusements were of draughts, cards, dice and other fancies to the tune of the Harp plus a Piper for dancing, all supported with the supply of food and service by the local tenants.
In the outer court were wrestling and football. On good days there were Hunting and Hawking activities.   ref: TCD.vol III p. 118-121

The Chiefs Officers of the Household held hereditary positions, eg: the Marisahall Tighe and the Cup Bearer, the Bard a MacVurich, the Harper, the Piper being a MacIntyre or MacArthur. There were also positions of Physician, a MacBeth or Beaton, and the Armourer, a Smith, all of whom had a free cottage, ie: Croit-a-Chlarsair, the Harper's Croft.

During the reign of CharlesI civil commotions broke out which shook the kingdom with great violence.

The Scots were courted by king and parliament alike, but one man would rise to the occasion to lead the charge for the King, it was the Marquis of Montrose.

The Marquis of Montrose.
A history of the Scottish Highlands, Highland Clans & Highland Regiments.

MONTROSE and the ROYALIST cause.

Their chance for exerting their manly prowess came when the forces of Alastair MacColla, [Alexander Macdonald, son of Coll], advanced to join with Montrose for the royalist cause.

Alastair's earliest experience with the sombre Argyll was in 1639 when Argyll drove all MacDonalds who refused to join the Covenanter's army, out of Colonsay and took Alastair's father and two elder brothers captive. Alastair MacColla was away at the time and stayed with Stewart relatives in Ireland and Macdonalds in Antrim.

The auld enemy, the Marquis of Argyll for the Parliamentary forces had besieged Mingarry Castle in Ardnamurchan in Lochaber.

Alastair sent men with the 'fiery cross,' (two charred pieces of wood, daubed with goat blood), racing from glen to glen, from isle to isle, calling the clanfolk to gather.
John Moydartach, (John of Moidart), raised an army from the men of Uist, Eigg, Moidart and Arisaig, and marched to Mingarry.
They were well armed with guns, bows, swords, targes and fearsome large bladed Lochaber axes.
They forced Argyll to retreat to Inveraray Castle where John held the position until Colonel James Macdonald arrived with men and stores to relieve the garrison.

By their very loyal nature the Highlanders stood for the Royal government so when Montrose brought his small contingent into the highlands in 1644 he quickly gained support from the populace.
With each success swelling his ranks he entered Dumfries and declared the district for the King by raising the royal standard.

The men of Lochaber marched to join with Montrose at Blair Atholl.
They moved out in the winter of 1644 in three divisions under the respective leaderships of, Montrose, Alastair MacColla and one under John Moydartach.

The armies 'take' from the farms and towns of Lochaber: "Some hae meat an' canna eat."

They warred through the districts of Appin and Loch Tay on the way to Inveraray Castle and Argyll where both the Covenanters and Royalists sustained their troops by looting the farms for provisions.

Life was hard and one needed an inaccessable hide for family and stock when the armies moved and raided through the land.

On hearing of the advance of the Royalist forces, Argyll abandoned his clansfolk and fled in a herring skiff along Loch Fyne.

The people of Argyll did not give any resistance to the advancing army.

The army replenished its food-stocks, [from Argyll's herds], and moved to Kilchuimen [Fort Augustus], in January.

Gilleasbuig Gruamach, [Argyll], had meanwhile called for reinforcements from Auchinbreck, a Campbell relative, who was fighting with the Parliamentary army in Ireland. On the arrival of Auchinbeck, Argyll marched into Lochaber with 3000 men, putting to waste Glenroy and the Braes. The army made camp at Inverlochy, where the dour Marquis felt secure with his Parliamentary army, as the passes were heavy with snow.

Now we relate *one of the finest moments in the history of the folk of the Highland Clans – the march to Inverlochy.*

On being informed of the devastation of burning and killing wrought by Argyll through Lochaber, the three commanders of the Royalist forces, Montrose, Alastair Macdonald and Clanranald were so incensed that they decided to attack him.

Montrose decided on a bold tactic.

The plan was so audacious that it would take Argyll totally by surprise and thereby overcome the disadvantage of his superior numbers. It also demonstrated the high esteem in which Montrose held the Highlanders.

His tactic was to move the Highland army, at night, undetected by Campbell supporters and Argyll's scouts.

Montrose proposed a forced march in full battle gear and weapons, off the main route, through the snow, at night, over precipitous mountains, along deer tracks known only to local hunters. His confidence was in the fortitude and ability of the highland warriors. They then embarked on a feat of endurance unsurpassed since.

This is the recorded epic:-

"not by the wonted beaten path along the waterway, but by ways unknown to strangers and untraversed save by wolf and deer; along the rugged basin of the Tarff, down into Glenroy and past the Spean;

across the untrodden snow of that wild mountain land marched the army of Montrose, until at last from the brow of Ben Nevis (range) they saw reposing in the silver moonlight the frowning towers of Inverlochy." ref: The Clan Donald vol.II,p.332

Thus the bard, Iain Lom Macdonald[16], recorded this epic march of thousands of armed men, through 50 kilometres of the winter snow (as the raven flies) - in one night and one day.

Argyll was astounded when informed that the Royalist host had been sighted in the afternoon, and he hastily ordered his commanders to ready their 3000 troops for battle.
The 'heroic' Marquis of Argyll then retired to his barge, [called "Dubh Luideach" by the Macdonalds], anchored on the loch for victory or flight.

He was accompanied by Sir John Wauchope, Sir William Pollock, and Mr. Mungo Law, who had come to witness and report on the encounters against Montrose.

At dawn on Sunday 2nd February 1645, Candlemas day, Montrose mustered the troops for battle.
On his right was Alastair Macdonald leading his men and Lt.Col. O'Kain with his Irish regiment. On the left flank was Ranald Og Macdonald of Dunnyveg.

The centre was under the command of Montrose with the men of Athole, supported by the Macdonald Lochaber contingents, who were lead by John Moydartach, Angus of Glengarry, Donald Glas of Keppoch and other Highland Chiefs.
Col. James Macdonald brought up the rear with a regiment of Irish levies.

The Parliamentary army was drawn up in similar order. The wings of Lowland troops and the centre of regiments of Clan Campbell, and the brave Auchinbreck to the fore.

---

16 Iain Lom the celebrated Lochaber bard and politician, died about 1709 or 1710. He was commonly called " Iain Lom," or Hare John, on account of his never having had any hair upon his face, or from his acuteness and severity when occasion demanded freedom of speech. ref: Rev. A. MacLean Sinclair, of Prince Edward Island, who published an excellent collection of his poems and songs in 1895.

Montrose and the Lochaber host were at a slight disadvantage in numbers against the troops of Argyll and being fatigued from the forced march. But they had rested 'at arms' through the night and their morale was high from their remarkable achievement and the belief in their cause, whereas the troops under Argyll were aware of his choice of a safe position on the loch and his wont to leave the field whenever adversity struck.

Montrose, with troops in line of battle advanced at sunrise.
The left wing engaged the Parliamentary right followed by a fierce charge by Montrose's right into Argyll's left and centre.
The men of Lochaber had suffered under the machinations of Argyll for too long and wished to end his influence.

The Campbells in the Centre were swept away by the ferocity of the attack by the clansmen of Garmoran and the North Isles.
The gallant Sir Donald Campbell of Auchinbreck fell under the sword of Alastair in the heat of the battle.

The day was won, the Irish musketeers under O'Kain and Alastair Macdonald captured the standard of the Parliamentary army. Half the number of the Parliamentary army lay dead in the snow.
ref:TCD & HSH&HR
 Montrose had crushed the Argyle Campbells, who had taken up the sword on behalf of Cromwell at Inverlochy.

The strategy of the forced march over rough country covered in snow by the troops of Montrose and the men of the Clans Donald, stands as one of the most awe inspiring feats of endurance and ability attained by any troops.
Argyll was last seen with his observers fleeing the scene, sailing off into the distance down Loch Lochy.

The ruins of Inverlochy Castle in the 21st century.

Before the battle commenced, Mac-Cholla said to John Lom, " Make ready, John, you shall march along with me to the fight."
" If I go along with you to-day and fall in battle, who will sing thy praises to-morrow ? Go thou, Alasdair, and exert thyself as usual, and I shall sing thy feats, and celebrate thy prowess in martial strains."

The poet accordingly had a full view of the contest from his high vantage point.
Eoin Lo`m MacDonald had strong antagonisn to anything Clan Campbell which flames through in another poem on Inverlochy:

" Campbell's welcome at Inverlochy."
Warm your welcome was at Lochy,
Blows and buffets thickening round you,
And Clan Donald's groove`d claymore,
Flashing terror to confound you.

By the field of Goirtean-oar,
Who may take his summer ramble,
He will find it fair and fattened
By the best blood of the Campbell."

NOTE: The claymore and Halberd was equipment of Highlanders called to Battle.[17] The Halberd was a combination of spear, Lochaber axe with a hook to pull down a shield or armour, some with a spike to pierce a helmet.

Iain Lom Mac-Dhomhnaill was the first Jacobite poet, and for his historic political bardic accounts Charles II provided him with a small pension, thus recognising him as a poet Laureate.
After the Battle, Montrose and the Royalist army retired to Castle Grant where they regrouped for two months.

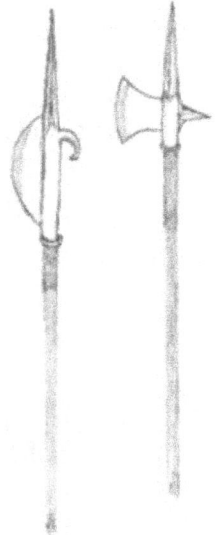

---

17 . the following provides the information of Acts which designated the fighting equipment a vassal must supply in 1597 when called to battle: "Hacquetbutis, bowis, havirshonis, swerdis, farlochis, and targeis" constituted the equipment which, in 1597, a levy from the shire of Talbert for service against the Border thieves, were instructed, by proclamation, to provide themselves with. Reference page 335 of "History of the Highlands and Gaelic Scotland" by Dugald Mitchell, MD. 1900

The clans regathered on September 1st, at Tippermuir, Montrose defeated the Covenanters, and again on the 12th at the Bridge of Dee. In rapid succession other victories were won at Auldearn, Alford and Kilsyth. All Scotland now appeared to be recovered for Charles, but the fruit of all these victories was lost by the defeat at Philiphaugh, September 13th, 1645.

KING JAMES VII of SCOTLAND and JAMES II of ENGLAND.

Charles II ruled Scotland and England after the English Civil war until his death in 1685 and as there were no heirs to succeed him, his brother James who was next in line was crowned King James VII of Scotland and James II of England.

Within the brief space of three years through his stance on Catholicism and open support of the French, James succeeded in fanning the revolutionary elements both in England and Scotland into a flame which may well have been his intent.

The English Parliament demanded James abdicate and on his sudden departure to Europe after the landing of William of Orange, they claimed he had deserted England and they invited William of Orange and his wife Mary, (James II's daughter), to take the throne.

In 1689 Parliament duly proclaimed them William III and Mary II as joint monarchs of England and Scotland. This was supported by the Parliament of Scotland.

The temper of general feeling became grave when the Highlanders who strongly protested by opposing the acceptance of William of Orange were labelled "the Jacobites" as of those supporting "Jacobus" the Latin for James.

In Scotland the supporters of the Stuart cause were mainly Highlanders and those for William and Mary were mainly Lowlanders, but these party lines were not clear cut as there was also a number of divisionary factors:

- the lowlanders were mostly Protestant and the Highlands had areas of Catholicism resulting in religious division.
- the Lowland people were more aligned with England than with Scotland.

- the Highlanders spoke Gaelic as their first language and the lowlanders English.
- English propaganda claiming that the Highlanders were uneducated and barbarians encouraged support to enforce political change.

All of these differences impinged on the membership of these opposing factions, so the edges were blurred and friend and foe might well come from the same village.

The actual rallying of supporters for the Stuart cause to regain the joint throne of England and Scotland was led by John Graham Claverhouse, Viscount Dundee.
In his role of Lieutenant general for James II, "Dundee" had seen Army service in Holland and France and had been given command of a troop of Dragoons on his return to Scotland.

This was to ensure that the populace followed the ordained religion of the Government, so this was an easy transition for John Graham Claverhouse with his ready made "troops" under his command as the nucleus of a rebel force.

He was aided in his cause by Sir Ewen Cameron of Locheil.

The scene is now set for actual confrontation between the Government troops and those of the rebel force who were for James and the Stuart cause.

The Government directed General Hugh Mackay of Scourie to take command of three Regiments of Foot and one Cavalry regiment to contain and capture the rebel force.

DUNDEE AND KILLIECRANKIE 1689.

'Dundee' learned that General Mackay of Scourie was marching with his army of around 4000 men to ambush the Jacobite troops so he commanded the Jacobites to make a forced march for Dalwhinnie, where he called on all supporters of King James to muster at Lochaber on May 18.

The situation escalated with both forces gaining recruits. Two further Government Foot battalions now joined up with General Mackay but on the 9th of June they encountered 300 MacLean highlanders marching to join the Jacobites and in the ensuing skirmish the Government troops were put to flight with MacLean gaining weapons and gear.

The political situation deteriorated over the next weeks with Dundee refusing the offer of a truce and the Government setting a reward of £20,000 for his capture.

John Graham of Claverhouse had gained popularity in leadership and he was now widely known as "Bonnie Dundee." He was now in control of Blair Caisteal from Stewart of Ballechin with highlanders from the Clans across Lochaber and further.
Among them were Sir Donald Macdonald of Sleat, Clanranald with 500 men, Macdonald of Aird and Valley, Alexander 11th Glengarry with 300, and MacIan with 100 Glencoe men in company with the Stewarts, Grant of Urquhart, Sir Ewen Camerons of Locheil, MacLeans, Frasers and a well known MacGregor named 'Rob Roy.'
His Standard bearer was James Phillip of Almericlose.   ref: HH&GS, p.532.

On gaining knowledge of the movement of the Government troops, now past Dunkeld and fast approaching with the intent to force a confrontation with the Rebels, Dundee called a council of war to discuss tactics.
One opinion was to wait until more of the Clans arrived but Dundee was of the opinion that the troops were well prepared and impatient for action.
They decided to 'make ready' for battle.

The Pass of Killiecrankie was an undulating mountain track winding for some two miles.

This narrow, wooded Pass was a contrasting scene of beauty and foreboding, the rocky gorge stark and eroded over the centuries by the tumbling rushing waters of river Garry with granite crags beetling overhead.

This, bordered by gnarled trees and flowering undergrowth, was a fitting entrance for Bonnie Dundee and the Highlanders to meet their destiny against the Government Troops on 29th July 1689.

The Jacobite army of 2400 men arrived and took up positions on the high ground.

General Hugh Mackay of Scourie lead the Government army of 4000 to 5000 out of Dunkeld at first light and reached the Pass of Killiecrankie before noon and continued "up the slope full of trees and shrubs" to establish his headquarters at Urrard House.

On his scouts alerting him to the Jacobite troops on the high ground and evaluating their position, Mackay issued the order for a 'Quart de Conversion' for his troops to make a quarter turn right and to march up the slope to take up battle positions facing uphill, on the roughly level terrace.

This was late July in Scotlands summer so the midges would have been in swarms around the Government troops in the open ground.

The Battle of Killiecrankie dispositions of the army under General Hugh Mackay is as follows:-

On their left was the party of 'shot' under Lt. Col. Landers, next the Regiments of Balfour, Ramsey and Kenmore. The Cavalry held the centre position.

On the right of the line was Leven's, Mackay's own and Hasting's regiment.

These troops were lined 3 deep across the 1,500 m battle line instead of the usual 6 deep formation.

Mackay decided that he had the superior force and held his position. The sun was at their backs.

The Jacobite force was higher at the 200m contour and Lieutenant General Viscount Dundee aware of the bonds within a Clan set his 2,400 troops in battle positions of their respective Clans:-

On his right the Macleods, the Irish under Col. Cannon, then Clan Ranald, Glengarry and the men of Glencoe flanked by Grants of Glenmoriston, while the centre was held by 40 mounted men under Walter of Craighie.

To the left stood Ewen Cameron of Locheil, MacLeans, MacDonalds of Kintyre, McNeils and Macdonalds of Sleat.   HH&GS p.534

With his lesser numbers Dundee deployed his Highlanders across a narrower front.

It was now late afternoon and the sun was in their eyes, so Dundee ordered his troops to hold their positions with sporadic sniper fire until the sun set.

There was much shouting of insults and exchange of lewd gestures as was the way of opposing troops in those days.

Our reader should be reminded of the practice of 'a Foot in each camp'.

Landed families indulged in the political exercise of having a member of the family on each opposing side to ensure their property remained with one of the winning 'family' as we have recorded in Stewart's Sketches, vol.1.p.63.

From those, we are privy to the conversation between General Hugh Mackay and the second son of Locheil who held a commission in his own regiment of Scots Fusileers as they viewed the dispositions of the Jacobite force:-

Mackay," Here is your father with his wild savages, how would you like to be with him?"

"It signifies little", answered the son of the chief "what I would like, but I recommend to you to be prepared, or perhaps my father and his wild savages may be nearer to you before night, than you would like."
HSH&HR, v.I,p.370

Mackay attempted to provoke the Jasobite force to engage, (because Dundee had the greater opportunity to retire than Mackay, if he so wished), by giving the order to open fire with their 3 leather field pieces which were light cannons reinforced with rope and encased in leather, but after some firing these disintegrated.   ref: HSH&HR, v. 1,p.371

The sun set after 7pm and Dundee ordered his troops to advance, the highlanders devested themselves of plaids and anything which impeded free movement.   Locheil discarded his shoes and ran barefoot.

They moved down the slope crouched behind their targes as protection from spasmodic musket fire.

Musket fire roared out from both battle lines announcing the start of the battle – a haze of gunpowder smoke filled the air.

The men of Scotland fired their muskets then disgarded[18] them.

---

18 the attackers could not stop to reload after the first firing, so they dropped their muskets, then

With fierce shouts of "dhaindheoin cotheir-aidh e", from Clanranald and "Caisteal Dowie" from Frasers, the Highlanders charged down the slope.

Targes with spiked boss on forearm and claymore at the ready, some with two-handed sword above their heads ready for that dismembering downwards slash.

Those with the terrible Lochaber axe of massive blade and spear point searching to carve a victim.

Only one section of the Government troops had time to fire three volleys before the Highlanders were upon them and some were still fumbling to plug their bayonets onto their gun barrel.

Due to the terrain the Highlanders veered to the right which gave Mackay and Levens men the opening to fire into their flank causing serious casualties.

This did not deter the Highland charge which penetrated the Government line stabbing with dirk, slicing bodies with the broadsword, hacking with the Lochaber axe, taking casualties themselves but scattering the Government troops.

General Mackay later relates that he galloped up the hill, "in all cases to disengage himself out of the crowd of Highlanders which came down just upon the place where he was calling to the Officers of the horse to follow him, spurre'd his horse through the enemy but none of his cavalry were with him!"

One can see the horse lunging and snorting with effort as MacKay spurred it up the slope to get away.

The centre was breeched and the Highlanders were amongst the government troops cutting a bloody path forward until they gave way and ran.[19]

Members of the victorious Jacobite army followed the fleeing English down to the baggage train, where they took possession of equipment and prizes.

---

charged the enemy – if they lived they returned to recover their musket.

19 ref: History of the Highlands and Gaelic Scotland, p. 530-537 give the account of "Killiecrankie.".

(2) Killiecrankie, the events of the battle were confirmed by a team from "Inventory of Historic Battlefields" who carried out a programme of metal detecting, geophyical survey, excavation and a topgraphical survey in 2003.   These accounts are also confirmed in HSH&HR, v.1,p.370 →

The rout was so complete that a fleeing English soldier, running for his life, leapt from a rocky prominence across a narrow cutting of the river Gary to make his escape.
This feat has been recorded by naming that point as "Soldier's Leap."

Mackay suffered heavy losses but was able to muster some of his troops to make a retreat back to Stirling.

The Jacobite army lost over 600 men including 'Dundee' and Sir Donald of Sleat, from an army of just over 2400. Any Highlanders answering the call to duty were required to present themselves with some protective dress for battle and the essential arms of targe, sword or axe and the personal dirk.

The Government lost 2000 troops out of a superior force of 5000.

The term 'redshanks' is sometimes encountered when researching .
This was used to refer to highlanders who wore cuarans,(footwear), made from deer skin with the red hair outwards, thus 'redshanks', which distinguished them from their lowland countrymen.

The Bard Aytoun describes the Highland charge:
        "The Charge at Killiecranchie"

>   " Like a tempest down the ridges
>   Swept a hurricane of steel,
>   Rose the slogan of Macdonald.
>   Flashed the broadsword of Locheil!
>   Vainly spread the withering volley
>   'Mongst the foremost of our band –
>   On we poured until we met them,
>   Foot to foot and hand to hand.
>   ~~~   ~~~   ~~~
>   Horse and man went down before us –
>   Living foe there tarried none
>   On the field of Killiecrankie,
>   When the stubborn fight was done."

ref: HH&GS p.535 .

Viscount Dundee was fatally wounded early in the battle when he stood in the stirrups, sword held high, urging the Cavalry charge forward and was hit by a bullet.

Banner of Alexander XI Glengarry carried at Killiecrankie.

Others such as Alexander Macdonell took command, leading their warriors from the front and ensured victory.
In relation to the disposition of the Jacobite army:

From "A History of the Scottish Highlands, Highland Clans and Highland Regiments," vol. I&II, p.370[20], wherein Keltie provides a detailed account:
"on the right he placed Sir John Maclean in two battalions. On the left he posted the regiment of Sir Donald Macdonald and Sir George Barclay, and a battalion under Alexander Maclean.
In the centre were placed four battalions consisting of the Camerons, the Macdonells of Glengarry and Clanranald, and the Irish regiment, with a troop of horse under the command of Sir William Wallace."

The battles and skirmishes fought by the Highlanders for the Jacobite cause with the intent to restore the Stuarts to the throne, continued for the next 60 years.

The painting by Harrington Mann of "The attack of the Macdonalds at Killiecrankie" from which our coverpiece is taken, captures the moment in that fierce charge by the Macdonalds into the enemy fire.

---

20 .[HSH&HR] A History of the Scottish Highlands, Highland Clans and Highland Regiments. Keltie, 1885

THE 'BETRAYAL OF TRUST' to the Sons of Iain 0g an Fhraoich.

The massacre of 1692 to "extirpate that set of thieves" had continuing repercussions over the centuries to 2014 as the rightful Chief fights for recognition. We unfold the the story of this Lochaber Clan known to a worldwide audience.

Angus Og of Isla ceded the lands of Glencoe to his natural son John, by the daughter of Dugall Mac Henry, Chief man of Glenco.
Dugall MacHenry claimed ancestry from Henry, the son of the Pict King Nechtan (Eanruig Mor mac Righ Nechtan), who settled in Kinlochleven in 1011.
They resided in Callart over the loch from Glencoe.

The 'Glen' was part of the lands of MacDougall until 1314 when Robert the Bruce came to power and in full control after winning the 'Battle of Bannockburn' whereby those who were for Edward of England forfeited their lands and King Robert granted these to those who supported his cause.

None was more supportive than Angus Og, Lord of the Isles, and in recognition of this, 'The Bruce' confirmed much of his lands and granted more including the lands of Glencoe which were bounded by Loch Leven in the west to Rannoch Moor to the east. Their land included mountainous fastness with secluded clefts ideal for confining cattle from raids.

The Chiefs of Glenco were known as MacIain [son of John] or Iain Abrach, after Lochaber, the region in which Glencoe lay. From the times of 'The Bruce' they had lived their lives by the sword and ignored 'sheepskin' agreements.
Had it not always been so!   Was it not true that they had fought many a skirmish over the years to keep their land and their right to live free ?

The chiefs of Glenco were never 'vassals of the Crown' until a late period of their history; thus whilst others around them complied with the edict of the Crown, the Glenco MacDonalds were able to evade official regulation due to their isolated mountain fastness.
This isolation was to finally prove their undoing, for, with no strong members of the Clan Donald close by to give support, and with powerful and unfriendly Clans as neighbours, it was only a matter of time, [a few centuries], before they were finally overcome.

The lands of Glencoe became part of the territories of John of Isla, Lord of the Isles, and passed from him to Clans of Argyll and of Appin who held them on behalf of the King of Scotland.

When the land passed from Donald to Stewart and to Campbell, the MacIains of Glenco held their land by some form of tenantry or vassalage to that chief, but there are no records available to define any type of agreement or arrangement.   TCD.

The independence and isolation of this clan, the destruction by burning of their homes and contents in 1692, and the later loss of the Charter chest taken from Invergarry Castle, left no records of their lives and it is only when their activities effect others that we can trace people and events.

This lack of their own written record has caused a most one-sided account of this clan, for even though they had their own seanachaidh to keep their history, the clanian of Glenco are mainly recorded by the written accounts of others. This is mostly by unfriends or long term feuding neighbours, thirsty for Glencoe land.

Mention of the clanian of Glenco:- In 1501 the Glenco men mounted a raid on Inchconnell [a Campbell stronghold] where Donald Dubh, heir to the Lordship of the Isles and kidnapped as a child by the Earl of Argyll himself, was imprisoned.

They traversed Campbell territory, broke into the prison, freed Donald and escaped back to their Glencoe lands; a bold engagement, which demonstrated their loyalty to Clan Donald and their outstanding courage and military strategy.

Documents record that in 1563 John Og Mac Ani Abryeht was in lawful occupation of Glencoe land, under Colin Campbell of Glenwrquhay.[Glenorchy]; he had 7 sons, John Og(2); John Dubh; Alex'; Archibald; Allan Roy; Ronald and Angus.

1590 - John Og (2), was the 9th. Chief of Glenco.

The MacIains honoured their tenancy agreements, as in the case in 1591:- "From a 'disagreement' between Campbell of Persie and Lord Ogilvie, [Campbell stabbed one of Ogilvie's guests], a feud developed between these clans to the extent that Argyll gathered the men of Glencoe, Keppoch and others, and despatched them to raid and plunder the Ogilvie's."

One had to recoup ones expenses, didn't one!

This was concluded with all the fervour and ferocity common in such forays to avenge hurt pride.

On the complaint from Lord Ogilvie, The Privy Council ruled against Archibald Campbell, Earl of Argyll, and his allies, in particular Allan Roy M'Ianoig, son to the Laird of Glencoe.
So the history of this clan is written through the petitions and complaints made against them.

Notwithstanding the claims made by rival clans, *it is most evident that the small but ancient Clan Donald of Glenco were fiercely independent, loyal to their Chief and*
Clan, lawful and disciplined within their own lands, well educated and adapt in the music and culture of their race.
The unity of this small clan was such that they held tenure of their Glen from the 14th. to the 18th century.

1599 must have been a good year for the Glenco clanian, as there were numerous complaints laid against them :-
(1) Complaints against Archibald Mac Coneill Mac Iain Abrich, and Ronald, Angus, Allan, and John Abrich in Glencoe, one charge being :-
"Allaster MacEan Oig and his men, under John Og MacEan Abrich, reft from David Craig out of his fold of Drumcharrie 'seven great kye' and a bull worth £140." TCD.
(2) In November the Duke of Lennox laid the complaint that Arch' MacConeill, MacIain Abrich, and Ronald, Angus, Allan and John MacIain Albrich of Glenco, raided into Ardincape woods and captured several MacAulas and others, then on to Strone and Auchingarth where they took 32 horses and mares and 24 kye.

Raids were part of the life and customs of those times and demonstrates the stamina, tactics and confidence of that small clan.
1605 - John Abrach, 10th. Chief, son of John Og MacIain.

In 1609 the petitions were against Allaster Iain Oig; and in 1610 against Angus MacIain Duy in Dalness and others; in 1617 to apprehend John Dow MacInnes and others; all for charges of murder of Stewarts.
Again only one side is heard and no final action recorded.

The Glenco men ranged far and wide, and Stewart of Ardvorlich found the need to shoot "a marauding Glencoe man" in about 1600.

The Isle of Munde in Loch Leven.
The burial place of the McDonalds of Glenco was on. 2014

THERE IS A STRANGE QUIET for the next 17 years.

The clanian of Glenco spoke Gaelic as their first language, but a number also spoke English and French and a few spoke Latin.
They grew their own corn and in summer and autumn they hunted for game and fished the rivers and lochs. Live-stock was of black cattle, horses, goats and sheep; the cattle being traded at the lowland fairs. Kippered salmon and skins were traded when the gabbarts from the Clyde brought goods to barter.

The MacDonalds of Glenco were noted for their bards, Raonull na Sgeidhe [Ronald of the Shield], then Aonghus Mac Alasdair Ruaidh, and later, Domhnall Mac Raonull [Donald, the son of Ronald], a grandson of Ronald/Ranald of the Shield.

In mediaeval times the parish of Eilean Munde encompassed Glencoe, adjoining areas of Mamore and Appin, and the Isle of Munde, which preserves the name of an early Celtic saint.   ref:Tombstone Inscriptions on the Burial Isle by Alex'McDonald.

The quiet is broken, and in 1635 the complaints are lodged anew.
A charge is laid against Allaster MacIain Abraich XI of Glenco, known as Alastair Ruadh, - sons, Alex'; Angus [Aonghas Mac Alastair Ruaidh].
In 1640 a party of Keppoch and Glenco MacDonalds were returning from a raid south and they had to pass through Campbell lands.
The tradition was that any raiding party passing through a neighbour's territory should pay 'toll' to that chief, *ie,* a percentage of 'the take.'

Of course these MacDonalds had no intention of paying any 'toll' to any Campbell and were travelling by diverse paths to avoid this.

The Campbells were attending a wedding celebration when the news reached them. They quickly formed an armed party and set out to 'cut off' the MacDonalds and to take their spoils.
The Campbell party met the MacDonalds above Margowan. A fierce skirmish followed with the MacDonalds the victors and 18 cadets of the House of Campbell fallen to the sword, with the loss of 2 MacDonald clan chiefs. TCD.

In the 'unrest' of the 17th century the Glenco MacDonalds, with others of Clan Donald, were for the House of Stewart and were there in the Wars of Montrose and Dundee from 1645 on.
The Glenco champion during these wars was Ranald of the Shield, the son of Allan of Achtriachtan.

In 1650 Alasdair MacDonald became the 12th MacIain by the old Gaelic ceremony in which he stood on top of a pyramid of stones surrounded by his warriors.
He was in his mid-twenties, a red-headed giant of a man, dark eyed with a fierce beak of a nose. He spent much of his youth being educated in France, so his two storied house at Carnoch would have been decorated with hangings of lace and objects of glass and of silver.

In 1655 the Glenco MacDonalds, with the Keppoch MacDonalds, raided through Glenlyon territory taking stock and goods.
Legend has it that as they returned driving the cattle and stock before them, they were delayed. A Campbell dairy-maid had broken the leg of one of the calves they had seized and this lame calf slowed the MacDonalds progress to Rannoch Moor. They were overtaken and the resultant skirmish left dead and wounded on both sides. *[we doubt that a group of raiding MacDonalds would have let a lame calf delay them, it would have been quickly dispatched.]*

Again there is no record of this fierce unit of MacDonalds from 1655 until 1689 when Alexander Macdonald XII of Glenco, as Chief, signed documents at Blair Athole Castle, pledging his support of 50 fighting men to the field.
This was in support of the first rising of the Jacobites in opposition to the ascendancy to the British throne of William of Orange and Mary.

Those loyal to James VII Scotland and II of England were lead by

Graham of Claverhouse, widely acclaimed as "Bonnie Dundee."
     Cameron of Lochiel brought his men.
MacIain of Glenco brought about 100 men to Killiecrankie and fought
alongside the Stewarts of Appin.
As a result, in 1690, both shared the same fate, a ruling from the Privy
Council 'that a force be sent to reduce them to obedience.'
This army of mainly men from the lowlands, Holland and Ireland were
lead by General Hugh Mackay, a highlander himself.
It is oft said that history is written by the Victor, but English accounts
of the Battle of Killiecrankie recorded as 'Memoirs' of the Battle, do
little for the integrity of English historians.

Bannatyne Club: One might come to the opinion that the following
account was a little biased in that Killiecrankie was a victory to the
Jacobites with a rout of General Mackay's army, the stated casualty
figure being exactly the opposite as given in the folowing account
from Major General Mackay at the Bannatyne Club, 1833 on his
experience at Killiecrankie –
*Memoirs of the War Carried on in Scotland and Ireland by Major
General Mackay:*-
"The enemy lost on the field six for our one, the fire to our right
having been continued and brisk, whereby not only Dundee, with
several gentlemen of quality of the countys of Angus and Perth, but
also many of the best gentlemen among the Highlanders, particularly
of the Macdonalds of the Isles and Glengarie were killed, coming
down the hill upon Hastings, the General, and Levin's regiments,
which made the best fire and all the execution."

Note: the confirmed account of the Battle of Killiecrankie on pages
89-90 :- The Jacobite army lost 600 men out of over 2400.
The Government lost 2000 troops out of a superior force of 5000.

In the district of Glencoe there were reports at this time of the
Keppoch and Glenco MacDonalds, returning from raids, despoiling
Glenlyon's property as they passed through.
It is obvious from the records of these numerous raids carried out by
the MacDonalds of Glenco, eg: from Glencoe into Glen Lyon; from
Glencoe down to Inchconnell [Loch Awe]; Glencoe into Strone and
Auchingarth etc., that for those with local knowledge, this 'wild
mountainous country' could be traversed with ease.

A map will show that Rannoch Moor provides access to Glen Coe,
Glen Lyon, Glen Garry and Glen Orchy and so on.

All of these actions and events set the scene for what followed in 1692, in fact the complaints and petitions over the years were the preparations to support the final act.

The Campbells of Argyll had used the MacDonalds of Glenco in their plots and counter-plots against neighbouring clans, *eg* the MacGregors when it suited, just as the MacIains had allowed their involvement when there was gain for them.

What the MacIains [to their final peril] were not concerned about was the political and legal machinations of the Campbells.

In 1692 Campbell of Argyll decided that the time was right for a move to be made against the MacDonalds of Glenco, in fact against all the MacDonald clans in that area, Glengarry, Keppoch and the like.

The Master of Stair initiated a devious plan to 'extirpate that set of thieves' which finally led to the Massacre of Glenco. He was aided and abetted by others in authority.

Glengarry was strong enough with his fortified caisteal to withstand attack and took steps to ensure he and his people were protected.

MacIain may well have been confident in the natural protection of his mountain fastness, but he did not allow for the immoral hypocrisy of politics.

Part of Stair's plan was to use the guise of friendship to gain entry to the Glenco stronghold so as to finally entrap the clanian before they scattered into their inaccessible mountain outposts. So he chose Glenlyon of Clan Campbell, to lead the operation, for he was a drinker, gambler, and poor manager, and by 1690 he was all but destitute.

He was related by marriage to MacIain XII of Glenco, and this was an important part of the overall plan which was used to gain entry and allow a troop of soldiers to be barracked in the mountain fastness.

Some of the Government Troops were highlanders and respected the code of hospitality; these were troubled by the way events were going and that they may be called upon to kill people with whom they had shared food and lodging.

Late in the evening before the massacre, there were some guarded and hinted warnings given to a few MacDonalds, probably to other Clan members visiting in the Glen.

In the early morning of 13th of February, 1692 the soldiers under Glenlyon attacked the sleeping households, killing clan folk as they went.

This was a BETRAYEL OF TRUST after accepting MacDonald hospitality.

They killed the Chief in his bed, they murdered his wife in the snow. As she lay in torn clothing, blood spattered and still, they stole her wedding rings - on and on went the slaughter. Some of their infamous tally amounted to,
* Macdonald of Inneriggan and nine others slain.
* Macdonald of Achtriachtan [principal cadet clan], and eight clanian slain.
* Alasdair of Glenco [Chief] his wife and others of their household slain.
* Old Ranald of the Shield who was struck down and left for dead, struggled to a house for shelter but was burned (with the others) when the house was put to the torch."

Tradition has it, as recorded by Finlay MacLeod, piper to Grant of GlenMoriston, that a party of the Clann Iain Ruaidh, [John the Red], who had property at Glenmoriston was visiting the Chief were given a warning that things were 'amiss.'
On the first sound of the attack, the following was recorded:-
"Oidhche mhuirt bha 'n Gleanna Comhann,
Bha droch gnothach ann,
's iad a thog an t-oighre
's ghabh greim dheth air ball."
"On the night of the massacre that was in Glencoe,
It was a bad business,
It was they who roused the heir
and took charge of him immediately."   ref. Prof. Matheson.

Other Macdonalds *of the family* would have quickly grasped plaid and sword and staying close to the 'heir', escaped along known paths into Glen Etive[21] and to Dalness and set off with the rescuers to their homes in Glenmoriston.

Others too had received subtle warnings which caused them to suspect treachery so they were awake and on watch. On seeing furtive movement of troops, they woke those close by and a large number escaped.

---

21 When the author first visited Scotland, as he passed the entrance of Glen Etive, on a fine sunny day, he had a physic experience, even though he did not know at the time what he was passing nor it's possible significance in relation to the tradition of his line; does this support the connection of Glencoe and Clanranald.?

Achtriachtan's brother and his eldest son, Young Ranald, son of Ranald of the Shield and Alexander II of Dalness, with about 150 souls of the clanian made their escape.

They trudged through snow and struggled over steep icy mountains, through narrow passes of iced rocks known only to the clanian of Glenco, some slipping to fall into into deep drifts.
Some sought succour with Macdonalds of Dalness or with Stewart relations in Appin, others went further into Ardgour, Kilmallie, and to Eigg, and some sought refuge along The Great Glen escaping along Glen Etive.

Old Ewen Macdonald was awakened to the shouts of soldiers breaking into dwellings and to screams of fear.

He woke the family, lifted young Ewan (b. abt. 1690) onto his back and with others escaped to make their way to Invermoriston Glen Urquhart.   ref:W.A. Macdonald, Invermoriston 1973.
They joined other Macdonalds who had settled in and around Glen Urquhart. Allan Clanranald died in 1505 and his wife Isabella married John Mor Grant, 1st.of Glenmoriston, their son Patrick Grant of Glenmoriston was half-brother to Ranald Gallda.

When the military mob had done with the killing, plunder and burning, they took all stock and drove them off, [as was their orders], effectively removing any chance for survivors to find food or shelter.
Alasdair XII of Glenco, and his wife, the daughter of Archibald the 15th.of Keppoch, were both slain, but some leaders and clanfolk escaped.

In a time of crisis the spirit of the Clan comes to the fore.

It shone brightly with the determination and resolution of the Highlanders to overcome their deprivation and the harsh weather, and to win through, as they trudged on and on through the snow.

Whether by a system of communication, or by chance of a passing trading vessel hearing the disastrous news, we know not, but information of the massacre and the plight of this ancient Clan reached far and wide even to the Isles of the Outer Hebrides.
The culture and tradition of the highlander especially relating to the close family bonds between members of Clan Donald and the spirit of blood relationship is so aptly demonstrated in the reaction to the 'news.'

Alastair Ban Mac Iain Vc Uisdein 'to the rescue'.

The Clan Donald history records the rescue in the following two short paragraphs, on page 222, vol.II , so we explain what those succinct paragraphs really mean.

"The sufferings of the Clan reached Monach Isle, west of Uist, and Alexander Macdonald, Tacksman of Heiskir, known as Alastair Ban Mac Iain Vc Uisdein, was moved by the sorrowful tale of his oppressed clansman.
He immediately gathered provisions, filled his 'birlinn' [galley] with meal, and set off, *steering through the stormy seas* to reach Loch Leven, on whose shores he deposited his welcome freight for the relief of the suffering Clanian."   ref: TCD v.II,p.222

It was February in the west of Scotland, coming to the end of the winter, " *the Glen was thick with snow,*" gales were sweeping in from the Atlantic.

Monach Isle lies in the Outer Hebrides, exposed to the raw power of the Atlantic Ocean. In fact, it is on the outer edge to the Outer Hebrides, on the west of North Uist.

On hearing the sad news, Alastair Ban,[fair Alexander], did not hesitate. He immediately called his clansmen to load the galley with bags of meal and spare woollen plaids. The cask of Whisky would have been standard sustenance.

The clansmen launched the galley into the rough seas, the crew rowed strongly to win past the breakers and to gain sea-room.

They shipped the oars and sprang to grasp ropes and the sail cracked full from the gale-force wind as they set out from Monarch Isle.

Alexander steered between North Uist and Benbecula, then below Skye *across the Atlantic Ocean, " the stormy seas ".*

Imagine the open galley in an ocean gale, a boat about the size of the Trans Tasman yachts, but without the deck coverings or hatches and having no navigation aids.
The mast bent from the force of the gale, the sail was so taut that it was solid, the ropes squeaked from the strain, the whole craft creaked and groaned as the boat's timbers worked against the force of the winds.
The deck was awash from the towering seas and the crews' heads just dots amongst the foam.

Alastair Ban was a solid figure on the steering platform, golden locks wet with spray, his face set and eyes fixed into the distance of the *"stormy seas."*

Legs astride, his back braced against the stern post, strong arms and hands gripping the rudder arm under his hunched right shoulder.
His henchman Dugall Ruadh on his right.
They made landfall at the Point of Ardnamurchan on the mainland, then sailed up the Sound of Mull and tacked into Loch Linnhe, at last into more sheltered waters.

The measured lift and dip of the 26 oars set their pace up the loch to Oinch, then into Loch Leven to steer towards the group sheltering about the fisherman's bothy.

The galley was beached on the sands and the provisions delivered to the desperate Clanian, suffering exposure and deprivation.
Alastair had taken the challenge and triumphed.

Yes, " *he set off, steering through the stormy seas.*" ref: TCD v,II,p.222

'Fair Alexander' and his clansmen sailed to the assistance of the MacDonalds of Glenco, to Clan folk under threat of annihilation by the King and by the heads of a vengeful, opposing Clan.
He and his gallant crew well knew that if the enemy came upon them, they too could be killed with the rest, or imprisoned and later executed.

So here is the example of one man, confident in his ability, with a clearness of purpose, overcoming the dangers of the elements, and the possibility of capture and execution, using everything under his control to bring food and aid to members of his Clan –   *"Challenged he triumphed."*

Stair's devious plan has all but succeeded over the centuries, for even today as this book goes to print, the direct line to Mac Iain Glenco is fighting for recognition through Lyon Court as the rightful Chief of Macdonald of Glencoe, as we will show.

THE RAISING OF THE STANDARD- THE ACCESSION OF GEORGE I, in 1714.

This was an unhappy event for Great Britain as discontent soon pervaded the kingdom.

All the King appeared to care about was to secure for himself and his family a high position, which he scarcely knew how to occupy, to fill the pockets of his German attendants and his German mistresses. First to get away as often as possible from his uncongenial islanders whose language he did not understand, and to use the strength of Great Britain to obtain petty advantages for his German principality.

The Clanfolk with other Chiefs petitioned George I on his becoming King, but their address to the Monach was neither read nor recognised and this lack of regard for the Highland Chiefs and Landholders was the direct cause of the rebellion to follow.

At once the new king exhibited violent prejudices against some of the chief men of the nation, and irritated, without a cause, a large part of his subjects.

Some believed it was a favorable opportunity to reinstate the Stuart dynasty.

John Erskine, eleventh Earl of Mar, stung by studied and unprovoked insults on the part of the king proceeded to the Highlands and placed himself at the head of the forces of the house of Stuart, or Jacobites, as they were named.

He organised a gathering at Castle Aboyne on 6th September 1715 of the Chiefs and nobles of the Clans, gentlemen of Scotland, and any followers of the House of Stuart and proclaimed James the rightful King of Great Britain.

The insurrection, both in England and Scotland, began to grow in popularity, and would have been a success, had there been at the head of affairs a strong military man.

Nearly all the principal chiefs of the clans were drawn into the movement.

SHERIFFMUIR:

The 'Rising' in 1715 by Charles Edward Stuart was in support of his father, James VIII of Scotland and III of England,thus the general term of 'Jacobite' for all supporters.

The leaders of the insurrection in Scotland were the Earl of Mar and James Murray the son of the Earl of Stormont who gathered their men at Perth on 28th September 1715 and fortified the town with 14 cannon scavenged from Dundee, Dunottar and whereever.
They were joined by further groups of Highlanders.

When news that a ship with supplies of munitions had come under the attention of Government officers at Burntisland off Fife, the Master of Sinclair acted immediately.

With 400 horse double mounted with footsoldiers, he galloped through the evening to arrive outside the port about midnight. The thunder of 400 horse, the jingle of harness and clatter of arms awoke and terrified the villagers as they passed.
Sinclair directed the Cavalry to encircle the outskirts of the town, whilst the 400 Infantry under command, double quick-marched through the streets to the wharf and took the ship. Then unloaded the ordnance and munitions into carts and rejoined Sinclair and the Cavalry to be escorted back to Perth.
This venture ensured a full supply of arms and ammunition for future campaigns.

On 4th October Mar commanded Drummond of Balraldie and Rob Roy Mac Gregor to take the Castle of Inveraray, but gave no direction for decisive action.

Again there is an unexplained period of inactivity on the part of Mar who was hoping for the arrival of "The Chevalier" when he should have directed an attack on the weakened Argyll and then garrisoned Stirling, but he wasted precious time.

In November Highlanders from the noth of Scotland joined the insurgents at Perth to increase the army to 12000 men.

Allan Clanranald XIV was one son of Scotland who answered the call 'to rise' in 1715.

Allan was not only a seasoned campaigner but with the 'second sight' which foretold future events.

When he left his stronghold of Castle Tioram, the 'head-house' of the Lordship of Garmoran since the 13th. Century, and called the men of Moidart to follow him to join the Earl of Mar to fight for Scotland he had a premonition that he would never return from the fighting ahead, never to tread the heather of Moidart again, never to smell the salt spray from the battlements and that the Castle of the Clanranalds would fall into the hands of the hated Hanoverian Troops.

To prevent Tioram being garrisoned by English Troops, he used the threat of a curse and ordered Dougie MacIsaac to torch the castle as soon as the main body left.

Allan, XIV Clanranald led the men of Moidart out of the Castle, the Piper playing a pibroch.

The torch was put to the stacked kindling and the fire took hold.

Behind them the towering smoke from the ancient home of their race casting a solemn shadow over the land.

They marched on to join the growing army at Perth.

Caisteal Tioram burns, 1715.

After more inactivity, a Council of War was called on 9th October when General Gordon arrived with his troops. From this, Brigader Ogilvie and the Master of Sinclair led a body of 3000 Highlanders and 8 squadrons of Cavalry on campaign to take Dunblane.

Argyll's scouts sent him information of this advance so he organised the Government army of 4000 forward to take positions on the rising

slope above the rough terrain of the Sheriffmuir.
Mar and his army arrived later and camped at Kinbuck within sight of the Government forces.

Early on the 13th the Commanders of the Jacobite army held a Council of War which ended quickly as the Highlanders were frustrated by the delays and inaction of Mar over the past months.
They could not be contained, not to open an engagement with Argyll, so they made ready for battle.

Both armies were disposed in battle order in two lines, but due to the undulating ground were unsighted.
The Jacobites front rank of 10 battalions under Clanranald, Glengarry, Gordon of Glenbucket, Brigadier Ogilvie, Sir John MacLean of Duart and the two brothers of Sleat. Their second line was commanded by the Marquis of Tullibardine, the Marquis of Huntley, the Earl of Seaforth and Panmure, Viscount Strathallan, Drummond of Logie Almond and Robertson of Stuan. Cavalry were positioned at each flank with a rearguard of 800. All the Clans of Lochaber were represented.

The 4000 Government troops were commanded on the right by Argyll, on the left by General Whitham and the centre by General Wightman.
The Scots Greys were among the horse contingent. re:p.571 HH&GS

On the command 'ADVANCE' the Scots charged forward in four columns over the rough ascent which caused them to veer to the right. The terrain caused the Government line to also veer to their right, thus exposing the left flank of each to gunfire from the opposition.

The Highlanders fired a volley from pistols which was returned by the enemy with heavy casualties to both sides. One Highlander who fell mortally wounded was Alan Muidertach –

Glengarry shouted "REVENGE-REVENGE!" and the MacDonalds charged forward.
The targe with vicious spike held up high to deflect the rifle bayonet of the enemy, then slashing across the chest with broadsword. Another stabbing to the hilt with dirk, followed by a beheading blow with short axe.

Altogether a fierce, bloody, business.

The Master of Sinclair later described the fury and devastation of their charge:-
"when the salvo was fired they started to their feet, most threw away their fuzies, and drawing their swords, pierced them everywhere with incredible vigour and rapidity.

In four minutes time from receiving the order to attack, not only all in our view and before us turned their backs, but five squadrons of Dragoons on their left, commanded by General Witham, went to the right about and never looked back until they had got near Dunblane."

It was different conditions at the centre and left flank – the Stewarts, MacKenzies and Camerons had fired an attacking volley but were held by return fire from the Redcoats and on joining battle gave no advantage to either side.
The hand to hand fighting continued with some heavy casualties to both sides, each loosing and regaining ground - the desparate fighting of exhausted troops.

Both Commanders withdrew: "Argyll recalled and reorganised his troops into a defensive position behind stone enclosures at the bottom of Kippendavie whilst the Earl of Mar had already positioned his forces of about four thousand men at the crest of that hill.

Mar did not use the superior position to advance on Argyll but allowed him to retire with his remaining force towards Dunblane, much to the chargian of his Jacobite Commanders, but he retired his troops to the Roman camp at Ardoch, and there bivouacked."   ref: HH&GS p.573.

This caused Gordon of Glenbucket to exclaim:
" Oh for an hour of Dundee!
 Now, if ye speir wha wan the day,
I've tell'd you what I saw, Willie.
We baith did fight, and baith did beat,
And baith did run awa', Willie"

Allan was proved correct in his premonition. He fought valiantly in the Battle of Sheriffmuir in 1715, his two handed sword slashing and stabbing the foe. He was in the thick of battle giving no quarter and was wounded a number of times.
He died some hours later.

THE ENGLISH LEARN A LESSON.

The English government had found the roads, or rather tracks, throughout the highlands were inadequate for the quick deployment of Troops and decided to improve their defences.

They commissioned General Wade to map the main route to Inverness and to develop a military strategy.

He built new forts along this route, at Fort William, Fort Augustus and Fort George, with a new metalled road to link and service them.

This also linked Blair Atholl and Crieff to Ft. Augustus.

Col. Wade's military roads from Ft. George to Crieff.

After the 1715 Raising, General Wade built the Military road to follow the previous bridle and walking pathway from Inverness to Fort William. A second road from Inverness (Ft.George) looped in to Dalwhinnie and back to Ft. Agustus. A road linked Dalwhinnie to Crieff and to Dunkeld.

This was a major and permanent operation as these roads were from 16foot wide to 10 foot wide with sturdy stone bridges constructed at river crossings.

The soldiers encamped at sites every 10 miles – these expanded over time to roadside inns named 'King's Houses,' some still in evidence today.

These roads not only linked the major towns but also improved the droving routes from Inverness to Crieff and subsidury roads along the way.

The downturn was that these northern cattle had to be shod after Col. Wade's construction as the metalled (stone) surface injured unprotected hooves.

The main market was later shifted to Falkirk and in 1777 over the time of 3 markets, 30000 head were sold. They reached their height in 1850 with the sale of 150000 head.   ref. I.F Grant 'Highland Folk Ways' p.68-71

A defensive strategy was all very well but this would not be enough, for a road may be used by anyone for access or ambuscade or ignored for an alternate route.

That was the case when whispers circulated that a 'move' was afoot.

THE CALL TO ARMS:
"The Rising of '45," under Charles Edward Stuart.

They're gathering at Glenfinnan! **they're gathering at Glenfinnan!** the word spread from glen to toon to glen.   The air breathed danger and excitement when the news came that **" Bonnie Prince Charlie has landed**,"[22] and had walked through Moidart from Glenuig to Kinlochmoidart, and at Glenfinnan had called the Clans to arms to support his claim of 'King.'

Clanranald at the head of Loch Shiel in his galley "Aileach."

When the call went out to join with the Prince, MacDonalds from Moidart and the Clans of Lochaber answered. Others travelled down from the north. Most of those who rallied were sons of the families who were 'out' in 1715.

John/Eoin was no stranger to sudden attack or of a sally forth to recoup cattle taken.
Born in 1730 "near Inverness," being the grandson of Dougall Mackdonald b.8.6.1656 "in ye other side of the watter" (from Petty) and by DNA matching on the Black Isle. By tradition a relative of those "who were there that night" of the massacre at Glencoe[23] and escaped along Glen Etive with Alexander and others.

---

[22]The Prince stayed in the house of Angus MacDonald of Borrodale after landing from Eriska on 25th. July, 1745.
[23]Supported by the author's psychic experience as he passed Glen Etive for the first time, (it was a fine sunny day), but, when opposite Glen Etive, his scalp tightened and the hair of his head tingled.
It is well documented that when descendants first visit, or pass by, an important place of their ancestors in Celtic Scotland, they may experience some 'particular/peculiar' feeling.

John saddled the garron and helped his father to gather provisions of meal, dried venison and a girdle on which to cook oat cakes, and packed all in one bag.

The other bag held a spare plaid and repair gear, these he swung up behind the saddle to hang each side of the pony.

John was about 14 years old and as he did not have facial hair he had not reached 'manhood' and was not included in war parties.

His father took sword and targe from their concealed storage, leaving the gun for John, [if need be his father would win a gun after the first skirmish], He left with the instruction that it was John's duty to provide for the family and to defend family and farm from assault by any free roving villains, but to retreat into the hills if attacked in force.

John's training in the use of Arms was underway by the Rising of 45', for it was never known when the clansfolk would have to defend their farms from raiders or political adversaries. The one weapon he would always carry was his sgain dubh, the 'black knife.' This was carried in a sling sheath under his right armpit, where it was not obvious and was in easy and instant reach of his left hand. Today the ceremonial sgain dubh is in the stocking.

John would have been trained in the use of the Targe, a small round wooden shield covered with toughened hide, reinforced with strips and studs of iron. It often had a spike or blade protruding from its central boss so that it could be used for attack as well as defence and was held on the forearm through two leather loops attached to the back.

The other common arms were the dirk and the sword, the dirk could be used with the targe, or used instead of the targe, that is, as a parrying short sword in conjunction with the claymore or broadsword.
This being the adapted claymore not the huge two-handed claymore of the earlier Scottish warriors.

John enjoyed the sport of deer stalking which gave good co-ordination of eye and limb. It developed stamina from climbing the mountains and patience for the watch and sight of a stag, then taught strategy for the final stalk and kill with the short yew bow and arrow.
The traditions of stalking and killing of the red deer went back to Fingal - Finn mac Cumhaill.

Dancing provided relaxation from the day's toil and training and gave agility and timing so essential to the swordsman.[24]

Other boyhood training was how to make and use a bow, to fletch arrows with goose feathers, to repair equipment, all the basic skills and knowledge required of every male member of the clan.

This enabled him, no matter his status, to fulfil his responsibilities in those times of territorial skirmishes and wars, when raiding was still a part of every day life or death.

The battles fought and won by the Highlanders with Bonnie Prince Charlie are mostly forgotten so we bring one early battle to the fore which demonstrates the feeling of support the general populace had for their Bonnie Prince.

The Prince started his march in 1745 with about 10 supporters but as they progressed to Edinburgh with pipes and drums.
Highlanders quickly gathered whatever arms they had and joined the growing band which numbered over 2500 men by the time Edinburgh was reached.
This patriotic small army marched on toward England and met up with an equal force loyal to George II under Sir John Cope at about 4am on 21st September.

The Highlanders, yelling their war-cry and brandishing pikes, swords and hooks charged into the English troops front line.
This sudden onslaught caused injury, then panic , then flight of the Hanoverian army giving a decisive victory to Prince Charles Edward Stuart.

It was the Battle of Prestonpans and was the first of many victories.

The battles fought and won by the sons of Scotland, and the accounts of 'Bonnie Prince Charlie' and his advisers, or ill-advisers, are well documented, as is the last Blàr Chùil Lodair (Battle at Culloden), which was a disaster.

---

[24]The noted historian Alastair Cameron writes that there was a school for fencing about Glenuig, and an armourer/blacksmith who could forge and work iron to the excellence of the famous Andrea Ferrara sword blades; other reports have the fencing school teaching new techniques of a relaxed stance but with superior defence positions which conserved the strength of the swordsman without compromising skill.

Cumberland lead the English forces with the express purpose to defeat Charles Edward Stewart, to decimate the Highland Clans, to destroy all armaments held by the Scots and to subjugate the Highlanders so that they would never threaten England again.

This they did on the boggy ground of Culloden Moor with their superior numbers and equipment and the deciding tactic which countered the famed 'Highland Charge.'

The word of the gathering of the opposing forces spread through the population. The pandemonium of the battle, the smoke from the burning farms and the noise of rampaging troops, alerted John and the family to quickly gather what provisions they could carry, to load precious goods onto one pony, then to flee into the hills and heather.

The Hanoverian troops were still high with the lust for killing and pillage after the 'Battle' with Cumberland's instruction to waste the highlands.

After Culloden, Hanoverian troops roamed the countryside. These were made up of German mercenaries, troops from the Lowland Clans and Clan Campbell, English Foot, Normans and Anglo-Saxons, etc.

The killings and burnings had started.

The farms at Craighouse on the Black Isle and at Draikes and Fisherton near Petty were in immediate danger as troops burned and looted the farms surrounding Culloden then along the Great Glen at Abriachan and Urquhart. The farms to the east and around Dores were at the mercy of the main body of the English troops, as Wade's road ran along the east bank of Loch Ness.ref:Lord Mahon's"History of England"v.III, p. 308-311.

In May of 1746 the HMS 'Furnace' sailed up Loch Nevis and Captain Fergussone put ashore a landing party who burnt all the houses including Barrisdale, then turned the guns of the 'Furnace' on the highlanders who came out to attempt to extinguish the fires.

He then ordered the 'blowing up' of Kinlochmoidart House by a barrel of gunpowder transferred from ship to shore. He had already laid waste to Eigg and Borrodale House (he was almost over zealous). Troops looted homes, slaughtered the cattle and hunted the people.

The surviving Kinlochmoidart family fled to Glenforslan.

Prisoners from this and earlier battles were 'transported' to America and the Indies and sold off as slaves.

A descendent writes: "Angus McDonald fought in the battle at Culloden Mor was captured and with his brothers John and Daniel and a sister Mary were sold as slaves to a landowner in Maryland, USA."

The assaults on family and the looting of stock and possessions from their farms and homes caused some of these MacDonalds to seek refuge with kin living in more remote districts such as in Moidart.
There were also vacant crofts, for some did not return from the battlefield. The clansmen who survived returned to find their homes burned to the ground, and many a 'Laird' hid out, living in a shepherd's bothy.

After the 'Rising of 45' the Crown passed a number of 'acts'. John was about 17 years old when the Act of Abolition and Proscription of Scottish Dress was passed in 1747 and the carrying of arms, speaking gaelic, playing the pipes, wearing the kilt, were outlawed.

These Acts had far-reaching effects on the life and culture of the highlander as they removed the Chief's feudal power over his clansmen. This made the Chiefs landlords, now dependent on their cattle and rents and not on the number of clansmen they had as followers, and resulted in the Tacksman, Goodman and Tenants having their rents raised.

Commissioners were appointed to manage the forfeited Estates.
These Commissioners who managed the forfeited estates brought in changes, ie: the granting of longer leases of 21 years, where preference for tenancy was given to kin of the previous occupant.

The introduction of new methods of crop rotation was encouraged.

It was largely due to them that the potato became a staple crop in the Highlands, which Clanranald had introduced into South Uist in 1743.

In exposed districts the winters were so cold that it required a specially designed and constructed dwelling to protect the inhabitants.

Thus the 'Black house' evolved, and far from being derided as the result of poverty, it was in fact the result of ingenuity and a knowledge of thermo technology, called necessity, in those days, which developed the ideal construction to resist the below freezing temperature and winter gales.

The dwellings had double walls of local stone[25] filled with sand or soil as insulation, cavity brick construction.

The roof tree was of wattle branches, covered with thatch which gave further insulation, held in place with plaited ropes and stone weights. With a wall or central fireplace they became very snug, protected from the ravages of highland winters. NOTE: the crofter owned the roof tree and the thatch.

The stone walls of a few of the stronger constructed old houses are still standing to-day, a reminder to local clansfolk of their 'kin over the seas,' others are just a heap of stones.
The winters were harsh so before the onset of snow, some beasts were slaughtered and the meat salted down, any spare cattle were sold at market and only basic stock were kept, as these had to be sheltered and fed.

The small crofter sheltered his cattle at one end of the family dwelling while the tenant farmer might have separated byres built at the end of the dwelling. The Tacksman might have the byres totally separate to the dwelling, as with 'Innes a Chulun', the latter being a much more comfortable lifestyle.

In a long harsh winter, cattle would be 'bled' and this mixed with oats to make the nutritious black pudding. If the winter was prolonged some of their breeding cattle would have to be eaten. These might be replaced in the spring by raids on the stock of other clans.

Of course the keeping of arms was forbidden within the Act of Abolition, but the highlander, if he was not actually using them, had been concealing his arms, wealth and cattle from the invader, or the Crown, since time began.
After the ravages following Culloden in 1746 and the loss of family and land, the men of Clan Donald from Inverness to Appin, were left with few assets, and the clansfolk had to rebuild and look to new sources of income or shift to safer or isolated districts.   mac p7.

---

[25]Good building stone was so scarce that older stone block buildings would be scavenged for material to build new Forts or Estate homes etc.

SOME LOST THEIR ANCESTRY.

Charles Samual McDonald writes of the history of his family after Culloden, because there is no family record before that date.

" My earliest ancestor to come to the USA from Scotland was Angus McDonald (McDaniel), he fought in the battle at Culloden Mor for Scottish independence and was captured there. He, with his two brothers John and Daniel and a sister Mary were 'transported' to America and sold as slaves here in the USA to Van Swearingen (a Dutchman) in Maryland.

After Angus won his freedom he moved to Virginia with his wife Anna Thompson (McDonald) where his son John was born.
John married Van Swearingen's daughter Rachael Swearingen.

They had about nine children of which William McDonald was one.
He married Sarah (LNU) in South Carolina and then moved to Georgia where William died.

All of the family of Hiram McDonald one of his sons and Hiram's wife Caroline Gassett McDonald with their children moved to Alabama.

Hiram fought in the Civil war and was captured in the Battle at Nashville.
He was taken to Rock Island Prison in Illinois. He died in prison."
ref: Charles Samuel McDonald, ID BW7NX

CULLODEN REMEMBERED 250 years on.

1996 at the Clan Donald marker, Culloden Moor:-
Angus MacDonald, Glasgow; Rob Parker, Clan Donald Centre; Glengarry; Lochgarry; Clanranald; James McDonald, USA; Malcolm McDonald Esq, Aust.; Norman H. MacDonald, Edinburgh.

In 1996 the 250 year anniversary of the Battle of Culloden was celebrated with a Church service and ceremony on the field with the attendance of the Clans involved in that battle.

Clan Chiefs, Armigers and Clan leaders honoured the fallen by the laying of wreaths at the respective Clan Marker stones depicting their place on that day.

ONE WAR STOPS, ANOTHER STARTS:

Skirmishes and battles with the English had always been a part of the highlanders life, but folk required food and in isolated districts such as Moidart the folk grew their vegetables in common plots in the 'run rig' system. The beds fertilised with kelp, were alternated between crofters so that all had the chance of a 'rich' bed.

The continuing wars in Europe in the 1760s caused a lack of basic chemicals resulting in the rudimentary processing of kelp to manufacture the basic chemicals of potash and soda for use in the glass and soap industries.   ref:TCD vIII,p.142

This was cut from the rocks with hooks or gathered along the shore and dried to a certain degree on the beach and was later burnt between layers of peat in trenches dug in the ground and stirred with an iron rake until the ashes reached a fluid state.
It required experience and skill to maintain the correct temperature to obtain the optimum result.
When cooled the residue condensed into a dark blue or a whitish mass which was quite hard. This contained basic chemicals of salts, potash and soda, but mainly soda. ref - 'A History of the Scottish Highlands' by Dr. Isabel Grant.

When the processing of kelp started to earn good money, they substituted this with bracken when making "lazy beds", where the soil was fairly deep and moist.

The author with a frond of kelp from the sea flat at Tioram.

"The bracken was cut in July when at its richest ~~~ ditches were opened about six feet apart and the soil from the ditches put on the bracken so that it had a covering of six to eight inches of earth over it."
"This was left for nine months to decay till spring came round again ~~~ holes bored in with a "dibble" and seed potatoes dropped in."
ref: *"A Hundred Years in the Highlands", Osgood Mackenzie, p. 154*

THE INTERNATIONAL SCENE.

Culloden was only one segment of the Crown's grand plan in world events and by 1754 William Pitt the English minister had strategies in place for the embarkation of Troops to North America to oppose the French Army stationed at Quebec and surrounding districts to drive them from Canada.

In 1755 the political situation between Britain and France had worsened, so the Black Watch regiment, and others, were brought up to their full complement.

Officer appointments were published and Recruitment Parties roamed the Highlands seeking men for Regiments to fight in America.
They were in the dress uniform of the particular regiment and canvassed the towns of Fort William, Fort Augustus and Inverness in Scotland, and had 'recruitment money' to spend.
To serve with the Cadets and leaders of their Clans, and with this show of comparative affluence of a warm, clean, bright uniform and a well fed countenence would have had a major influence on the Highlander.

The farms beside the River Ness, along the Great Glen down into Appin and elsewhere were burnt out when the farming communities suffered severe reprisals after Culloden in 1746-47. They had to start afresh in the postwar depressed economic climate and in general had little chance to improve their lot, so by 1755 the men of the highlands eagerly took up this chance to enlist and to "take the King's shilling."

Those who could purchase a 'commission' did so, and others simply joined as soldiers, [some were 'pressed.'] [26] with the ambition to win prizes of war in Canada.

They had to take any opportunity offered.

---

[26] In this time of vying for religious power, all serving in the English army had to 'profess' the Protestant religion.

The Officers came from all clans:- 1756 saw promotional appointments in the (later) 42nd Royal Highland Regiment when they arrived at New York of: Major Grant to Leiutenant Colonel, Duncan Campbell of Inveraw to Major; Thomas Graham of Duchray with James Abercromby of Glassa and John Campbell of Strachur to Captains.

The second Division of the British army under the Earl of Loudon sailed for Halifax in June of 1757 with additional companies with 700 recruits to a total of 1300 men, all from the Highlands with officers, James Murray, son of Lord George Murray, James Stewart of Urrard, Thomas Stirling, son of Sir Henry Stirling of Ardoch as Captains and Blair, Barclay, Campbell, Mackay, Menzies, and Mills lieutenants.

ref: Hof SH, HC&HR,VII, p.337

An account recorded regarding the first Highlanders to arrive at Halifax when on their march to Albany they attracted much attention from the local Indians who hurried to view these new arrivals who they claimed as brothers because their dress was of a similarity to theirs!

ref: History Scottish Highlands,Highland Clans & Highland Regiments,V.II, p.336

Duncan MacDonald Colonel of the 57th Regiment of Foot, was nephew of Alexander III of Dalness, a cadet branch of Glenco, who resided at Fort William to 1726.

Ranald the 17th., second son of Donald,was appointed in 1757 to a Company in Fraser's Highlanders to serve under Generals Wolfe and Amherst.

Allan Stewart of Appin served in the same regiment with Ranald the 17th., as a Lieutenant.

"Archibald Montgomerie, brother-in-law of Sir Alex' Macdonald of Sleat in Skye, raised 'Fraser's 78th. Highlanders' and led them in Canada under Colonel Amherst. William, the 4th. son of Donald, served as a Lieutenant."[27]

"Alexander, 5th. of Kinlochmoidart, entered the army and received his first commission in the 42nd. and later became Lt. Colonel of the 2nd. Battalion of the 71st. serving in America; he was invalided home in 1780." ref: HSH&HR V.II, p.337

Pitt had advised Parliament and the Lords of the Admiralty of the requirement to establish a standing army to meet Britains strategy to be the dominant nation in the world.

---

27 HSH & HR – "The History of Scottish Highlands, Highland Clans and Highland Regiments" by John S. Keltie, F.S.A. Scot. Published 1885.

THE HIGHLANDERS IN NORTH AMERICA.

In 1757 Regular Officers with recruitment parties based at Fort William, Fort Augustus and Fort George had orders to 'obtain' recruits to meet Brigade numbers.   Their 'net' spread far and wide.
One so 'recruited/pressed' at Fort George was John McDonald of a local family across the water who had relatives residing in the Glenorchy to Lochaber districts who were 'recruited' at Fort William.

By the 1750s some of John's relatives resided on the MacLean of Ardgour Estate Inverness-shire, in Kilmallie Parish, so we will follow his army service with the 15th Regiment of Foot with his fellow Highlanders in the wars in Canada which would ensure that Nova Scotia was British and not French, though its future would be of Gaelic speaking Scotsmen.

Able bodied soldiers serving in the British Army at the cessation of their 'time' were offered grants of land, as this was cheaper than shipping them home. This aided the Government's politics by providing ready made "civilians of occupation."

John's 'enlistment' into General Jeffery Amherst's companies about 1757, was possibly from Fort George, near Inverness.
Some wives travelled with the Officers and Troops whilst in England, but only a 'balloted number' travelled on active service. ref:W.O.,5/45.

Captain (Rtd.) E.A. Gray, Military Historian says,"The British Army of the period at which John McDonald served was a brutal institution, which had not the slightest interest in soldiers parentage, their wives or families. Wives contrived to follow their men to escape the abject poverty of the times."

John and the highlanders from Lochaber would have been immediately kitted out with uniforms of dress and work and issued the equipment of a private soldier.
What luxury! A cocked hat, a scarlet coat with yellow facings to cuffs, collar tabs and skirt turnback. An under jacket buttoned down the front with a white neckachief, red breechers, white stockings and black knee boots. Some had not owned such clothing since the Crown had banned the wearing of the woollen kilt under threat of death. One old soldiers trick to keep the scarlet coat clean was to wear it 'inside out' when in dirty situations!

The new soldiers of Amherst's 15th Regiment marched through Scotland and England, receiving training of marching in formation and drill exercises along the way. Their destination to be billeted in army camps at Maidstone on 29th October 1757. From there they were ordered to march from Winchester for Southampton on 8th January 1758

Colonel, later General Jeffery Amherst.

John McDonald with the lads from Lochaber sailed for Nova Scotia with the 15th Regiment under Colonel Jeffery Amherst in January of 1758.

This was part of a fleet of 157 ships carrying 11000 troops, and the ordinance stores ships, with their baggage, equipment, arms, cannon and wagons etc.

What a sight the fleet in full sail made. The individual 'Man-o-war' recognised by the figurehead at the bow, some in gold but most in bright colours. The ships were also painted to give a splendid appearance as the Captains were generally from landed gentry or had earned prize money from previous victories, and there was great pride and status in the 'turn out' of their ship.

Each gun deck was a band of black with the inside of the gun covers painted red, there was either a yellow or royal blue band above and below the gun deck, or these colours might be reversed – the exterior of the stern galleries would be of bright colours and some with gold relief, but all quite grand at the commencement of the voyage.

General Abercromby reported on the 28th April 1785, that after 11 weeks of sailing the seas, the 'Prince Frederick" and the 'Juno' had arrived at Halifax with Amherst's Regiments after sailing through a savage storm which broached one of the Transports and demasted the 'Prince Frederick.' They used replacement masts carried by the 'Le Arc en Ciel' to continue.

Here they joined other Regiments, *ie*. Colonel James Murray, Major James Murray and Archibald Montgomerie, under joint command with General Wolfe.[28]

Captain James Cook was there in command of the 'Pembroke' which was a 60 gun 4th rate ship of the line. In a few years time in 1768 he would sail from England in the renamed 'Endeavour' to search for the "unknown south land" and in 1770 map the east coast of Australia, the land to which descendents of these same highlanders would emigrate in the late 18th and 19th centuries.

The task of the British Army was to drive the French from Canada by taking the Fortress at Louisburg and the fortified Town of Quebec and the trading town of Montreal.

Wolfe was an experienced soldier and a strict tactician. He initiated some restructuring of the British army under his control, in tactics, disposition in battle, uniform and hygiene, after suffering heavy losses against the French/Indian attacks in the earlier campaign.

The British Army had found the traditional uniform restricted movement as it caught in briars and bushes and the clothing was of too heavy a material for the humid summer weather. Wolfe changed this for the scouts and the forward units. The coat skirts were cut off and lighter material was used. The traditional 'cue' or pigtail pulled the skin of the face back and tight and was unhygienic so orders were issued that these be cut off.

This was most unpopular but had to be obeyed.

The light infantry and grenadier units were issued with a tomahawk as a utility weapon, being most useful for clearing a path, chopping wood for a fire and in silently killing the enemy and were directed how this should be carried with other equipment.

Directives were issued as to the rations and ammunition per man, medical inspections, procedure for embarking and disembarking the transport ships. Wolfe was most methodical.

The troops were drilled as to formation marching, movement as a unit, a company or a regiment, for attack and defence. They were exercised in the town and harbour in battle scenarios and Wolfe issued procedures to meet various situations.

---

[28]It is interesting to note that one gains a broader 'picture' by reading both "A History of the Scottish Highlands, Highland Clans and Highland Regiments" published 1885, and the diary notes of the Officers serving in those Regiments.

The war was now being fought using two tactical fronts, the traditional open battle positions of battalions and the new concealment and attack from ambush.

1758: The 175 strong British fleet arriving in North America. with troops and supplies.

LOUISBURG:

Col. Jeffery Amherst had sailed from Portsmouth on 16th March in H.M.S."Dublin" with Captain George Rodney, but was delayed due to weather conditions and only arrived, fortuitously, on 28th May when Vice Admiral Boscawen was leaving Halifax with a force to attack Louisburg.

Amherst was able to join that expedition with the local rank of Major General with orders to 'take Louisburg' the French Fortress on the St Lawrence reputed to be "the greatest battlement in North America."

This fortress overlooked the entrance to the estuary of the St.Lawrence River, the pathway to the major objective of Quebec and had to be 'silenced.'

The fleet of 11000 men sailed into Gabarus Bay on the 2nd June 1758 just west of the small peninsula on which the fortress of Louisburg stood proud and formidable.

Major General Amherst's tactics were to direct an attack on three fronts, the brigade under Lawrence to attack 'White Point', a mile from the fort, with Whitmore attacking at 'Flat point.'

The second front was with the 28th Regiment against 'Lorambec' and the third was for Wolfe to lead his brigade against 'Freshwater Cove.'

The weather was adverse for any landing so Amherst used the Naval guns to bombard the French emplacements.

Amherst launched his attack at first light on the 8th June and even with fine weather many boats and men were lost in the heavy surf.
All went according to the battle plan in the first instance but the French were well prepared with the placement of 10 cannon and swivels in concealed forward batteries.

They had scouted the British approach and held back until those troops were committed to the attack, then opened fire from cannon blasting a swathe of grapeshot through the advancing ranks leaving bloody paths of wounded and dying troops.

John and the 'Lochaber lads' were in the second flotilla of small boats rowing through surf for the landing site, when French cannon targeted the closer boats smashing and drowning their occupants. John grasped his rifle with one hand and clutched the boat thwart with his other, his face a mask as he looked at Dougall.

He would much rather be face to face with a screaming, tomahawk waving, face-painted French-Canadian than helpless in a ship's boat. There would be little chance in the sea when weighed down by full kit and equipment.

Wolfe gave the order to 'withdraw' but Major Scott with 10 men had gained a foothold on a craggy point sheltered by a spit of land and were returning the French fire.
The order was rescinded to one of 'advance in support' and the British were able to continue the landing with a greater force. John and 'the Lochaber lads' jumped from the boats into the surf and waded to the shore under continuous fire from the French, but were able to advance and return fire from hastily built barricades.
The French batteries were finally overrun and the area surrounding the fortress secured.
Amherst organised roadworks over the boggy ground and John with his mates experienced the dirty work of a soldier, knee deep in mud and the backbreaking work of carting great lengths of planks to form the track for the transport of field fortifications.
The British bombardment was heavy and continuous.

Three French 'ships-of-the-line' were set on fire on the 21st and with this final loss Governor Drucour surrendered Louisburg on the 26th July, 1758.

ref:'A History of The 15th Regiment' p.138 - 141

The fortress of Louisburg.
Courtesy 'The British Army a concise history' published1979, p.46.

THE BATTLE OF QUEBEC: September 1759.

The advance against Quebec was a different engagement, Wolfe who was in poor health, had three tactical problems to solve:-

- To overcome the Canadians at Point Levi, which overlooked the anchorage and Quebec and threatened any British shipping.
- To safely navigate the St. Lawrence River with its unchartered shoals and submerged rocky outcrops.
- To find a way onto the Plains of Abraham to allow him to form up his Regiments and artillery to attack the fortified town of Quebec.

On the 29th June a battalion quietly crossed in the darkness and set up a defense in Beaumont Church at Point Levi. Monckton followed the next morning with three brigades and caught the Canadians between fire from the Church and his troops. The advance continued with Fraser's 78th Highlanders directed to clear the village resulting with Monckton controlling the high ground at Point Levi and able to protect the British ships in the basin.

Durell delegated Captain James Cook the task to chart the river and shoals – Cook sailed with great care up the river in the 60 gun 'Pembroke" with a crew in the ship's boat preceeding, a sailor with a lead line sounding the depth and type of bottom.
Cook charted the river with notes on shoreline and landmarks, placing markers and buoys to guide the Fleet. They were occasionally fired upon.
He lead the exploratory parties seeking a break in the steep banks and cliffs to afford a landing for the following army to reach the Plains of Abraham.

The convoy of seventeen sloops, five frigates, troop transports and ships stocked with stores, equipment and baggage had a most inauspicious start. The day of the 4th of June was, cold, wet and miserable.

The bay had large ice floes from the spring thaw floating among the ships with a few bumping against the hulls, this new and startling experience was viewed with stony silence by 'the lads from Lochaber'. Sailors fended them off with poles and boathooks but the icy wind allowed some of the fleet to leave the harbour, only for this to drop, forcing the Fleet to anchor.

The next morning with a freshening wind at the break of day the fleet left the harbour and by afternoon sailed past Newfoundland on the starboard bow.

They sailed through the Gulf of St.Lawrence during that night and in the early morning the ships floated lower in the fresh water of the St.Lawrence river into their 230 mile voyage to Quebec.
John and his highland comrades may well have thought this was now a pleasure cruise as the weather had changed for the better with water birds flying past and the cavorting antics of porpoises and seals swimming beside the ships.
Their safety was in following the marker buoys along the river.

About two weeks into the voyage up the St. Lawrence the peaceful scene was broken by the fury of a violent storm with ferocious winds smashing down trees, renting sails, and torrential rain swamping the decks and washing down the hatchways . Then it ceased just as suddenly with an eerie stillness to be replaced by the 'clank clank' of the pumps sucking out the rainwater in the holds, another experience for the Lochaber lads manning the pumps.

Light Infantry Lookouts were stationed on the fighting platforms on the masts of the 'Ships of the line', to keep watch for any movement or reflection in the woods bordering the river which warned of the sudden rifle shots from Canadian woodsmen. It was a competition to see just who could shoot whom first – this was war.
Warning beacons flamed from high points through the nights telling of the fleet's progress.
Finally the fleet reached the Quebec basin and the reality of the war between Britain and France was brought home with avengance.

The ships of the fleet had only just anchored when they witnessed a boat launched from the shore and carried by the current toward the British ships, suddenly there was an explosion and it burst into fire. It was a 'fire-organ' coated with oil and tar and combustible waste with a gunpowder charge meant to collide with the anchored shipping and to spread fire throughout the fleet.

The charge had been set off too early and a crew of British sailors in a ships boat were able to throw a grapple hook and chain onto the 'fire-organ' and tow it aside to burn out in the shallows.
A few suffered burns.

Vaudreuil now ordered the French naval ships to sail down river and attack the British Fleet, but this was but a token gesture as they formed a line of attack and fired off their cannon in defiance. They then tacked about and sailed back up the river to safety in the shallow tributaries of the St. Lawrence.

At last the expeditionary force under Durell and Cook sighted a fall of earth and rock which had breached the cliff face at Anse au Foulon, where it might be possible to make a landing and scale the landfall to reach the Plain above – p.147

Wolfe ordered a Pioneer party to make a track up the fall and to secure the exit onto the plain, then to await darkness and to guide following troops.

This was no easy task as men slid down on loose shale or fell to the rocks below when a boulder came free under their grasping hands, but the determined elite infantry won through.

There was much activity on the river, ship's boats transferring troops from ship to narrow shore , a cannon dismantled and hoisted from the man-o-war onto the rocking ship's boat, with many a sailors curse from fear of capsize.

On reaching the shore came the risky unloading and the arduous task of hauling cannon and supplies up the slope by ropes and pulleys, with many a fall and curse.

Wolfe quickly put plans into effect for a body of troops to climb the cliff face in darkness and to haul up equipment for an immediate assault party to attack the French Battery at Samos.

The troops had quite a struggle with the steep incline, the loose shale, some undergrowth and the nuisance of a couple of French Pickets firing on them, which alerted of the French command.

Louis-Joseph Marquis de Montcalm in command of the main French Forces, fearing a night attack, ordered all the French guns to open fire.

This was returned by combined cannon fire from the British 74 gun ships of the line and the nimble Frigates darting as escort to blast any French 'fire-ship', floated toward the British Fleet.

The night sky was alive with the flash and thunder of exploding gunpowder and the breeze full of the stench of its smoke as the firepower from the British warships smothered the French emplacements.

The French Battery of four twenty-four-pounders and one thirteen-inch mortar were silenced.

By break of day Wolfe's soldiers were at the top of the escarpment with further troops hauling more equipment up the slope.

Full light gave the lookouts at Quebec the unbelievable sight of the British Regiments formed for battle, two ranks of 'scarlet' and 'green' stretching across the plain, in lines parallel to the walls of Quebec and about three quarters of a mile clear of them.

It was most foreboding! The British troops stood straight, silent and unmoving in the dawn light.

Montcalm questioned his sight when his officers reported the presence of the British Regiments.
He immediately called for reinforcements of troops and cannon, but to no avail, Vaudreuil and others wanted the cannon as protection for themselves.

From the history of The Regiment:
" On the right of the front line were the grenadiers with the 28th Regiment on their left, on the left flank was the 47th Regiment with the 43rd on their right."

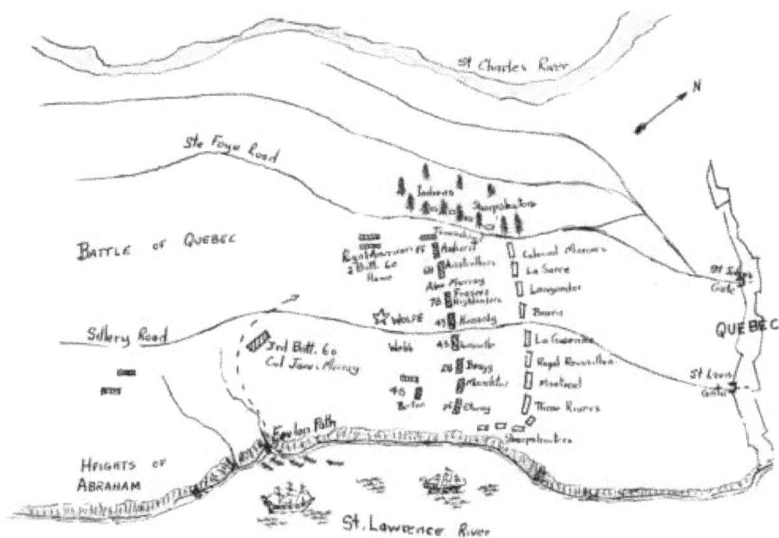

BATTLE ORDER - Regiment positions for the 'Battle of Quebec'.

"The 15th and 35th Regiments and a battalion of the 60th formed up behind them as the second line, and a little later the 58th and 78th marched through this second line to strengthen the front.

A battalion of Royal Americans were left at the top of the Anse au Foulon to guard the landing-place. Colonel Burton with the 48th Regiment stayed in reserve."

Montcalm made the first mistake, instead of waiting for reinforcements he ordered the French Troops to sally forth and meet the attack of the English and Scots regiments.

In the attack on Quebec, the 15th were a regiment on the English left, in a very vulnerable situation to prevent any flanking movement by the French.
John McDonald with the 'Lochaber lads' checked their powder, and with a grin and a muttered "comhla ri che`ile" (together), they waited, waited, for the order to fire.

The blast of cannon, the woosh of the ball, the screams of horses and men smashed and bloody, declared that the Battle had begun with heavy cannon fire from the walls of Quebec.

This initiated heavy fire into the British left flank from Indian and

French-Canadian sharpshooters in the nearby forest as a diversion.

Some of the 15th were wounded.

15th Regiment at Quebec, from painting at the 15th Regiment Museum, York.

The main body of the French advanced, firing on the British front.

Wolfe had ordered double shoot to be loaded by his front line troops and ordered them to hold their fire until the French had advanced to within 40 yards. The British line's courage held, and they held their fire until the order came at last "FIRE".
The 78th Highlanders in the front rank of the British army fired double shoot into the mass of French troops and as the front rank knelt to reload and the second rank immediately fired. There was utter carnage, the front ranks of the French were blasted to the ground.

Volley after volley blasted between both front lines and the heavy gunsmoke made it difficult to see the enemy.
But 'something'was out there, so they fired, and fired again.

For rapid fire, the infantryman held his musket under his left arm, took a cartridge and bit off the twisted paper end and spat it out. He then ran some gunpowder onto the flash pan and closed the pan and then inserted the open end of the cartridge into the muzzle.
He dropped the rifle butt hard against the ground to bed the cartridge down, the paper acted as a seal to prevent any powder spilling past the ball. They then swung the rifle up to the shoulder, pulled the trigger and the flint struck the 'flash pan' igniting the cartridge. The gun fired and the half inch ball would shoot a distance of 150 yards.
The attack increased on the left flank where John with other troops

came under this heavy fire from the French-Canadian and Indian sharpshooters positioned in the forest bordering Ste.Foye Road.
They suffered heavy casualties but held their ground and returned fire as reinforcement of Light Infantry was brought forward from the rear.

The French army broke and fled. Montcalm had lost all by his rashness and Quebec was won for Britain.

One of Wolfe's reports on an early engagement at Quebec reads :-
" Amherst's (15th) and the Highland Regiment, by the soldier-like and cool manner in which they performed would undoubtedly have beaten back the whole Canadian army if they had ventured to attack at that time."   ref: 'A History of the 15th (East Yorkshire)Regiment, 1685 1914.'

THE TAKING OF MONTREAL: 1760

The war for Canada was coming to a close for the victorious British Armies as any remaining French troops, now weakened and ragged, made their way to Montreal alone, without the Canadians who had silently left to return to their farms in the backwoods.

Amherst now mustered his forces to make the final move to 'take Montreal.'
"His force moved on Montreal from three directions, he himself down the St. Lawrence from Lake Ontario, Brigadier Haviland by way of Lake Champlain and the Richelieu River from the south, and Brigadier Murray up the St. Lawrence from Quebec.
Distances were vast and communications non-existent."
                    ref: "The British Army, a concise history," p.55.
Brigadier Murray with his 2500 men, now fresh from rest and good food on board ship sailed up the St. Lawrence for Montreal.

The voyage was so peaceful with birdsong and the flowers and fruits on the trees bordering the narrow river and the relaxed manner of the sailors, that one could only wonder that hostilities might be but a few miles away.
The ships dropped anchor at the island of St.Therese below Montreal

General Amherst was the only brigade to suffer delay from adverse conditions:
The spring thaw had started and the river had large blocks of ice floating downstream.
But not to be deterred Amherst's army commandeered boats and

canoes and entered the dangerous torrent.

John and his fellow highlanders found the ride down the St.Lawrence both exhilarating and terrifying with the river in spate, fast flowing rapids around rocks, with floating obstacles of ice and debris.

Their lack of experienced boatmen cost the British the lives of 100 soldiers when some boats capsized, throwing the troops with full packs and arms into the freezing water of the Cascades and Cedars rapids.

ref: p.182- 183, 'A History of the 15th Reg.'

"Amherst's Army running the St.Lawrence Rapids" by Capt.-Lieut. Thomas Davies.

Late on the 6th September they had reached Lachine close to joining forces with Murray and Haviland.

The Battle for Montreal was hardly a battle at all, under adverse weather conditions, John and his compatriots struggled through the mud and slush, wet, cold and hungry to surround the town.

Vandreul signed the surrender on 8th September ending the rule by the French of Canada.

THE ARDGOUR ESTATE and its HISTORY:

One of those "recruited" was John McDonald with McDonald relations who resided in the Glenorchy to Lochaber districts and by the 1750s some resided on the MacLean of Ardgour Estate Inverness-shire, in Kilmallie Parish.

ARDGOUR FROM PREHISTORIC TIMES:

The MacMasters were the traditional owners of Ardgour lands prior to the MacLeans driving them out in about 1432. The Ardgour estate was bounded to the north by Loch Eil, to the west by Loch Shiel and to the east by Loch Linnhe which protected it from incomers in general. As these blocked any arterial road through the region and to the interior, traditional access was by perimeter tracks fed from boats trading the locks.

Little is known of the region save for a few archaeological sites of prehistoric origin, again on the periphery, being a cairn at Duisky, a cist at Clovullin, a cairn at Corran and the fort at Loch nan Gobhar near the Loch Linnhe shore, which establishes prehistoric occupation.

ref: Jennifer G. Robertson MA PhD Archaeological survey.

The isolation of the early settlers was interrupted when the Norse Vikings raided the Western Highlands and established strongholds where galleys could be repaired and crews rested.

Place names indicate some Norse occupation especially 'Inverscaddle' which could be 'Scat-Dail' or 'Skan Dale', and 'Eilean nan Gall' or 'Island of the Strangers' demonstrate that the Norse sailed the waterways and controlled the region, collecting 'rents or taxes' probably of produce.

A 67: Acts of the Lord of the Isles.St. Andrews, 6 January 1508/9 (RMS, ii, 3284), granting the lands of Ardgour to the MacLean.

COMMENT: The lands were to be held by Ewen (MacLean) for the service of one galley of 22 oars 'quotiens regi videretur expediens', with remainder to a series of named heirs.

Therefore those who had holdings in this district under the Lord of the Isles prior to 1508 and 1613 when the Lord of the Isles granted Ardgour to the MacLeans, were MacDonalds and they continued to hold land on the (later) Ardgour Estate after this, until it was resurveyed into crofts pre 1802.

Duncan Campbell was factor of the Ardgour Estate when Donald MacDonald of Drimintorran, married Flora Campbell who was a sister to the Factor – this was Donald's second wife. Donald, the first son to this union succeeded to Drimintorran.   ref: p.262- 267, 'Clan Iain Abrach.'

We accept IGI records and the Ardgour Estate papers, that Dougal Macdonald, born about 1755-8 and married to Peggy Livingston in 1788, would have had a share of a farm on Ardgour estate and later one of the 1802 crofts at Blaich in Kilmallie, beside Loch Eil outside Fort William was a close relative to John of the 15th Regiment living at Corran at that time.

Croft Rental account from Whitsunday 1813 to 1814 records 'Dugald Macdonald holding Croft No. 2, paying £12/7/2 rental for the year.
It also shows Croft No. 26 held by Alexr Kennedy's widow and Dugald Macmillan paying £8/7/2 rental for the year.   ref: Croft Rentals

His son John born in 1791, married Amelia MacLean on 12.12.1816, and is recorded in the Census records of 1941with the croft at Blaich, and his son John born 1819 holding Croft No. 18 in the 1851 Census.

In a letter to tenants of the Ardgour Estate dated 31st August 1850, Colonel MacLean of Ardgour writes of his first connection with his friends about 1780 when they were scattered in the glens and on farms upon the estate, holding from a fourth, an eighth, and some a sixteenth. The arable land divided into many parts, with lots drawn for every season, so that no man should sow the same land for two years following.
He continues: After the first French War he examined this uneven system and devised a fairer division which would be advantageous to both the tenant and the landlord.
In 1801 he had four farms along the shore of Loch Eil surveyed and sub-divided into separate allotments, each consisting of arable land, or land easily improved into arable. With each of the allotments, the pasture of four cows, there followers, and a certain number of sheep.

The entries in the Rental Records to Whitsunday 1814 as shown by the numbered crofts on the following map of Blaich that tenants were from from numerous clans:
1.Kennedy; 2.Macdonald; 3. MacMillan; 4.MacLean; 6.Cameron; 8.MacIntyre; 18.MacPherson; 17.Livingston; 25. Fraser and MacColl, etc.

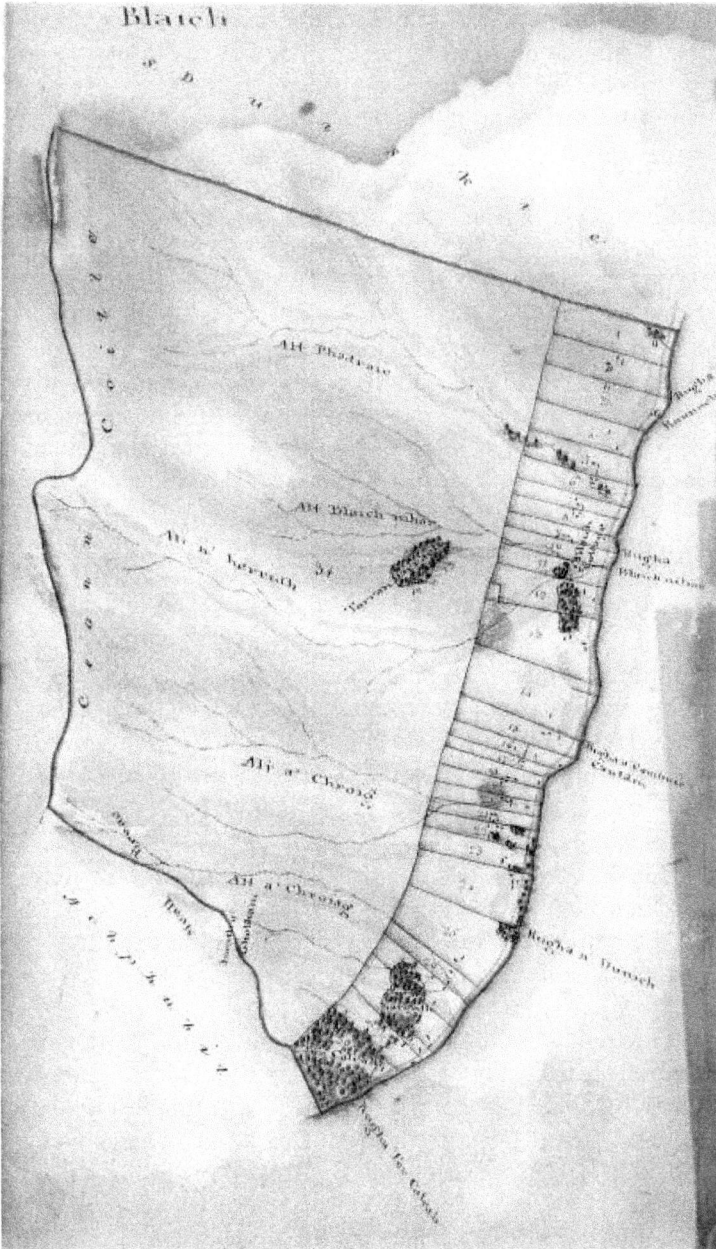

Map of 1802 with Blaich crofts 1 to 30 along Loch Eil
Courtesy: Fiona Maclean of Ardgour.

The crofts were drawn by lot by the tenants. Hill rent was gratis for three years, when stone houses, head and side dykes were to be finished.

This system proved to be an improvement except for the management of the tenants' sheep which was later changed with the whole of the sheep under the same mark under one shepherd, under the control of three men chosen by all. The plans were finalised in 1801.

THE DEMOGRAPHICS OF THE REGION are altered.

Whilst Colonel MacLean was looking to improve the conditions for Ardgour residents in 1780, the political situation and increased rents had initiated action by leaders in other areas of Lochaber and in neighbouring Moidart which would move families and alter the demographics of the region.

The Bishop of Edinburgh and the Bishop of the Highlands with Glenaladale initiated a scheme to migrate people from Lochaber with a long ancestry to the area, across the seas to Prince Edward Island.

One such family was that of Donald Mor MacDonald born about 1690 who was the son of Alasdair which connects him to Clan MacIain Og born about 1560 of the Glenaladale family. He lived on Kinlochmoidart property and moved to Eilean Shona in the 1700s.
He was out in the '45 and is mentioned in Clanranald records.
He died on Eilean Shona in 1748.
The Clanranald Estate had been forfeited to the British Government after 1745 which then held all papers for the Estate and would have appointed a Commissioner to handle all business and collect rents. These families of Clanranald did not return till after 1780.

In 1748 the Clanranald records state the tenants paying rentals for the Baillie farm on Eilean Shona were James MacDonald and Mary MacDonald each paying £44 per annum for 11/2 farthing of land each. Mary was the widow of Donald Mor MacDonald and James was their son who had been left the half right of the farm on his father's death.

James of Baillie farm had a brother John who left to reside in Perthshire and married.
His sister Margaret married John Ban MacDonald from Ulgary, Glenmoidart and had issue of a daughter Marjorie who married a Macpherson from Smirisary and one of her descendants married Angus MacDonald of Samalaman who was a well respected

genealogist and has descendants living in Glenuig.
It seems James of Baillie married before 1754 with a family of seven children.
His eldest son is thought to be Alasdair b.abt. 1754 on Eilean Shona who later married Janet Macdonald in about 1780.

Janet was from the family of Alasdair OG who had a farm at Kylebeg with issue of Rory, Charles, John, Donald, Angus and of course Janet.

Glenaladale looked abroad and purchased land on Prince Edward Island in 1770 and cut this into lots to lease. This would effect a major shift in the residents of Ardgour and Moidart.
In1772 folk from Lochaber sailed on the 'Alexander' to lease these lots from Captain John MacDonald VIII of Glenaladale.
They were followed by others and by 1790 the family of James MacDonald, who rented Baillie farm on Shona, sailed, leaving his land vacant.
These communities of Moidart who were encouraged to leave by Glenaladale and the Bishops were not evicted.

John Ban MacDonald from Ulgary married Margaret MacDonald the sister of James MacDonald of Baillie farm.
Their daughter Marjorie MacDonald married a MacPherson from Smirisary and another married Angus MacDonald of Samalaman whose descendents remained in Glenuig.
Alasdair Og of Kinlochmoidart had a farm at Kyles beg and married Janet the daughter of James MacDonald of Shona, she had brothers, Rory, Charles, John, Donald and Angus.

In 1782 the rents had been increased and land was at a premium in the Highlands, times were hard and Alasdair had received positive correspondence from Canada. So finally, Alasdair Og of Kyles beg with Janet and family sailed for Prince Edward Island with a large group of Moidart and Lochaber MacIsaacs, Gillies, McEacherns, Camerons and others in about 1790 on the ships, 'Lucy', 'Jane', and 'British Queen'.
Rory was recorded on the 'Lucy'.
RESEARCH: from the book "FAIR IS THE PLACE" by Mildred and John Colin MacDonald and researcher Catherine Gillies nee MacDonald

It is accepted that family members of John McDonald of the 15th Regiment moved onto Kinlochmoidart farms when relatives migrated to Nova Scotia.

MS3983 f 74 – lists of tenants of Kylesog and Kylesmore who made Kelp on Shores of Kinlochmoidart for the 1784–5 crop.

Kylesog:
Ewan Macdonald
Angus MacInnes
Neil roy MacInnes
Alexr Macdonald
John Macdonald

Kylesmore:
Ewan Macdonald
Dougald MacPherson
Alexr MacPherson

f 78 was a Rental of Kinlochmoidart Lands, 1786

Ulagary, one penny
Rory McDonald
John McDonald
Ewen McDonald senior
Angus McDonald
Ewen McDonald junior
John McPherson
Donald McDonald
Dugald McDonald

Dugald Macdonald son of John of the 15th Reg. was Tenant on Kinlochuachdrach with Duncan McVarish in 1807. Alexander Macdonald is listed as tenant in 1808.

In a letter to Major Robertson dated 7th July 1808, (MS3984), it refers to Dugald Macdonald as a Merchant trading out of Glenuig as far as Dunbartan. ref: MS 3984, 1807-14, f 64-65.

He is recorded as assisting with an investigation 1836 into 'Shellsand.'

THE TROOPS RETURN.

Fraser's Highlanders were disbanded in 1763 and returned to England; some of the 15th Regiment returned to England in 1763 also; but the main body returned later, when relieved by the 8th King's, in July 1768.

In 1768, after 14 years in the 15th.Regiment of Foot, fighting in Canada, John returns to England to the Royal Hospital Chelsea for treatment as he had wounds received during the Battle of Quebec.

John was officially discharged at age 40 on the 15th June 1770, as an out-pensioner of the Royal Hospital, Chelsea; his pension was probably nine pence [sterling] per day; John would have been 'well off.' ref: Capt. A.E. Gray Military researcher.

Fort William had an Invalid Regiment of veterans stationed there in the 1770s who carried out 'light' duties. Family living on the Ardgour Estate were close at hand.

Colonel David Stewart of Garth wrote in 1822:-
"While the country was portioned out among numerous tenants, none of their sons were allowed to marry till they had obtained a house, a farm, or some certain prospect of settlement, unless perhaps, in the case of a son who was expected to succeed the father."

To all expectations, John is now a man who has no claim on any property, for, on being recruited into 'the King's Service' in 1756, he had been passed over for any heritage and disappeared from all family records, as either dead or missing, or, "gone to Canada."

The economic situation of the times meant that if a wife lost her husband through any circumstance, especially foreign service, the only honourable way forward was to marry again. As the mortality from childbirth was high there were just as many men needing a new wife for their children.

WO. 116/6 records his discharge papers :- "John McDonald, wounded in the shoulder was discharged from the Royal Hospital Chelsea, on the 15th. June, 1770, [after 14 years service, at age 40], as an out-pensioner of the 15th Regiment, born near Inverness." Research has examined "born near Inverness," which would encompass from Drakies to Nairn, but 2017 DNA has connections to the Black Isle across the water from Petty.

John, as a soldier in a British regiment was discharged from the Royal

Hospital Chelsea in June 1770 as an out-pensioner receiving from 9 to 12 pence Sterling, per day.

John's pension of 9 pence per day = 63 pence, or 5 shillings 3 pence per week.

This amounted to £1 pound 1 shilling [sterling] a month, was a goodly sum.

As Scot's money was worth about one tenth of English money, so the comparative value of Johns pension was the equal to £10/10/- in Scots. This pension was sufficient to allow John to provide for a family, to rent land and to prosper. ref.Capt.G.

John carried out light duties in the Royal Corps of Invalids at Fort William in Kilmallie where he maintained contact with Lieutenant Allan Stewart of the 76th. and others who had fought beside him at Quebec.

Kilmallie was a Lochaber parish of Inverness and Argyll shires, the largest parish in Scotland. It contains the burgh of Fort William, and the hamlets of Leanachan, North Ballachulish and Oinch in its Inverness-shire, and of Ardgour, Banavie, Blaich, Clovulin, Corpach, Duisky, and Garvan in its Argyll shire, section.

Johns return to civilian life after 15 years of harsh military service and social deprivation would have been a total reawakening, as all had continued normally in Kilmallie Parish and John's life was the abrogation.

Long evenings of a 'wee dram' and a lengthy blather, now ensured that he was in contact with both MacDonald and Stewart relatives in Ardgour and Glenorchy, as information of mutual interest on family relationships and financial standing was exchanged between them.

One of the relatives of this group was John Stewart, sometimes recorded as Miller and sometimes as waulk Miller, but always as of Edindonich.

Edindonich House is a two story L- shaped building of natural stone. It was originally part of a large sheep farm at the end of the village of Stronmilchan on the lower reaches of the river Orchy.

The land still has water rights to the stream some 75 metres from the building which was necessary to drive the mill wheel.

This was a Waulk mill where the 'fulling' of the tweed cloth was completed after weaving.

The cloth was especially dampened and the women would sit around a large table with a length of damp tweed cloth, pushing and pulling at it, 'waulking' the cloth.

John Stewart married Elizabeth Campbell and as a Miller of Edindonich House in 1756, he was a Stewart of some consequence indeed, as his wife would have some connections with the Breadalbane family as the tenancy of the Mill was from the Earl of Breadalbane, whose Factor was John Campbell of Achallader.

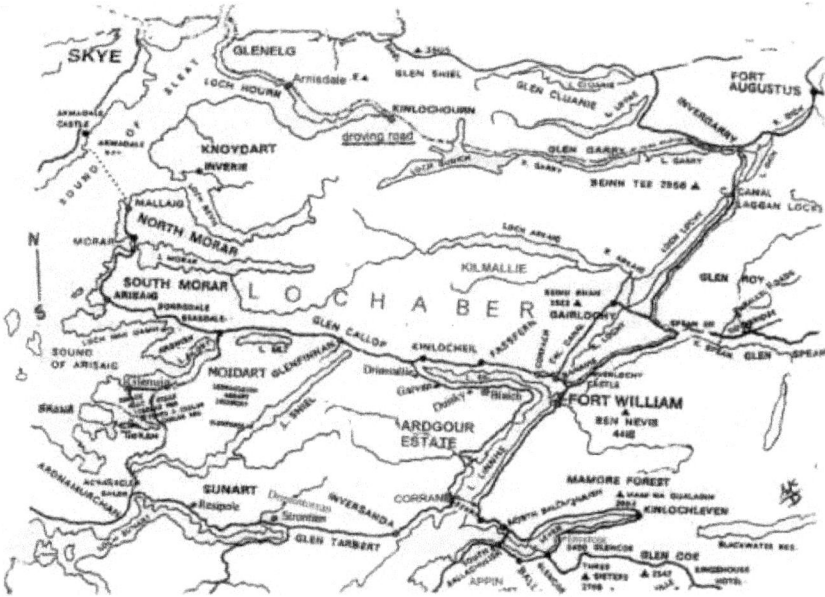

The Western Highlands of the Lochaber region which includes the inner Islands of Muck, Rum and Eigg and Arisaig, Knoydart, Morar, Moidart, Ardgour, Kilmallie and Ardnamurcham.

THE "TANGLE O' THE ISLES" - of Stewarts, McNabs, Campbells, and MacDonalds.

The Glenorchy Church is 150 metres from Edindonich House and is built on land once owned by Donald McNab of Barachastalan, who gave his location as Clachan Dysart, originally a place of Druid worship.

In this churchyard may be seen the engraved grave slabs of the Campbell's of Breadalbane.

About 1430, Sir Duncan Campbell of Loch Awe acquired the lands of Glenstrae and Glenorchy. He gave the lands of Glenorchy to his son Colin who married Janet Stewart so he became Sir Colin Campbell of Glenorchy and was a Knight of Rhodes and fought in the Crusades, Sir Colin was the ancestor of the House of Breadalbane.

In 1567 Sir Colin Campbell, 6th of Glenorchy, bestowed Achallader on his natural son Archibald, but the Fletchers rightly refused to leave their land.

Sir Colin's son Duncan finally acquired the land of Achallader.

Campbell of Achallader was the first factor and Chamberlain to the 1st Earl of Breadalbane in 1686, and his son John Campbell of Achallader was the Factor and Chamberlain to the 2nd Earl of Breadalbane from 1736.

The changes to land tenure were being felt by the early part of the 18th century and a few of the Chiefs of Clans introduced agricultural and industrial initiatives to improve production and to develop small cottage industries for their tenants.

The Earl of Breadalbane sponsored the use of water power to establish Mills, ably assisted by his Factor. John Campbell who was highly respected as a farmer and scholar brought prosperity to the Glen by his progressive methods. He died in 1791.

One of these Mills was Edindonich at Stronmilchanjust, Glenorchy. John Stewart married Elizabeth Campbell and was the Miller of Edindonich, Glenorchy.

John is not recorded as paying rent for the Mill, so we see him as the Miller for the Earl of Breadalbane, he then rented the Mill to tenants.

The state of Scotland's economy was so depressed in the mid 1770s that when his relative Lt. Allan Stewart, late of Fraser's Regiment, returned from fighting in America and told of the fertility of the land and the opportunities available for those who had the will to work, John and relatives were willing listeners who became willing emigrants.

Beside John Stewart, other members of the same family who sailed were : Allan Stewart, 44, late Lieutenant of Fraser's Regiment, Apine [Appin] and his servant Donald Carmichail; Kenneth Stewart, 40,late Ship's Master, Apine, his wife, family and servants; Alexander Stewart, 35, Gentleman Farmer, Apine,[Appin], and his son Charles.
Farmers and agricultural labourers who decided to emigrate, unanimously declared," that they never would have thought of leaving their native country if they could have supplied for their families in it."

Tradesmen who decided to emigrate did have some prospect of better wages in Scotland but their principal reason for leaving was that, " their relatives were going so rather than part with them they chose to go along."
Men from Appin told of thirty-three merk land turned into sheep walks.

In 1775 John Stewart, Miller Edindonich, now Clothier, his wife Elizabeth and most of their family, with employees, relatives and neighbours of Glenorchy, sailed on the ship 'Jupiter of Larne,' for Wilmington in North Carolina; Samuel Brown, Ship's Master.

Part of the family stayed in Scotland.
Daughter Mary had married John McIntyre in Glenorchy, son John, now 17, was already living and working with relatives elsewhere, and Donald who would have been 8 years old in 1775, had probably been fostered with kin, so as to maintain the family line in Scotland, and he married Christina ..?, in Appin in 1788.

The voyage from Scotland to America varied from one to two months depending on the weather, but it was the unscrupulous Captains and crew who preyed on vulnerable passengers.

On some ships, instead of the agreed supply of meat, meal and biscuit, the Captain saved/made money by stocking old and soured supplies, the food being so bad that children died and adults were quite ill.

The voyage for the Stewarts went relatively well because they were a large family group and so were well provisioned and able to look after themselves, which also protected them from abuse by crew.

The family arrived to a country in unrest, a country in political turmoil, which within a year of their arrival was in a state of War.
They had traded the hardships of their native land for the hardships of a country in a Civil War of Independence from Britain, Carolina was in the thick of some of the most bitter early fighting.

To obtain 'Grants of land' on the Cape Fear river, new arrivals had to take the oath :-
" ~~~~ in the support and defence of his Majesty's Government."
ref:The Highland Scots of North Carolina, by D.Meyer, Ph.D., p. 67.
This immediately put them in the opposing military camp to the local, fervent patriot for Independence.

Some would have been aware of the unrest in America at the time, but, the general assessment was that these were localised incidents.

Lord North spoke of, "the rebellious people of Massachusetts," so they had no idea that there would be outright War with Britain in 1777.
What they also did not know was the writings which denigrated the Scot :- " The Scots are regarded by many Americans and Englishmen as naturally despotic, they are strangers to liberty themselves and wanted the rest of Mankind to live under the same slavish notions that they had done," wrote Landon Carter. ref:sc,'The War of American Independence.'

These writings were aimed at stirring up the populace against the Earl of Bute in particular. Bute had been first Minister in 1762-3 and he was believed to still be controlling policy long after he had left office, and against Britain in general.   sc.

Landing in 1775, in a country in political upheaval, did not allow the new settlers to establish foundations of trust and community solidarity before the War was upon them.
Worse was to come: In 1776 John Stewart was with Allan Mc Donald of Kingsburgh in a company of Highlanders under General Donald McDonald, who mustered at Cross Creek, to form and march to join Government Troops at Cape Fear. Their march would cross Moore's Creek and pass by the town of Wilmington.

Lt. Allan Stewart, who sailed with John Stewart and other relatives, was one of General Donald McDonald's staff, and is mentioned in a book on Flora McDonald which tells of the trials experienced in North Carolina and her return to England.

THE AMBUSH:
Colonel Richard Caswell mobilised his Minute Men and with other Patriot militiamen marched to take up a fortified position at Moore's Creek Bridge, where they removed the floor boards of the bridge and greased the main bridge girders.

The Loyalist Highlanders led by Colonel Donald McLeod attacked across the bridge framework and were decimated by rifle and artillery fire, with 50 killed and 880 captured.
Those captured were thrown into the common jails of the colony, their families alone and unprotected. The muster rolls were also captured so those who escaped were identified and.
The American 'troops' were local Militia and citizens who were individuals rather than professional soldiers and at times difficult to control, as when they indulged in looting the possessions of residents in the vicinity of a skirmish with British troops or Loyalists.
This unruly behaviour caused an oft angry Washington, trying to stop plundering, to quote to his troops, "why did we assemble in arms? was it not to defend the property of our countrymen?"   sc.

In May of 1779 the back country of Carolina was aflame.

This caused Nathanial Greene the American Commander in the South, to state," the Whigs and Tories pursue one another with the most relentless fury, killing and destroying each other whenever they meet."

John Stewart tried to look to the safety of his family but he may have waited too long before acting as that area of Scottish settlement was overrun by marauding and looting Militia bands.

One of the 'new migrants' was Flora McDonald who was in the same grave situation as John Stewart's family, because her husband, Allan of Kingsburgh, had been taken prisoner at Moore's Creek Bridge. Zealous patriots then forced Flora to leave their plantation on Mountain Creek.
Flora and her children negotiated to leave North Carolina under a flag of truce, to return to Scotland in 1779 after spending only four years in the Colony.   THSNC, p.74.

When told of this and the assault to members of his family, John decided to send Janet and her sister Margaret back to Scotland on the same ship to arranged marriages, Janet to John McDonald and Margaret to John Stewart in Appin. pr

In the book Flora reports, "I and three young ladies and two gentlemen set sail," this was on the 'Lord Dunmore' a letter of marquee ship of 24 guns.
British ships sailed with ease between Britain and America up to 1779, because Britain had superiority of 'Ships of the line.'

There are ample records of members of Scots families returning to Scotland from America to marry. The experience of Culloden and its infamous aftermath and the similarity of this situation in America would have caused them to reconsider their position.
These 'young ladies' of 16 years had been subjected to capture and assault by marauding bands of Militia; therefore an arranged marriage with a suitable gentleman back in Scotland, was the most secure option for their future.
In Janet's case, John McDonald was 49 years old, an invalid soldier, with a secure pension, of a known family, so he was acceptable to John Stewart for his daughter. The arrangement would have been of mutual advantage to both parties.
Thus due to events and circumstance, in 1779 John McDonald of the 15th. Regiment married Janet Stewart.
Marriages were arranged between families to maintain lands and tenancy, to keep the Family line of inheritance secure,[29] and in general to provide a future for a daughter.

After their marriage John McDonald and Janet Stewart resided in Corran, Kilmallie where Macian of Glencoe had houses.
This was part of the MacLean of Ardgour Estate where his cousin Dougal Macdonald, had a croft at Blaich.

So one of "the Lochaber Lads" who fought in Quebec had returned home to a future life with relatives in his beloved Lochaber.
A son Dugald was born in Corran on 10-3-1782[30] .

---

30. In celtic Scotland an heiress was either married or put in a Convent by the age of fourteen; marriages were arranged for daughters of well connected families as soon after puberty as was convenient.
31 The exact birth dates recorded in the OPR's show these families to be 'well to do'; other children in the district were christened in groups when the Minister visited.

John of the 15th Regiment died about 1786 believed buried on the Isle of Munde, in the Nether Lochaber section, Loch Leven in Glencoe. It is accepted that ages and dates can differ by 10 years in a persons records of that time and in regard to the indistinct engraved date on his grave stone.

The late 1700s and early 1800s were periods of activity in the Kilmallie shire along the great Glen as there was the traditional productive activity of fishing out of Fort William and Glenuig and from Loch Shiel. The cattle markets at Corpach Canal and Fort William traded wool, skin, hides and kelp.

In 1803 there was the construction of the Caledonian Canal which joins the lochs of the Great Glen for 100 kilometres connecting Fort William at Corpach at the head of Loch Linnhe on the west to Inverness on the east by 29 lochs, 4 aqueducts and 10 bridges.

It passes through the Parish of Kilmallie which includes Fort William, North Ballachulish and Oich within Inverness-shire, and in the shire of Argyll it has Ardgour, Banavie, Blaich, Clovulin, Corpach, Duisky, and Garvan.
The boundaries west are Ardnamurchan and Glenelg, then northeast by Leanachan, Kilmonivaig, south by Lismore and Appin and southwest by Morvern, very extensive indeed and home to a population of McDonalds.

It is a mountainous region and has Scotland's magnificent Ben Nevis to the East of Loch Linnhe at 4406 feet with gneiss and mica slate the predominant rocks, with granite, porphyry, quartz, hornblende, limestone and fine marble also present.

Extensive deposits of roofing-slates have been quarried at North Ballachulish and mineral deposits of lead ore, with a high proportion of zinc and silver, are within the parish.

Stands of native pine forests and plantations covered a large area.

MOIDART LIFESTYLE and families who later migrated to lands afar.

Dugald, son of John of the 15th, enjoyed life as a youngster hunting and training until he was old enough to go out and earn a living.
He had connections with Clan Ranald relatives and with Duncan son of Archibald McDonald at Glenuig and also with MacLeans of Ardgour.
Dugald is first recorded as tenant on the Kinlochmoidart family croft of Kinlochuachdrach with Duncan McVarish in 1807, but the farm was of poor pasture so he showed enterprise in 1808 to engage as a Merchant in Glenuig, trading in sheep, cattle, kelp etc, and of course Uisge-beatha, [whisky].

In a letter to Major Robertson dated 7th July 1808, (MS3984), it refers to Dugald Macdonald as a Merchant trading out of Glenuig as far as Dunbartan, with John Campbell, (recorded as Dugald Macdonald, MS 3984, 1807-14, *f* 64-65). Dugald is recorded as having resided on Kinlochmoidart property from 1807, and after marriage in 1809 moved onto Kinlochmoidart farms on Kyles Mor when relatives migrated to Nova Scotia.

This was in the Clanranald country of Lochaber, a land of rough terrain and high mountains where ice glistened on the peaks, and deer took refuge in their ravines; these were the Garbh-chriochan [the Rough Bounds.]
Theirs was the land of purple [heather] coloured hills, misty with rain in summer, and of deep snow in winter, of beautiful spring days, of long deep lochs gouged from the earth by ice age glaciers, with salmon in the quiet waters, of glens and coastal meadows for barley, oats and the grazing of cattle, and the western sea for fish and kelp.

In winter there were times of icy gale-force winds, snow and sleet, raging seas and snow blocked passes, a time to be in the stone walled dwellings, with the peat fire burning – in other seasons the warm gulf stream flowing past Skye gave a temperate influence to the weather.

It was a land of harsh climate and rough terrain, a land where only the strong of mind and body could prevail, a land where 'the water of life' was needed to warm the blood, where only the music of the 'bagpipe' could carry through the long, deep glens – where only the thick, home spun, woollen 'feileadh mor' [tartan plaid], could protect the body from the winter storm, where only the binding of Clan kinship could prevail against all odds, this was the home of the Highlander.

Donald Mor MacDonald (1690s-1748) son of Alasdair, of Baillie farm on Eilean Shona:
It seems James of Baillie farm (son of Donald Mor MacDonald) married before 1754 with a family of seven children. ref: FITP. p.17

James held the tack of Baillie farm until 1790 when he sailed for Canada.

Other early MacDonalds from the Western Highlands who migrated:
Donald MacDonald (*Domhnuill mhic Roanuill mhic Uillean mhic Calum*) "Donald, son of Ranald, son of William, son of Malcolm" from Moidart had sons of John born about 1740, Angus, Rory Ban MacDonald and Donald. The *slionneachd* of Donald gives his line back to the 1620s
They are recorded as "the Bogainn MacDonalds" so named because of their seafaring ability. ref: FITP, p.19

Eigg is close to Arisaig and was repopulated by Clan Ranald folk in the late 1600s – also it is written that folk from Glencoe went to Eigg after the Massacre.

This family lived on Eigg and left the Island in the 1780s to sail for Canada to settle in Nova Scotia in the Jidique district of Cape Breton. Their other brother Donald migrated to Pictou Nova Scotia in 1791 and also his married sister Mrs. MacDougall.

"Some time after 1800, John MacDonald of Glenuig, a foxhunter and a man of means, applied for a croft in Caolas[31] , alleging that he was the nearest relative in Scotland to Colonel MacDonald, and much nearer than James MacDonald of Caolas." NB: a *croft* is an area of land for grazing or crops.

This application would be some time after 1804, as Colonel MacDonald last of the direct line, died at Santa Lucia in 1804.

The claim as to relationship was upheld by the estate factor Mr. Alexander Campbell, who recommended that MacDonald be given the croft, and added that he had sufficient stock to be successful.

---

[31] Today, the ruins of 6 dwellings show Caolas Mor as a toon, [a small village] with evidence of 'run-rig' cultivation, and the walls of the more recent Custom House with mortared walls and square corners.

This would be the same John Macdonald recorded(f163 NLS) on 2/2/1836 as Tachsman of Craig in a shared Report on 'Shellsand' with Dugald Macdonald Kyles More. It is understood Dugald and John were of 'the family.'

Also in 1804, Alexander MacDonald family of McEachan, sailed to Prince Edward Island. John Mc Eacharan was tenant in Kyles Ian Og and Kyles Mor in 1748-49.

So, at 25 years of age, by 1807, Dugald moved to reside on Kinlochmoidart property after Clanranald kin had emigrated to Prince Edward Island.

NOTES TO MS 3948 of papers 1807-14 f 64-65 - LETTER OF 7/7/1808.

This letter of 7/7/1808 to the proprietor at Dalilea from the factor Alexander MacDonald throws some light on the early trading by Dugald Macdonald in Kinlochmoidart:-

"He is actively involved in the trading of kelp and seemingly sheep and is engaged with John Campbell in loading Shell sand for Dumbarton. It would also seem that his cash flow was somewhat stretched."

But with all of what the Factor reports, he himself had advanced finance to Dugald and "but I believe I will be soon paid."

It is of interest to note that Dugald Macdonald, a Merchant in Moidart, has trade connections as far away as Dunbarton and possibly with the markets at Falkirk.

Others mentioned in 1808 are: George and James Stewart, McEachen, Mcpherson and Young Macdonald the Wright.

Today, the only evidence of the bustling toon (small village) of Caolas More in the 1800s and before are the ruins of five dwellings, now only heaps of stone on hillocks, and the dry-stone walls of the sixth dwelling of three large rooms with external doorways.

These encircle the 'run rig' furrows of past cultivation in the hollow of the hills. The ruins of two more dwellings are across the burn.

In the late 1700s the Government ordered the local people to build an Excise House of local stone as dwelling, storerooms and offices for the Excise men.

Using celtic logic, the locals built a fireplace in every room to encourage these Officers to remain indoors.

They sited this House opposite and in clear sight of the home of a known smuggler across the strait on Shona Bheag so that he would know when the Excisemen left on patrol and could inform the locals who distilled whisky.
It was named "Autigill"- [the place where people come to connect.]

Legislation of the 1780s imposed Excise duty on any and all whisky distilled by licensed manufacturers with the added authority to close down and destroy any illegal still.

Whisky, or Uisge beatha, the 'water of life,' required certain ingredients and conditions:-   pure, sweet, mountain water filtered through layers of ageless peat, an even, cool temperature for fermentation, secluded area away from robbers and the authorities, a lookout vantage point, a close quiet anchorage, a quantity of good quality malt barley grain, and a drying kiln.

The only evidence today of the 'Toon', is the ruins of six dwellings, the walls of the Excise House at the south east, two drying kilns, one in the narrow defile through Torr More, the other in the open meadow.

On the other side of the hill are walls of the dwelling of 'Innes a` Chulun' with its two separate byres, as well as holdings for cattle, sheep and goats.
All of which demonstrate the size of that community.

Multiple roomed dwelling Kyles Mor, Moidart

From a Report on Kinlochmoidart to the Commissioners of 1755:-
"The country supports the breeding and grassing of cattle, a little oats and barley as well as a few potatoes are grown. It produces little meal but a great abundance of beef, goats and a little mutton and as much butter and cheese as serves its inhabitants.
White fish is plentiful all along the coast. The black cattle are sold to drovers or at markets in Falkirk and Crieff. While the horses are sold at the Fairs at Inverness or the Moss of Balloch.
Supplies of meal were shipped from Banff and Aberdeen Shire or from the islands of Egg and Muck which also supplies potatoes, plus a quiet trading of barley from Uist with return goods of Whisky etc.
Kelp processed to ash is sold to Traders who arrived from Ireland and Liverpool."

It can be seen that such trading created much movement of shipping from the north and east coasts of Scotland, west to the Hebrides and Ireland and south into England. there would be work for the shipbuilders of Port-a-Bhata.

The black highland cattle were part of the Highland scene from at least the 13th Century when the earliest report relating to Cattle was found on a map. In 1259 a map noted cattle in the Highlands and 14th century records for Scotland show exports of hides and skins and wool.
Each autumn, Cattle were brought down from the summer shieling to be sold before the severe winter when cattle had to be fed and sheltered.
This dictated that the strong breeders were kept and the rest either sold off to the Drovers or taken to the nearest local market at Canall [Corpach Canal] or Fort William

Cattle were driven from the north of Scotland down the walkways of the Great Glen but after the Military roads were built the cattle were shod to protect their hooves from the stone surface.
From the Hebrides cattle were carried in small open boats to the mainland and others were swum across from Skye to Glenelg then walked to the small local markets where Drovers bought them or negotiated directly with farmers on pledged payment after sale.
This droving route continued on to the markets at Corpach where the numbers swelled from the local black cattle.
They drove these ever increasing herds to the main Fairs at Crieff and Falkirk, where they either purchased more stock or on-sold to others.

By 1723 approximately 20,000 were sold there annually. These main Fairs had peddlers, play-actors, stalls, beggars and traders.

Moidart had such a strong cattle trade that some were sold at the Corpach market, but others joined the herd droving south through Kinlochmoidart and Sunart to be transported by ferry at Corran and on to Stirling.

The main market was later shifted to Falkirk and in the year 1777, at 3 scheduled markets 30,000 head were sold. They reached their height in 1850 with sales of 150,000 head.   ref. I.F Grant 'Highland Folk Ways' p.68-71

THE AFTERMATH OF CULLODEN.

After the Battle of Culloden the well known surviving supporters of Prince Edward Stewart, the Chieftains and Tacksman of Lochaber, had to flee from Cumberland's troops, for if captured, they would be imprisoned or hung, so this left the main farms in in the districts without principal tenants.

At the same time in 1746, the Crown appointed Commissioners to administer the 'Forfeited Estates' and Factors to supervise local tenancy arrangements. A number of the appointed Factors were Campbells as that Clan had supported the English at Culloden.
Family members of Donald and Reginald now had to take action to retain lands and crofts which had been managed by the family for generations.

Ewen Ban was a tenant of Ulgary before The Rising of 1745, and when he returned from the fighting, he and John McDonald took up tenancy on the Moidart croft of Issiroy [Inchrory] in 1747 and had the lease renewed in 1764.
It is recorded that "on 11th September 1764, Ranald MacDonald, Younger of Clan Ranald let by Tack the half merk land of Inchrory (Issiroy) to Ewen MacDonald, John MacDonald and John Corbet.

Mary Corbett, John Corbett's daughter, married Angus Mor McDonald of Port a Bhata, and their son Donald married Marcella, daughter of Dugald McDonald in 1837. [Donald's DNA is of Cranachan]

In 1908 an interview of Father Joseph MacDonald, priest to the parish of Boisdale in Cape Breton reports, "Father Joseph's own people left from Moidart – he is of the Corbetts of Port a` Bhata at the head of Loch Moidart and has a brother Father Ronald OD ~~~ the mother of these two priests was Mary Corbett and their father was Donald MacDonald of North Side East Bay, Cape Breton."

NB: In 1931 a James MacDonald of North Side East bay in Canada, [Seumas Mhic Domnuill Bhan Vich Dhomnuill Bhain na Coire], reported that he was related to Corbett on his maternal side.

1996 -The author and the wreath at the Clan Donald marker.

The Scottish Record Ofice collection of the Forteited Estate Papers, 1745, includes the documents of the Barons of the Exchequer in Scotland concerning all those estates forfeited in 1747 as well as estates annexed to the Crown in 1752 and managed by the Board of Commissioners. File: Thesis, University of St. Andrews.

THE DISTILLING OF UISGE BEATHA, the water of life
(whisky).

The very early common beverage for the people had been a rough beer or wine but Uisge Beatha had the great advantage of being tastier, it 'kept' well, had many uses and the product and its equipment were easy to transport.

The 'creation' of the Water of Life was an art form known to a select number and required the process of germination, fermentation and distillation, and finally ingestion.

In relation to the distillation of Uisge beatha of fresh water, barley grain, drying kiln, a secluded site, an access for boats. 'Innes a Chulun' had all of these except for the barley grain, this was shipped in from Uist and Tyree.

Pure, sweet, fresh water was taken from the brook, 50 yards from the dwelling, recorded as 'Allt na Innes Chulun' which drains from Loch Innes Chulun.

The malt barley grain was soaked in burn water for three days to start germination, then the grain was spread out. When the sprouts were about half the length of the grain, the germination process was halted by spreading the 'green malt' over the heated floor of the grain-drying kiln and carefully raked until the sprout was withered.

The grain drying kiln was in a defile by Tor Mor of a round bowl within a round stone wall, topped with turfs, with a paved flue from the outer wall running under the bowl.
The drying kiln had various uses: (1) regular agricultural pursuits, (2) part of the whisky manufacturing process

This dried malt was then placed in casks with pure mountain water to allow fermentation.
At the completion of fermentation the 'mash' was emptied into a still which was heated, the steam distilled in the cooling coils and the fluid with an alcohol content of from 20 to 60 percent collected. The 'Water of Life' was casked and sealed.

The final product of Whisky was then traded as back loading with the birlinns bringing in the barley grain from Uist and Tyree.
Uisge beatha had many uses, as a curer of ills, a reliever of pain, an antiseptic for wounds, warmth on a frosty morn or an icy night, enjoyment in the evening. It was truly "The Water of Life."

The Pot Still used widely:

The Kiln in the defile, stone wall, flue and bowl.

A Pot Still ranged in size from 25 cm to 52cm high and from 14cm to 27cm round, the larger still holding 2.5 gallons or 12 litres.
A ¼ bushel of barley (9.8 litre volume) weighs 11.75 pounds so a mountain pony could easily carry a cask of barley mash, a cask of water and the pot still to any secluded location, where the preparation and distillation could take place.

In the years of Excisemen, a bounty was paid on reporting an illegal Still so the local whisky manufacturer turned 'honest.' When the copper distilling 'coil' of his Pot Still had worn out, the smuggler would report finding an 'illegal copper coil' and would receive the 5 pound bounty. He would then purchase a new copper coil.

Smuggling was a risky 'trade' as Excisemen were posted throughout the highlands and a wisp of smoke in a lonely glen oft pointed to a hidden Still.

Ancestors examine the drying kiln in the defile.

Innes a`Chulun - ruins of byre and dwelling, 1996.

Illustration of the daily life on a croft in Moidart, 1836,
by M. McDonald.

SONS AND DAUGHTERS OF THE HIGHLANDS look to their future.

The sons and daughters of Scotland who emigrated on the 'William Nicol', 'Midlothian' and the 'British King' came from Inverness-shire and Argyllshire, that is, from Lochaber, Appin, Skye and Mull.
They were of Clans Ranald, Glengarry, Keppoch and Glencoe, the only way to these clan areas in Scotland was over the high mountains, or by sea to the west coast.
These were the highland districts of Scotland, areas of rough terrain and high mountains where ice glistened on the peaks, and deer took refuge in their ravines, these being the Garbh-chriochan.

The original McDonald families who emigrated to Australia and settled around Canberra and east across the Manaro to the coast came from Moidart, from the area known as Kyles / Caolas, a small coastal plain, and across the North Channel from Port-a Bhata, and from Glen Moidart and they were gaelic speaking Roman Catholics.

Some of the crofts or meadows in Caolas/Kyles were, Craig beg, Caolas Beg, Caolas Mor, Allt a' Ghille, Innes a' Chulun and Eignaig.

The farms and crofts of Ulgary, Assary, Issiroy, Lednacloich, Glenforslan, Duilad and Kinloch were to the north-east of Caolas, along Glen Moidart.
Shonaveg, Kyles, Eignaig, Smerrasary, Samalaman, GlenUig, Irine and Allasary, were districts in 'Moydart' in 1800 and are still identifiable in Moidart today.

The walking track from Glenuig passed through Caolas Mor and communicated with Eilean Shona,[the Isle of Shona] by a causeway across the North channel called 'Caolas Ian Oig', to the croft farms of Shona Beg and Port-a-Bhata, where more family members lived.

At the junction of the South channel, between Shona and the mainland and Loch Moidart, is Castle Tioram, the original stronghold of Mac 'ic Ailein Clanranald.

The climate was adverse, and clanfolk with any health problems died at an early age and men could not marry until they could support a wife.
So most married at a late age, thus only the strong survived as this is reflected in records showing parents with children up to 30 years apart.

The harsh conditions and lack of medical assistance resulted in the loss of infants at birth, and children in their early years; dysentery, pneumonia, diphtheria, smallpox and other fevers were endemic and virtually untreatable.

Pennant, in his account of a journey to the Hebrides about 1722, speaks of many of the natives suffering from an affliction known there as 'MacDonald's throat.'
These bronchial and chest conditions would certainly affect the susceptible population by age 30, especially if their diet was poor and weather/living conditions adverse.

An account from the book "Old Scottish Customs" is headed 'The Cure of Disease' and relates to various remedies and cures.

One of these cures refers to the disease called 'Claeach' which effects the chest and lungs; they continue :- " it was also called the MacDonald disease, because there were particular tribes of the MacDonalds who were believed to cure it with the charms of their touch and a certain form of words, no fee was given. The Highlanders' faith in the touch of a MacDonald was great."

Not withstanding the above accounts, conversely, those who were not affected, or who overcame throat and chest infections and diseases, and the sword, lived on to an old age, to at least 80, some to over 90 years.

The clanfolk of Moidart had some mountain ponies and raised cattle and goats, they also cultivated some grain crops and later they grew potatoes for their own use and some whisky was manufactured.

The name Muydeort [Moidart] is of Norse origin for 'mud fiord' which is obvious at low tide with the exposed brown sea-weed, kelp beds.
Arisaig is Norse for Ari's bay, which shows Norse occupation of parts of this area in the times before Somerled's domination.

In the 1760s kelp gave a useful income, originally as fertiliser but due to shortages from the war and the nature of the Chemical industry it provided a further resource in the manufacture of basic chemicals of potash and soda for use in the glass and soap industries.

This saw the price rise of kelp to £20 per ton in 1772 and some Tacksman became rich.

This was later burnt between layers of peat in trenches dug in the ground. When cooled the residue condensed into a dark blue or a whitish mass which was quite hard.

This contained basic chemicals of salts, potash and soda, but mainly soda.
In a list of those who processed kelp in 1784-1785 are Ewan MacDonald of Kyles Ian Og and Ewen MacDonald of Kyles Mor.
As this was a privileged concession it is logical to deduct that Ewan Macdonald of 'Innis a`Chulun' at Kyles Ian Og, was a Tacksman.

The kelp trade expanded quickly as the war with France continued and the kelp industry provided a good income, the finished product was shipped out from Porst an Dunan.
ref: Dugald Macdonald is mentioned in MS3948 1807-1814 re kelp shipments

'War and Peace' both influenced the economy and the war with France certainly had a serious effect, but when Wellington won 'The Battle of Waterloo' in 1815, (and there were many Highhlanders who fought in both the French and British armies), the market with Europe was lost to local trade.
Peace destroyed the market for kelp as a more refined chemical was available from Spain.

The situation within the British Isles set the populace looking for ways to improve their lives.

FOLKLORE OF THE WESTERN HIGHLANDS – cults and religions.

We are aware through archaelogical excavations and DNA forensic evidence that the early folk of Scotland travelled from Europe across the landmass and later the narrow straits of the later named North Sea and brought with them their various 'gods,'many superstitions and stories of the 'netherworld.'

The most advanced and influencial of these was the Druid religion whose Scholars trained for 20 years to learn of Law, Healing, Mental transference, the Netherworld, the Stars and seasons and more, and to retain all this knowledge orally.

Some of this knowledge was retained by hereditary priests and circulated over the centuries after the Romans had outlawed their ceremonies and systematically destroyed their followers.

The Druids were followed by missionaries of the 'Culdee church who usurped much of their practices and festivals, then came the 'new' deciples of the Cistersions. Each used or built on the site of the previous 'religion' because this was the "holy place", this was the place where the populace had always gathered, this was the place where their fathers' fathers had gathered.

This was where everyone placed their votive offerings to ward off evil spirits and supernatural beings, or paid homage to an especial god, or watched a Druid ceremony, and with the coming of the Church paid to view a Holy relic or to have prayers said by the Priest.

As few people could read or write, the Oral tradition of preserving folklore and genealogy continued through travelling Bards and the family elders so that years later Observers recorded tales of wisdom, supernatural happenings and local events which were still spoken at the winter ceilidh and around the evening fireside in the Western Highlands.

Of traditional folklore is the properties of the ROWAN TREE:
The Rowan tree has a distinguished place in celtic folklore and the linguists give the definition as from the Old Norse name of 'raun or rogn.'

The rowan ranges from a bush to a 50 metre tree which grows in a range of soils and will even grow in the fork of a tree if the seed is dropped by a bird.

The tree has a white flower cluster in May and red berries in winter which can be used for a compost or a drink and the dried berries for a protective necklace or amulet.

> " The Holy Rowen Tree."
> In the yard there grows a Rowan.
> Thou with reverent care should'st tend it.
> Holy is the tree there growing.
> Holy likewise are its branches.
> On its boughs the leaves are holy.
> And its berries yet more holy.

Excerpt from 'The Kalevala' of the 1800s, a compilation of Finnish folk lore.

The wood is strong and dense, ideal for a walking staff or stick as used by the Druids which also defines the trees related magical properties with 'rune' sticks carved from its wood. It is used for foretelling events by casting the runes and reading the design as these had magical properties.

This tree was recognised as providing protection from witches and evil spirits and in Scotland one would see a rowan bush near the door or beside the walkway from the dwelling so that occupants could touch the bush for good fortune or protection from evil as they passed by.
The faith in the rowan tree to keep the family safe from witches and evil spirits is reflected in the Scottish folk song "Oh Rowan Tree" of happy family life through the seasons under the rowan tree.

Since the time of the seanecheal and the bard, Scots history and folklore has recorded many strange and mystic ' happenings' relating to the foretelling of events through people with the gift of 'second sight', and of miscreants being mysteriously punished for their misdeeds, to the extent of death, when they have transgressed certain traditions of the Clan.

These ' happenings' are mystical or strange only to the 'incomers' or people of non celtic ancestry.

To the indigenous celtic highlander or the direct celtic descendent, there is nothing 'strange' at all in the foretelling of events or in the visual witnessing of an emotional experience of someone close to the 'gifted one.'

The gift of 'the second sight' is not a thing of the past, for today there are numbers of celts who are 'fey', i,e, have 'the second sight,' who experience moments of insight and communication with members of their clan.

LOCAL FOLKLORE, as told by Tearlach McFarlane.

MORAR - THE GREY DOG .

"There was Dugald McDonald, of close kin to McDonald of Morar, this Dugal had a staghound of which he was most fond, so that when he had to go to War he instructed that his folk care for the hound.

The young chieftain returned a few years later and on inquiring about his dog was told that the staghound had swum to the nearby island to have a litter of pups and never returned. By now the pups were full grown wild dogs and a danger to every living thing, so that no one would venture onto the island.

Dugald laughed at this and said his hound would recognise him and protect him and he intended to swim across to be reunited with his faithful hound.

He ignored all their protests and walked down to the shore then swam across the narrow strait and landed on the island. The wild dogs picked up his scent first and attacked him before his faithful hound could protect him.

When he did not return, a group of men armed with clubs went across and found his torn body. They brought him back and he was buried in the burial ground beside Loch Morar.

That night the howling of a hound was heard and the faithful hound was seen at the grave. It stayed at the grave of its master until it too died.

One would expect this to be the end of the story, but no, many years later Dugald's brother lay dying and through the door came the ghost of the 'grey dog' and gave a howl.

From this the man knew that his time had come and he passed away that night.

Since that time other members of the family had similar experiences, but more often than not they would not see the dog but others looking after them or visiting them would.

One of the family had been living in Glasgow for many years when she took ill in her old age. A neighbour came to visit and remarked that she had to step over a large dog lying across the doorway.

"What was it like?" asked the old lady.

"Oh, a big grey dog with long hair."

"Ay, she's come to see me before I go," said the old lady as she knew that her time had come and she passed away soon after."

" Now the following happened up here at Glenfinnan, at a place called The Gatehouse, where a brother and sister died within 24 hours of each other, and the dog was seen at the scene, not by family, but by neighbours.

It has been seen in Nova Scotia. MacDonalds of that family who emigrated have seen it regularly over there.

When I visited Nova Scotia I went to see Dugald McDonald named after his forbear, but he had died a couple of weeks before and the 'grey dog' had appeared to his neighbours."

THE MIGRATIONS OF THE MEN OF ALBA – thoughts in the 1600s.

Highlanders of Northern and western Scotland were seafarers from the earliest of days and none more so then those of Clan Donald with their fleet of Galleys under the Lord of the Isles. These Scots sailed and traded far and wide from the Faeroes to the Mediterranean.
Trade became more organized and Scots invested in overseas ventures as merchants set up trading houses from Spain to Sweden, from Rouen to Russia and their families settled there.
Business was well established in Europe in 1366 when John, Lord of the Isles, went as envoy to Belgium to negotiate trade of Scotland's wool to finance the King's ransom.

Even in the mid 1600s there were thoughts of settling Australia, then not so named. If the King had felt in a better mood when he read a certain petition, Australia might have been an extension of Scotland. For in 1624 Sir William Courteen petitioned James Ist to colonise Terra Australis , but the King knocked him back!

The first organized migration came with the opening of shipping to the Americas and settlement in Jamaica sponsored by the Government and then later to what was to become Canada. Scots were the backbone of the Hudson Bay Company and in the later timber and fishing industries of Canada.

The next influence for immigration came with the change in land tenure.
In the 17th century, land was apportioned to family relatives of the Chief of the Clan and sublet to other kin.
Testament dative records of 1684 with the inventory of goods belonging to Euin Mc Dugald Vc Innes in Ulgary, 51 great cows 10 others, horses, sheep and goats, etc, amounting to £909/6/8.

In the 18th century it was a different story. After Culloden due to their support of Bonnie Prince Charlie, most of the Clans traditional land had been forfeited to the English Crown which then appointed Commissioners[32] of Forfeited Estates selected from their supporters,

32 Reference: The Scottish Record Ofice collection of the Forteited Estate Papers, 1745, includes the documents of the Barons of the Exchequer in Scotland concerning all those estates forfeited in 1747 as well as estates annexed to the Crown in 1752 and managed by the Board of Commissioners. File: Thesis,

who then leased out the croft farms, generally to family sometimes to favourites.

Conditions soon deteriorated whereby people could not earn enough to enjoy an acceptable lifestyle. The main chance for highlanders to earn anything was to join the army. Fighting was something they were good at!

THE LATE 1700 MIGRATIONS- AMERICA WAS THE CORNUCOPIA.

In comparison to the hardships they were suffering at home, America was described as "the land of plenty" and was the initiative for the second early migration from the Highlands. A number of Highland Chieftains migrated with members of the clan to Nova Scotia and North Carolina.

Something like 20,000 Highlanders migrated to America between 1763 and 1775.

The sea voyage in the late 1700s was one of high risk, not just from the vagaries of the weather, but from corrupt officials, Captains and undisciplined seamen.

Owners of cargo and/or passenger sailing ships made a lucrative trade plying from the British Isles to America with immigrants and returning with goods.
 The outward journey was one of adverse conditions, as America was due west from the British Isles.

After collecting passengers from ports in Scotland, Britain or Ireland, the Captain was faced with the prevailing winds blowing from the west, forcing him to tack southwards against the buffeting waves to the Tropic of Cancer to then pick up the prevailing winds from the east to take the ship westward to the coast of America and north to Washington or Halifax.

Depending on the season, the average voyage took six weeks but if winds or weather conditions were adverse then the voyage could be as long as twelve to fourteen weeks.

University of St. Andrews.

Captains who plied this trade were in general a most corrupt type, ever ready to cut corners and extract monies from whatever situation, so they only provided the bare essentials of food rations for passengers so the longer the voyage the less food was available and conditions became drastic. Passengers were forced to pay extra monies for food to survive, thus the captains made higher profits on that voyage.

The return voyage from North America to Britain could not be compared with the outward journey. The Captain had the following westerlies behind his ship so could almost sail directly across the Atlantic Ocean between 30N and 60 N.
Immigrants suffered many dangers when crossing the Atlantic.
The food was cooked over an open fire on deck, and lanterns were used for light so there was an ever danger to the ship.

The other major danger was from shipwreck as these were unknown waters for the most part with a lack of lighthouses on rocky landfalls, and in winter there was danger from icebergs. 1834 was a disastrous year with seventeen ships wrecked in the Gulf of St. Lawrence with the loss of 731 immigrants.

The "Alexander" sailed in 1772 with 210 highlanders for Charlottetown and sailed up the Hillsborough River to land at Scotchfort.

These folk were of a scheme initiated by the Bishops of Edinburgh and the Highlands assisted by John Macdonald of Glenaladale to resettle people of the Catholic faith from South Uist to Canada.
Glenaladale's brother Donald travelled to the Island of St. John to purchase land and then have this surveyed ready for tenants from South Uist, Kinlochmoidart and Glenaladale in Scotland.

The "Nancy" sailed from Dornoch with 200 pasengers for America in 1773, only one of the 50 young children on board survived the trip. Just think of the tragedy as a little bundle of canvas slid overboard into the Atlantic Ocean.

During the voyage seven babies were born but all the mothers died and only one baby lived so only one hundred of the two hundred passengers who embarked survived the voyage – this mortality rate was blamed on the poor food supplied, "foul water and uncooked, musty, black oatmeal."   ref:'The Highland Scots of North America' p.17

By the time Officials in New York began examining the charges brought by the distraught Highlanders the ship had weighed anchor and left port.

It was common for women passengers to be intimidated and abused by Captain and crew and young men travelling alone were robbed of money and belongings.

The "Jamaica Packet" sailed in 1774 bound for North Carolina. These unfortunate emigrants suffered crowding below decks where they were confined for nine days during storms at sea and their conditions deteriorated to an isolated existence in odoriferous waste.
The only ventilation was through cracks in the deck above, which also allowed sea water to run through as each heavy wave crashed on the ship.
Instead of wholesome food as contracted, they received a weekly supply of: one pound of spoiled pork, mouldy biscuit, two pounds oatmeal and brackish water. Their main sustenance was raw potatoes which they had with them.

The "Jupiter of Larne" sailed in 1774-75 for Wilmington, North Carolina.
The Ship's Master was Samuel Brown; the Collector, Duncan Campbell and the Controller, Neil Campbell.

By the end of the 1770s the ecomomics of the majority of the clansfolk in Argyll were so depressed that people were forced to examine every avenue which might improve their lot.
Soldiers returning from the Wars in America told of available land of such fertile soil, that yields of three crops a year were common.
They told of a place where a man's toil returned ample reward in harvest or value, whereas in Argyll, as elsewhere, a man could not raise enough produce to feed his family, nor earn sufficient from trade or trading to progress.

Men from Appin spoke of thirty three merk land turned into sheep walks.
So it was that in 1774-75 many of the inhabitants of Glenorchy and relatives of Appin decided to imigrate to North Carolina. They sailed on the ship 'Jupiter of Larne' for Wilmington, North Carolina.
The Farmers and labourers who emigrated, unanimously declared," that they never would have thought of leaving their native country if they could have supplied for their families in it."

Some Tradesmen who emigrated did have some prospect of better wages in Scotland but their principal reason for leaving was that, " their relatives were going so rather than part with them they chose to go along."

David McDonalds description of the emigrants on the 'British King' as "relatives and neighbours" is the same as used by those on the 'Jupiter of Larne' and is obvious by their names, occupations and place of origin, as 138 people either paid their passage or assisted relatives less fortunate.

One family who sailed on the "Jupiter of Larne" landed in the middle of the American War of Independence to experience major hardships was of:

John Stewart,48, Clothier, Glenorchy is number 1 on the Ship's list and is followed by most of his family as listed in Parish records when he was Miller of Edindonich from 1756 to 1771. Mary the eldest daughter, of 19 years, stayed in Scotland and married John McIntyre in Appin.

Donald, born 19/5/1767, is not included on the list as it is believed that he stayed with his sister Mary, or was fostered to a relative so as to maintain the line in Scotland, and he married Christina ..?, in Appin in 1788.

Beside John Stewart, there were three other Stewarts of some standing who also emigrated, so it is logical to deduce that these four were of the same family.

The three other Stewarts of some standing on the ship were as follows:
No. 51, Allan Stewart, 44, late Lieutenant of Fraser's Regiment, Apine [Appin] and his servant Donald Carmichail.
No. 81, Kenneth Stewart, 40,late Ship's Master, Apine; his wife, family and servants.
No. 54, Alexander Stewart, 35, Gentleman Farmer, Apine,[Appin], and his son Charles.

Some would have been aware of the unrest in America at the time, but, the general assessment was that there was localised incidents.

Lord North spoke of, "the rebellious people of Massachusetts." But it is doubtful if they would have thought that there would be outright War with Britain in 1777.

What they did not know was the writings which denigrated the Scot.

" The Scots are regarded by many Americans and Englishmen as naturally despotic, they are strangers to liberty themselves and wanted the rest of Mankind to live under the same slavish notions that they had done," wrote Landon Carter. ref: sc, The War of American Independence 1775/83.

These writings were aimed at stirring up the populace against the Earl of Bute in particular, Bute had been first Minister in 1762-3 and he was believed to still be controlling policy long after he had left office, and against Britain in general. sc.

Landing in 1775 in a country in political upheaval did not allow the new settlers to establish foundations of trust and community solidarity before the War was upon them.

From 1775 the situation steadily deteriorated with daily forays by American Militia against British troops and local 'loyalists' and advances by British troops against Militia outposts and 'revolutionary' bands.

The result was armed and plundering groups moving through the country 'shooting and looting.' The family of the citizen and settler alike were under constant threat of robbery, assault and death.

The American 'troops' were local Militia and citizens who were individuals rather than professional soldiers, and at times difficult to control, as when they indulged in looting the possessions of residents in the vicinity of a skirmish with British troops or Loyalists.

This unruly behaviour caused an oft angry Washington, trying to stop plundering, to quote to his troops," Why did we assemble in arms? was it not to defend the property of our countrymen?"

Likewise in June of 1777 the Commander of the British 40th. Foot decried   " the most shameful practice of Maroding and plundering," that prevailed in the Regiment.

British ships sailed with ease between Britain and America up to 1779, because Britian had superiority of 'Ships of the line,' but from 1779 the Navies of France and Spain steadily gained in numerical superiority.

In May of 1779 the back country of Carolina was aflame. This caused Nathanail Greene,[the new American Commander in the South], to state,

"the Whigs and Tories pursue one another with the most relentless fury, killing and destroying each other whenever they meet."   sc.

There are ample records of members of Scots families returning to Scotland from America to marry as the experience of Culloden and its infamous aftermath would have caused John Stewart to look to the safety of his family.

He was too late, as that area of Scottish settlement was overrun by marauding and looting Militia bands. Such an assault on members of his family would have been ample reason for sending Janet back to Scotland to an arranged marriage.

The economy had changed from the exchange of goods between crofters and the paying of rent in kind, by labour and produce, to having to pay in coin.

Traditional Clan lands were sold and clansfolk had new, often absentee, landlords and these were the changes which resulted in some cases of eviction from traditional land, and later titled 'the Clearances', which a couple of writers sensationalised as happening to all people who emigrated.

In 1782 the first sheep farmer from the Borders was employed in the Glengarry estates and a series of evictions took place from these estates in 1785.

In 1786, 500 Glengarry folk from Knoydart emigrated to what is now Ontario, Canada.

A number of Highland Clan Chiefs did endeavour to assist their clansfolk in the transition from croft farming by creating alternate cottage and local industries and assisting in resettlement.

In some cases they lead their people to North America to settle.

Cotters, the workers on the rented crofts, were encouraged to resettle to areas of developing industry, but in some cases this reduced them to a life of squalor in the Industrial tenements of major cities.

SCOTTISH EMIGRANT SHIPS – trading to Canada and America.

In 1790 the ships:-

Jane; Lovely Nelly; Lucy; and the British Queen sailed for 'The New World'.

In 1801:-

The Sarah; Nora; Hope Of Lossiemouth; Good Intent and The Dove berthed at Pictou, Nova Scotia. The Marco Polo; St. Lawrence; William Tell; and the Clarendon arrived in 1808, some to Canada and some to America

THE HIGHLANDERS – warriors, musicians and bards.

In 1791 a group from the Lochaber region sailed for Canada to settle at Cape Breton.
They lived on the Island of Eigg which has its own history of resettlement in the late 1600s and of welcoming displaced folk from Glencoe after 1692, Eigg being part of Lochaber off Arisaig on the mainland.

A few landlords may have been pleased to lose a number of crofters, because they themselves needed ready money to pay for goods and produce but this was not the common view.
Contrary to the opinion that all landlords engaged in "The Clearences," a large number of landholders feared the emigration of local people from their districts because they were losing their readymade workforce and they themselves were in as dire economic circumstance as everyone.
These landlords tried to keep local people on the land.

THE CALEDONIAN CANAL:
The situation was so grave that the Government decided to start some Relief Work projects. They engaged engineer Thomas Telford and his associate William Jessop to develop plans for the construction of a canal with a system of locks to join the east coast at Inverness to the west coast at Corpach as an encouragement to foster water transport and trade. Construction work commenced in 1803.
The Caledonian Canal of 100 kilometres with its system of Lochs was completed in 1822 to be used by barges and pleasure craft.

2014 – The peaceful scene of the entry to the first loch of the Caledonian canal at Corpach with Ben Nevis in the distance.

THE START OF THE 1800s MIGRATIONS .

The early 1800s saw the next major migration and this to Australia.

Again, contrary to some writers who would have Australia populated by convicts and their progeny, whereas convicts suffered a relatively high death rate and a few escaped to live in the bush. Of those who gained release a large number left Australia to return to England or went to the American goldfields and elsewhere.
As womenfolk were in the minority they had their 'pick' of suitors, so an ex-convict or 'ticket of leave man' was last on their list. The much talked of "convict population base of Australia" is another myth of the politic writer.

There followed 'pioneer free settlers,' some of whom were 538 Scots who up to the 1830s were mainly self financed agriculturalists, merchants and ship owners, as well as half-pay officers and Tacksman all seeking land offered by the Government, and trade.

1815 and there is Peace between Britain and France.

This period after the European wars was a time of hardship. Peace destroyed home markets and commerce failed, with the loss of local industry such as from kelp, more Landowners turned to larger sheep farms which worsened the situation as there was less land available for small farms and crofts.
This exacerbated the land problem as highlanders discharged from the armies wanted and needed land to support them and their families and added to this was a series of bad harvests.

The other private, or rather cultural hardship, was the Excise Act where the home distillation of Whisky 'the water of life' was outlawed in the 1780's with the imposition of a heavy Licence.

On the other side of the Highland Line great changes were also taking place; new techniques for smelting ironstone in 1828; the coming of the Railway in 1830; shipbuilding on the Clyde.
The population of some large towns of Scotland, increased with industry, but the greatest influx of people was on the Clyde - in the middle decades of the 1800's some hundred thousand Irish workers migrated to Scotland to work for low wages rather than stay in Ireland and starve.   rm.

This too affected the available work and income for the Scot who lived below the Highland Line and the loss of their jobs was the basis for confrontation between the Scot and the Irish, not the religious question of protestant or catholic.

In August of 1832 Cholera broke out in Inverness-shire and four years later in 1836 there was a famine; causing social and economic hardship.
The time had come for clansfolk to look further afield and to follow those Scots who had migrated to Australia between 1815 and 1832.

These were the elements which set the scene for people to leave home and family.

They were encouraged by Government Selection officers and Land Agents who toured the Highlands seeking people of the necessary skills and industry willing to emigrate –

David McDonald, one of those who emigrated in 1838, tells of the stories told of the availability of land and the high wages paid in Australia, and quote, "these agents described the many advantages of settlement in Australia, that many families, well to do, were induced to emigrate."

The 'First Fleet' in Botany Bay, 1788- *M.McD*

AUSTRALIA might have been the "NOVA SCOTIA" of the southern hemisphere –

IF JamesI had felt in a better mood when he read a certain petition which might have made it an extension of Scotland.
In 1624 Sir William Courteen petitioned the King to colonise Terra Australis but the King knocked him back!

So let us look at the facts for those times -
Yes, there were evictions from crofts, there were resettlement from crofts to areas of developing industry, there was a change from non productive croft rental to sheep farming. But, the majority who emigrated did so by practical choice because of the depressed industry, low wages and recent famines.
They emigrated to gain a better lifestyle of fairer wages and available land.

To review the book "The Long Farewell" by Don Charlwood which tells of the voyages of emigration to Australia through diary records and other research.
The essential elements of the hardship and experiences of people emigrating to Australia and America in the mid 1800s is well told by Charlwood and gives us a fuller picture of what the early builders of the Australian nation had to withstand

In so doing, one must consider the whole 'picture' *ie* the internal politics of Britain from 1745 and its international policy from the 1750s involving France and North America.
The first emigration from the Highlands was influenced by:
(1) the aftermath of Culloden (1746) with the subjugation of the people and devastation of the land by the English.
(2) the conditions wherein people could not earn enough to enjoy an acceptable lifestyle.

The voyage from Scotland to America or Australia was not something to take lightly but the Highland Scot was not one to fear adventure. In considering the social attitudes of the peoples of those Nations without appreciating the international machinations of the British Parliament in world affairs, *ie*, the War between Britain and France in Canada 1756-1763 followed by the American War of Independence until 1777 and then the War in France concluding in 1815, should have been brought to the notice of their readers.

To state that, "north America, by contrast, was private-enterprise country, founded by merchant venturers, populated by people paying their own way. It is not surprising that the North American ethos contrasts with that of Australia," is certainly a loose statement when originally both were settled by 'venturers' obtaining land Grants from the British Government. Also prisoners from 'Culloden' were transported to America and sold to farmers as workers to serve a sentence.

The slave trade used by the early American 'venturers' for cheap labour should not be ignored either.

In regard to Australia. Granted that convicts were transported to Australia as a Government 'workforce' to serve out their sentences, but the 'pioneer settlers' up to the 1830s were self financed agriculturalists, merchants and ship owners, seeking land and trade.

In 1813 the Blue Mountains had been crossed and the merino sheep industry, introduced by John Macarthur in 1797, expanded onto the inland plains.

Timber and wool were shipped to England and word spread of the natural riches enticing more self financed settlers to emigrate.

This expansion in sheep numbers and a lesser extent in cattle grazing required a workforce of shepherds and supporting trades.

This initiated the Government emigration policy to Australia, simply to sustain the growing industries and blossoming trade from Australia which reflected in the earning capacity for the British Government and gave her a strategic position on the Eastern Trade route.

It should be noted that "government assisted passage" required the people receiving this to sign up for employment for the first 2 years in Australia, so the "assisted passage" did have a "payment" attached.

Grazing improved to such an extent that by 1850, there was 16,000,000 sheep producing wool for export.

Later in the 1830s the voyage to Australia was the better simply because it was under the scrutiny of Government officers and under Government Regulations, but even these came under strain when Ships were in great demand to carry people to Australia during the time of the Australian Gold Rushes, in Bathurst 1851, and anything at any price would do.

The one aspect of a seafaring voyage was that of sea sickness.

What was not appreciated was the effect, below decks, of multiple people being seasick at the one time for days on end with no one to assist or look after those incapacitated, as all were affected and the crew was too busy in the rough conditions to help.
I leave the imagination to conjure up the situation.

One quoted Diary entry writes that English passengers refused to travel on Ships with Scots as the Scots were dirty and smelly.
Weren't they all !

In the period under discussion the level of hygiene, or rather lack of it, was sadly common to English, Scots and Irish, to high society and working class. People still questioned the overuse of water and the opening of windows as instruments which encouraged disease and illness.
The death rate among children was due to their exposure to communicable disease and their low immunity to these diseases.
Highland children had little immunity from living in the clean country air of the Highlands so were very susceptible to the common diseases of the crowded English cities. They stood no chance against the influenzas and unknown "fevers", or the common measles brought on board by passengers and crew.

England did not simply transport ALL their convicts from the 'Prison hulks', it seems they were rather selective as to who they transported to Australia.
Convicts transported had a higher literacy standard than convicts left in England, which supports a selection process to provide a basic structure to ensure a good start for the Colony.
The Government needed a ready workforce to construct roads, bridges, and a Town, ie Government Offices, buildings for local commerce and industry, fortifications and all the ancillary Tradesmen.
They also needed clerks, and all this immediately.

There were other considerations.
There was competition from France and other countries looking to explore and settle 'The Great South Land' for commercial gain, so England had a vital interest to set up facilities to protect her shipping and as a staging post for the Eastern Trade routes.
Convicts suffered a relatively high death rate and of those who gained release a percentage left Australia to return to England or went to the American goldfields etc.

The main movement of people from Scotland was as emigrants, so that 10% of all emigrants to Australia up to 1900 were Scots.

Scots formed 10% of emigrants up to 1900 and were encouraged by Government Selection officers and Land Agents who toured the Highlands seeking people of the necessary skills and industry willing to emigrate and settle the land.

They told of the availability of land and the high wages paid in Australia, " these agents described the many advantages of settlement in Australia, that many families, well to do, were induced to emigrate."

Scots who had emigrated to Australia before 1832 came as free settlers, but most after this to 1850s took the offer of Government assisted passage to save money which they would later use to purchase produce and stock or to set up a business.

All arrangements were conducted by the Government agents who followed set Regulations.

They were Scots of all callings, some being - younger sons, half-pay officers, tacksmen and the like, because as they were 'not the heir or the spare' they were not going to inherit anything, so a career or land grant in Australia was their best prospect for the future.

Settlers from Scotland were to the fore in banking, medicine, education, engineering, administration, the military, coastal shipping, skilled trades and grazing.

The voyage in sailing vessels was long and uncertain, hazardous due to storms at sea, life threatening from disease and general illnesses brought into a contained environment on board ship and the lack of medical cures to treat them.

One author states that in 1847 John T.Towson proposed 'Great Circle Sailing' as the fastest route from England to Australia and that it was not until 1850 that this route was used.

We will show that in 1838 the Captain of the "British King" used the 'Great Circle Sailing' route on the voyage to Australia.

SOCIO ECONOMIC CONDITIONS in the western highlands late 1700s – 1800s :

In 1782 the first sheep farmer from the Borders was employed in the Glengarry estates and a series of evictions took place from these estates in 1785, 86 and in 1787.
In 1786, Father Alexander MacDonell of Scotus led 500 Glengarry folk from Knoydart to emigrate to what is now Ontario, Canada.

Political affiliation played no small part. The 5th Earl of Selkirk opposed British Capitalism and its sanitizing of the Gaelic culture, and in 1803 assisted 800 Skye folk to emigrate and settle on Prince Edward Island.

This situation continued to deteriorate and emigration was a way out for the Estate Holder and a lifeline for the local folk, who had been forced onto a narrow coastal strip on Skye.

EMBARKATION of the "William Nicol" from Oransay in 1837 for Australia.
The local news account:-
"Isle Oronsay has for some days past presented a busy scene.
Last week, the William Nicol of Glasgow, arrived in the bay for the purpose of taking on board the emigrants.
Monday the 3rd was the day fixed for the embarkation.
At an early hour on the day, Dr. Boyter, the government agent for emigration, attended.

The Doctor was accompanied by Mr Bowie, the Commissioner for the McDonald Estates.
In the course of the day, Glengarry, Mr. Sellengston of Lochalsh, and various other gentlemen connected with Skye and the adjoining mainland, came to Isle Oronsay to witness the interesting scene.

The embarkation was soon commenced, and all was finally completed on Wednesday evening, when the 322 emigrants were all comfortably settled on board the ship:

Of this number 104 were under 7 years of age; and, judging from appearances, there is likely to be a considerable addition to the passengers before the ship reaches her destination.
On Wednesday afternoon, at the last muster of the passengers, every family was presented with a Bible.

The ship was fitted up in the most commodious manner possible, and all who visited her were satisfied that the comforts of the immigrants had been most minutely attended to. Indeed as to this, the poor people expressed themselves in the most grateful terms. The provisions laid in are of the first quality.

Dr. Roberts, Surgeon of the Royal Navy, accompanied the ship as Superintendent Surgeon, and what pleased the people most of all was to find that a large and airy part of the ship was laid off as a hospital.

An emigration is at all times an unpleasant scene to witness. On the present occasion, however, it was in many respects the reverse, for such was the eagerness of the poor people to be taken on board that all who presented themselves could not be received.
This to many was a source of great disappointment, Dr. Boyter, however, was firm in his refusing to take one more than the ship could comfortably accommodate, and several families were in consequence felt behind, with the hope, however, of being taken away by the next ship.
On Wednesday dancing commenced on board to the enlivening notes of the bagpipe and kept up till a late hour.

Early on Thursday morning the ship weighed anchor and sailed and on passing Armadale Castle she was saluted with 12 guns.
The salute was returned from the ship followed by three hearty cheers from the emigrants.

All on board were loud in their expressions of acknowledgement to Dr. Boyter for the great trouble he had taken, and thanks were as liberally poured out to Mr. Bowie for the part he had acted in procuring for the poor Highlanders so great a boon.
The first ship has therefore sailed with éclat, and as other vessels are to follow, it is earnestly to be hoped that in process of time the poor Highlanders may be removed to a scene where they can not only be useful to themselves, but also prove an important acquisition to the colony to which they are to proceed." – From a Correspondent.

THE SHIP 'THE STIRLING' sailed from England in 1841 for Western Australia.

It arrived at Perth with Thomas Brown[33] and his wife Eliza Bussy as passengers
Thomas Brown's later life is public knowledge but his early life in Scotland is unknown save that he named his property "Glengarry" thus laying claim to Lochaber heritage.

This account demonstrates the privations and unknowns of that early period in Australia's history and the opportunities available to some.

In 1836 Thomas Brown married Eliza Bussy, the daughter of a wealthy man in Oxfordshire and in 1841 the family emigrated from England on the 'Stirling' to land in Perth Western Australia and leased the property of Grassdale in York, living in a bush hut without furniture or a fireplace.
This made it must difficult for Eliza to cope, especially with young children.
Conversely, he came with sufficient finance to purchase 400 sheep at top prices. In 1849 he was appointed to the Legislative Council that caused some discontent among some longer serving settlers.   ref. Ancient Landmarks, p.48.

We know that early immigrants were aware of the opportunities on offer in the infant state of Western Australia but were probably ignorant as to the history and geography of the area.

Early navigators had landed along the west coast from Bart Diaz in 1487, Menezes in 1527, Dirk Hartog in1616 and mutineers from the 'Batavia' were marooned near Red Bluff in 1629. Most found the land unproductive and inhospitable, but there was the odd report of 'good country' by a couple who sailed by in good seasons.

When Matthew Flinders sailed the north coast in 1803 he contacted 6 vessels with Malay Captains, part of a fleet of 60 Prows of the Rajah of Boni. These people, (who were Mohammedans), had been fishing the coast and landing and setting up camps well before the Dutch had first sailed the sea routes.

---

33 Thomas Brown is the grandfather of Dame Edith Cowan, the first woman elected to the Australian Parliament in 1721.

It is probable that some of these fishermen stayed and mixed with the local tribes as the explorers noted that: 'one particular warring tribe practised circumcision as an initiation.'   ref.Als p.43

Exploration of the Victoria District (Geraldton) area took place in 1848 with the finding of minerals and the Governor travelled there to inspect the 'find' and came under attack by natives.
Even so, the mining for a substantial sample of ore for Government analysis was undertaken and a small Garrison sent to the area of Champion Bay.   Dr Foley the Medical Officer, wrote glowing reports of the area but John Drummond told of the hot climate and of cannibalism to the north.
He befriended and studied the two warring native tribes in the area and also wrote of the cannibalism practised by the natives but it seems this was not a practice but done to an opponent as a ceremonial cult.

Gerald Lefroy said the conditions were so bad that he considered leaving.   ref.ALs p.40-43
Farmers around Perth had experienced poor seasons and suffered crop and pasture loss from fire due to the aboriginal practice of burning off scrub to drive out game for an easy kill, so the farmers were open to any opportunity for better land.   ref.ALs p.13

In September of 1850 "The Inquirer" reported that a Cutter would be sailing to Champion Bay with supplies for the new settlement and that Thomas Brown of Grassdale intended establishing a station at the "Northward." William and Lockier Burges had gained leases of 3 blocks of 20,000 acres to the north of Champion Bay and Thomas Brown had gained similar leases to the east of the Bay.

The "Inquirer" reports, "Thomas Brown was forty-eight years of age, (born 1802), and as he never spoke of his early years, speculation was rife as to his background

The party overlanded with their stock to the Port of Geraldton, 424 km north of Perth, in 1850, making the future droving track as they went to take up the first pastoral property in the Geraldton/Greenough area that they called "Glengarry" as it resembled the countryside in Scotland.
Thomas became interested in Horse Breeding when the trade of horses with India was strong and he planned a complex for this. The stables were built from the late 1850s onwards with the help of convict labour.

They consist of 4 buildings set around a quadrangle, a hayshed, buggy shed with tack room and kitchen quarters, a shearing shed and a two storey stables building.

Stables and lunging room were circular in shape, which is recognised as the only one in Western Australia if not Australia, at that time.

The family of Thomas and Eliza Brown had a definite influence in the development of Western Australia as they were pastoralists, writers, explorers, magistrates, parliamentarians and horse breeders.

Edith Brown was born at Glengarry on 2nd August 1861 the granddaughter of Thomas and Eliza and daughter of their son Kenneth and his first wife Mary, she was honoured as Dame Edith Cowan, the first woman elected to the Australian Parliament in 1921.

Dame Edith Cowan's portrait is on the Australian $50 note.
She died in 1932.

Glengarry Homestead 1910 "in the dry," courtesy Faye Smart.

The story of Thomas Brown and family was based on extracts from "Ancient Landmarks:" history of the Victoria District of Western Australia by Mary Albertus Bain O.P., 1911, University of Western Australia Press, 1975:

THEY SAILED THE OCEANS WIDE.

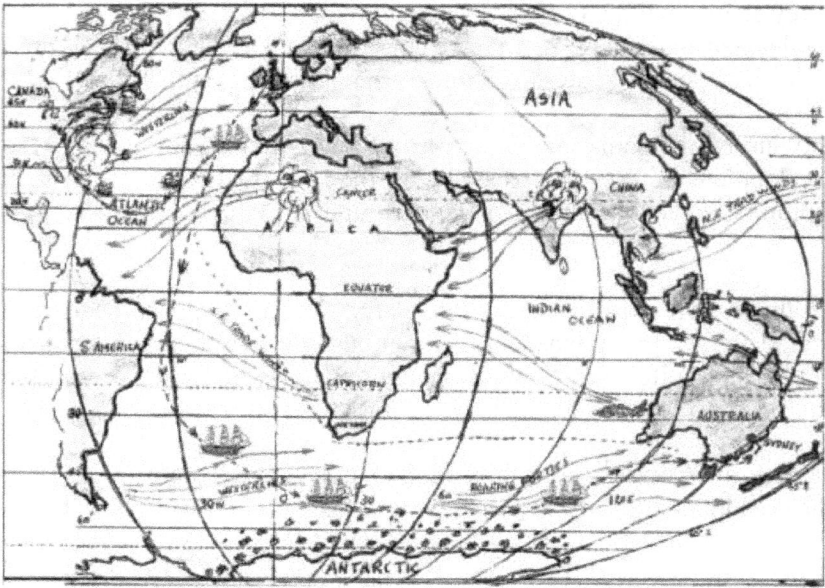

Diagram of the routes of the emigrant ships from the British Isles to America, Australia and Canada – reference   p.22, "The Long Farewell" by Don Charlwood.

Later in the 1830s the voyage to Australia was the better simply because it was under the scrutiny of Government officers and under Government Regulations, but nothing could alter the distance from the British Isles to Sydney Australia, it remained roughly 1300 nautical miles.

In the 21st century there are so many navagational aids for navagaters of international air services and ocean liners with the various satilite positioning systems available even on mobile phones, but how and what was available to the CaptainS of the ocean going sailing ships of the early 1800s who did not even have rudimentary communication as we know it, save for a system of flags.

They were required to calculate the latitude, longditude, ship speed, time lapses and sea depth by elementary methods.

The actual position of the ship relied on the basic calculations of the Captain and first mate.

If these were incorrect then shipwreck would follow.

1. Direction was by nautical compass mounted in gimbals to maintain the face of the compass to be level in all seas, and contained in a binacle (housing), at a height for the helmsman to read with a shielded candle for light.
2. Greenwich mean time was from the ships chronometer a highly technical instrument accurate to the second from which most calculations were made.
3. 12 noon on board the ship was calculated by using the Sextant to ascertain when the sun reached its zenith.
4. Longitude was then calculated from the time difference between the Ship's noonday time and Greenwich mean time using special tables as Greenwich was situated on 0 degree longitude.
5. Latitude was calculated using the Sextant to measure the angle of the sun above the horizon at 12 noon Greeneich time.
6. Speed of the ship was calculated using the "ship's log," a triangle of wood attached to a line which was calibrated with 'knots'tied at intervals. The 'log' was dropped into the sea and at the same time a 'sand glass' was turned. The 'knots' were called and measured against the 'sand glass', reading giving the speed of the ship in 'knots.'
7. Depth under the ship was measured by the 'lead line' which was a line with a hollow ended lead weight attached with markers of different colours and texture tied at various fathoms up to 20. This line was lowered till it reached bottom and the marker noted, so that when the 'lead line' was raised the hollow in the weight was examined to check on the type of bottom. If this was very important the hollow was filled with fat so that the bottom soil would stick to it.

There are as many differing accounts of voyages from Scotland to Australia as the differing lifestyle and characters of the passengers, so it is important to read widely to gain the true picture.

The voyage in sailing vessels was long and uncertain, hazardous due to storms at sea, life threatening from disease and general illnesses brought into a contained environment on board ship and the lack of medical cures to treat them.

A less mentioned hazard was debilitating sea sickness, when, during prolonged stormy weather with the ship almost pointing to the sky one minute and then plunging down the giant swells, the decks awash, seawater spurting through cracks and running into the scuppers, with hundreds of seasick passengers incapacitated below decks for days on end – the lack of sanitation services, no one fit or able to assist or to clean 'below decks' resulted in an appalling situation.

" The Emmigrants Lament"
Pure blue waters, of wonders to sing,
Birds aloft on out stretched wing,
Fluffy white cloud and steady sea,
Oh where but here would want to be.

Sudden wind with black clouds looming,
All has changed to threat and glooming,
Shriek of gale, crash of wave, crack of sail,
Two men at wheel, reef to sails to no avail.
Lodgings wet and dark the only witness,
Assault by terror of unknown and illness,
They huddle for comfort, shudder and scream,
Their plans for farms and family now a dream.

The 'cook house' fire was inundated by seawater as it was situated on the main deck for safety and was exposed to the elements as were the cages holding pigs, sheep and fowl kept for fresh food for the first class passengers.
 These broke loose and were washed overboard in the violent storms.

'Life lines' for the crew were rigged along the main deck to save them from being washed overboard from the tons of seawater smashing against and over the plunging ship as each monstrous deep ocean wave threatened to drive ship, crew and passengers to a watery grave.
In time all storms pass and calm returns.

Scots who emigrated to Australia before 1832 came as settlers to take up land .
After this from 1835 to the 1850s most took the offer of Government assisted passage with the agreement to work for a couple of years before settlement.

It would appear that the 'British King' was the first passenger vessel to use 'Great Circle Sailing,' as it was the first ship NOT to call in at Cape Town. This saved money from Port dues and time at sea.

Instead the Ship's Master Captain William Paton sailed the route south between South America and Africa to catch the Trade winds then curving to the east about the 45 parallel to pick up the Westerlies.

This allowed him to then make use of the Roaring Forties within the 40 to 50 degree latitudes to sail below Australia to (hopefully) pick up Cape Otway in Victoria and sail through Bass Strait.

This was one of the most dangerous sections of the voyge as there was more often than not wild weather with low cloud in Bass strait, and King island was between Otway and Tasmania, so the lives of all on board relied on the 'dead reckoning' of the Captain's navigation.

Once safely through Bass strait it was plain sailing up the east coast of Australia to their destination of Sydney Cove

David McDonalds account of the voyage does not mention any icebergs. The later, even faster route sailing in the 55 degree latitude was more dangerous from the any icebergs in those lower latitudes and many more ships were lost .

SOME SCOTTISH EMIGRANT SHIPS to Australia –
1837 – 1850s.

'John Barry' sailed from Dundee in March 1837 with 323 Scots.
This was one of the first ships organised to carry emmigrants selected by Dr. Boyter for the Government bounty system. The complement included engineers, masons, carpenters, farmers and shepherds, under the care of Surgeon Superintendent D. Thomson.

'William Nicol' sailed from Isle Oronsay in 1837 with 323 Scots.
This was a ship of 408 tonnage, built at Greenock in 1834, Ship's Master Capt. John Mc Alpine, Ship's Surgeon Dr. George Roberts RN., sailing from port of Isle Oronsay, Skye, on 6th July 1837.
John MacDonald, wife Sarah [nee Scott] and family, later of Thistlebrook Station in Australia, having been accepted by the Selection officer, Dr. Dunmore Lang, to emigrate were passengers on the 'William Nicol.'
Archibald MacDonald with wife Margaret MacDonald and family of Glenelg,(later of 'Burra') sailed with his brother John and brother-in-law Kenneth.

'Midlothian' sailed from the Isle of Skye in 1837.
Duncan MacDonald with his wife Catherine MacDonald, sister of Donald, daughter of Angus Port-a-Bhata, (later of Mohawk Station in Australia), and their family, as well as Robert Campbell, farmer from Lochaber, with wife Margaret nee Kennedy and family.

'Brilliant' sailed from Tobermory in 1837 with 311 Scots.
On the 'Brilliant' were three crofting families from the parish of Ardnamurchan, Alexander and Mary Cameron and their daughter. John and Margaret Gilles and six children. Donald and Catherine McDonald and four children. Alexander MacKillop, Locharber.

'Saint George' sailed from Oban in 1838 with 326 Scots.

'Boyne' sailed from Cromarty in 1838 with 286 Scots.
Of Peter MacPhee, (son of Allan MacPhee and Mary McColl, farmer Kilmallie), and his wife Jane McMaster, (daughter of Ewan McMaster and Jane Cameron), with children Duncan and Allan born Corpach Kilmallie.
Also Alexander McPhee b.1813 Corpach, son of Alex McPhee and Catherine McMillan. McPhees and Camerons were on the Ardgour Estate in 1814.

'British King' sailed from Tobermory in 1838, with 326 Scots to land at Sydney Cove 2.3.1839. Fifty percent of the passengers were MacDonalds from the Highlands and islands.
There were also MacKillops from Lochaber, MacLeans from Ardgour, Arbuckles, Campbells and Dugald Macdonald with his wife Margaret and family from Moidart.
48 families, a number being McDonalds, were transferred from the 'British King' to the 'John Barry' to be transported on to Port Phillip to land at Williamstown.
'James Moran' sailed from Lochinver on 10th October 1838 to land at Sydney 11th February 1839 – only one family of 14 McDonalds.

'Asia' sailed from Cromarty in 1839 with 268 Scots.
This ship carried a number of MacDonalds and McDonell. There were also John and Alexander Matthewson (Matheson) sons of Postmen with their wives, and Ewen and Catherine Kennedy.

'George Fyle' sailed from Tobermory in 1839 with 178 Scots.
'Henry Porcher' sailed from Skye with 21 Scots.
'Glen Huntley' sailed from Oban with 305 Scots, and arrived in Melbourne in 1840.

'Stirling' sailed from England to arrive in Perth, Western Australia in 1841.
This ship with folk from Scotland who included Thomas Brown with his wife Eliza Bussy were passengers. Thomas Browns later life is public knowledge but his early life in Scotland is unknown save that he named his property "Glengarry" thus laying claim to Lochaber heritage.

'Prince Of The Seas' departed Scotland on 24th November 1859 under Captain John Minor with passengers of 330 adult and 24 children to arrive at Port Phillip in Victoria on 20th February 1860

Some well researched and supported accounts:-
Scottish culture = Dr.Isobel F. Grant
"Botany Bay Mirages" by Alan Frost
"The Long Farewell" by Don Charlwood
"Caledonia Australis" by Don Watson.
"Ancient Landmarks:" by Mary Albertus Bain O.P.

FOLK FROM WESTERN HIGHLANDS EMMIGRATE to Australia.

By 1813 the Blue Mountains had been crossed and the merino sheep industry, expanded onto the inland plains. Timber and wool were shipped to England and word spread of the natural riches, so that more self financed settlers emigrated.

This expansion in sheep numbers and to a lesser extent in cattle grazing required a workforce of shepherds and supporting Trades, thus came the Government Emigration policy of Australia, simply to sustain the growing industries and blossoming trade.

The common skills listed by Highland immigrants were 'shepherd' or 'ploughman' and 'maid servant,' as most had been 'self employed' as a family group. A Macdonald of the direct line was listed as 'labourer' because Tacksman or wife were certainly not employment descriptions.

Government Selection officers and Land Agents, with a list of employers and jobs, toured the highlands seeking people willing to emigrate, with the health, honesty, skills and industry, which were necessary attributes for success in that new land.

David tells of the stories told of the availability of land and the high wages paid in Australia, and quote: "these agents described the many advantages of settlement in Australia, that many families, well to do, were induced to emigrate."

Dugald's father-in-law, Ewan Macdonald, was a tenant farmer of the family croft of "Innes a' Chulun" and he was also a whisky distiller, seemingly unaffected by the 'clearances' that were taking place, whereas Dugald had lived on Kinloch property as tenant on Kinlochuachdrach in 1807 and later as a Merchant out of Glenuig.
Now with a large family with six sons, he had to look to their future as the famine of 1836 was still fresh in his mind, so with relatives they decided to emigrate to Australia and were accepted by Dr. David Boyter, the Agent of Emigration of New South Wales, as meeting the criteria.
Dugald signed up to emigrate on the 'British King.'

Family members from the Moidart district had emigrated to Australia some years earlier and taken up land for grazing.

The government of the day needed families of good repute and with skills and trades, to migrate to Australia to work on the properties and assist in developing strong and viable primary industries.

Dugald must have met this easily, for he was over the acceptable age but the Selection officer corrected this, and also accepted Dugald and family without a nominated employer, for on the Disbursement list information he is recorded as of good character, healthy, able to read and write, but he had no employment arranged before they sailed.

The Moidart McDonalds received news that the "British King" would be docked at Tobermory after mid October 1838, to sail on 28[th,] the weather being favourable.

They had signed up, there was no turning back as it was all decided.

The extended families from Caolas Mor, Shona, Glenuig, and relatives in Ardgour had discussed the move to Australia when they gathered for the last two ceilidhs.
There had been some questions from MacIssac, who sailed later in 1852 about the ship information, and Angus of Porta Batha was curious about where the family might settle in Australia, and of course there were the decisions as to just what they would take with them.

On the day everyone gathered to help with the carrying of belongings down to Porst an Duin and to load them onto Angus McDonald's boat for the sail around to Tobermory.
There were only the essentials of kilt, clothing and blankets for each person and the individual personal effects and jewellery.

For the family they packed the family Bible with its records, cooking utensils, general tool kit of knives, needles, awls, thread and twine for clothing and leather repairs, and the accessories for defence and labour.

Of course there was the set of Pipes and a violin and the odd sheep dog.

It was here that the first and most important farewells were made, for this was their home and the home of families of McDonalds before them, so it was a quiet group who sat on the ship's thwarts and luggage, as the vessel sailed up the North Channel for the Isle of Mull.

They sailed down the coast to round Ardnamurchan Point on the port bow and into the Sound of Mull.

Ardmore Point came into view and shortly after they sailed into Tobermory Harbour and there was the ship which would take them to the other side of the world, the ship which would be their home and their only security from the elements for the next few months.

The activity on board ship and about the dock looked chaotic as cargo was loaded by davits from wharf to deck. Horse and carts, people and sailors, children and dogs, seemed to be one moving swarm.

They disembarked and unloaded their belongings, then joined the moving throng.
The journey was about to start.

"The sailing of the 'British King' from Tobermory was a highly emotional experience for those leaving their native land of Scotland and for the mothers, fathers and kin who farewelled them, undoubtedly seeing them for the last time."

The grief of parting was intense, but as Highlanders, the event was given due regard with Pipes playing and the 'water of life' freely drunk.

Some clutched a handful of earth as they boarded ship, many were weeping, but, as the ship weighed anchor the pipers played 'Cha Till Mi Tuille' that traditional pibroch, We Shall Return No More.

Final goodbyes were shouted from ship to shore, 'Beannaicheadh Dia sibh' [blessings with you] then a cheer from the ship, an answering cheer from the shore, another and another, bonnets were tossed into the air, and the ship sailed to the shout of 'Alba gu Sioruith', [Scotland forever].

AROUND 'THE CAPE.'

They sailed on the 'British King' from Tobermory, Mull, on 28th October 1838, accompanied by McKillops, MacLeans, Camerons, McKechnies and more. Note: Tobermory means it was named after a local spring.

The decision to emigrate must have taken much consideration, even without the changing conditions regarding land availability, for they would have been aware of the length of the voyage, months at sea, and the dangers included, contagious diseases, fevers, severe storms, shipwreck, but they lived in a time of hardship and the thought of owning farms in an abundant land was just too much of an inducement to pass over.

The 'British King' was a ship of 637 tonnage, 'well decked out' with a regular frigate deck from stem to stern of 124 feet, ceiling of 8 1/2 feet and width of 28 1/2 feet.
Ship's Master was Captain William Paton, with the total of 326 passengers under the supervision of Dr. Alexander Arbuckle.

"There was a wide promenade around the whole ship made airy and agreeable by the provision of air ports on each side."
Both of the 9 berth male and female hospitals were situated under the Surgeon's cabin from which he had immediate access by way of a hatchway.
A wind sail could be put to the top of the poop which funnelled wind down into the hospital cabins.

Each adult was provided with a clothes bag, a bed (hammock) and blankets, a knife, fork and spoon. The dining tables were affixed amidships. The 'British King' was looked upon as one of the most 'comfortable' ships of that time.

Stores to last five to six months were taken on board and consisted of arrowroot, biscuits, flour, meat, molasses, oatmeal, pork, port wine, sago, soap, vegetables, vinegar, water and medical supplies."
Besides the stores and baggage of passengers and crew, the 'British King' also carried a commercial cargo of soap, vinegar, whisky, ale, wine, Geneva, bottles, hand pikes, and other stores.

All passengers had to obey the Ship's Regulations, *eg* :-
. out of bed by seven.

. beds rolled up and in fine weather carried on deck.
. breakfast at eight.
. clean the decks at ten.
. dine at one.
. tea at six.
. all under fifteen years to be on deck at ten for inspection by the Ship's Surgeon for cleanliness.
. school lessons each day for those under fifteen.
. Divine service every Sabbath.
. washing days Mondays and Thursdays, no washing of clothes between decks.

The voyage took 123 days; the first non stop voyage from Scotland thus making a great saving from Harbour fees by sailing well past the Cape of Good Hope and not berthing at Cape Town, to arrive in Port Jackson on 28th February, 1839.
This did not mean total isolation for the full 123 days, for the Ship's Log records that the British King exchanged signals with a number of ships :-
. the Cassandra bound for Bombay on 5th December.
. the North Britain, from Sydney to Batavia on 18th.February.
. the Black Joke, from Launceston to South Australia, 25th.

For the parents it must have been of concern and responsibility, for the young men and women a great adventure, for the children a wonderful game.
David writes, "the voyage was a pleasant one, for there was no lack of pipers and fiddlers, and dancing in fine weather passed the time merrily."
He also mentions that when sailing in the tropics, they experienced a thunderstorm, or white squall, of such violence, that the ship's mainmast and bowsprit were carried away.
     David's comment was, "this delayed us considerably."
A LONE SHIP ON A VAST, WILD OCEAN: Imagine being one of 326 passengers clutching for dear life to anything solid as chests and belongings were hurled across the hold smashing and injuring. The noise of the shrieking wind and crashing gear, the towering waves, the driving rain. The monstrous seas washing across the decks and foaming under the hatch covers. The incessant noise, the terror and confusion when rigging, sails, spars, tackle and heavy pulleys came crashing down over the decks, covering and smashing all underneath, were frightening.

The barque, 'The British King'- a small ship on a vast ocean.

I have referred to publications which have biased accounts of how and why changes occurred in the culture of the Highland clans and in Land tenure etc, blaming all on Chiefs and 'the clearances', but I was still surprised at a BBC account of the Battle of Culloden and their superficial comments on the so called 'Highland Clearances.'

Contrary to what was stated from English sources and from Lowland/border accounts, my research has found:-

1. A small number of Highland Clan Chiefs did all within their power to assist their clansfolk in the transition from croft farming to large sheep farms, by creating alternate employment/industry; assisting in resettlement; paying for the ship's passage to Canada where land was available, and in some cases leading their people to North America to settle.
In Clan Donald districts Chiefs were migrating to Canada and North Carolina in the 1700s', not counting those who had been 'transported' by the English to Jamaica and America after Culloden. A few later became very rich from their own efforts.

2. Ships carrying Scots to Australia were on the whole well provisioned and relatively clean, and the term [from the BBC program] of 'Coffin ships' was not justified as a generalisation.
These ships were Government leased for the purpose of emigration.
If all ships were like the 'British King' as described in the Press of the day and by David McDonald, then they were of a good standard indeed.
Deaths certainly did occur on the voyage out, but in those times of epidemic diseases and fevers which had no cure, then a number of folk would die onboard some ships during a four month voyage, but that also occurred in many homes in London, Plymouth, Edinburgh.

3. Yes, in some areas there was inhuman treatment of tenants and residents wherein 'factors' acting on behalf of the English Government or the new owners of the land not only forced people to leave their native home but loaded them into overcrowded holds on ships with little provisions or personal belongings to sail for 'The New Land.'.

This situation was the result of long standing English policy to 'rid' the Highlands of the 'troublesome' highlander culminating in the extreme policy of the English Government after Culloden to:
* kill the highlanders involved in the civil war for their independence, which meant anyone, and to destroy farm buildings, crops and livestock.
* implement Acts of Parliament which forfeited the districts previously held by the Chiefs of Clans and to prohibit the wearing of the 'kilt' and the right to speak Gaelic.
* appoint Commissioners to administer these districts and to allot land to tenants.

The actual cause and effect for the two separate movement of people were:-

1) the voluntary decision to emigrate to Canada, North America and Australia to seek a life free from political oppression with opportunity to better their lot.

2) the 'clearances' of the crofts for sheep grazing and deer farms and the
forced immigration of the indigenous residents by non-resident landlords.

'LAND HO!'

There on the horizon was their new land, Australia; it was now February of 1839, four months since they had set sail from Tobermory. Some had died on the voyage, and there had been a number of births, but now that was all behind them. They were about to sail into Port Jackson, through the giant headlands guarding the quiet waters of this natural harbour.

The full passenger list of emigrants was inspected on board ship and welcomed by the Governor of New South Wales, Sir George Gipps, after which they were allowed to land.

On the 3rd March 1839 the McDonalds and countrymen landed from the British King in Sydney Cove, rowed in boats to a narrow jetty, which ran out from a shallow beach, the centre of what is now Circular Quay.
"Sydney at that time only extended to the foot of Brickfield Hill, and the extreme outside building was a small shed built on brick pillars styled 'Paddy's Market,' in which a variety of inferior and damaged goods were sold for auction.

The only houses observable outside of the city were four or five near together, and they were styled Newtown, which now remains as the name of the suburb.
Woolloomooloo Bay was a shallow sandy beach, and only a couple of small cottages were to be seen higher up the valley.'

On the day they landed there were seven men hanged for the massacre of a large number of blacks at Myall Creek. Talk was that over the past ten years no fewer than 360 persons had been hanged in Sydney, rather a rude welcome to new arrivals, but one that showed the Colonial policy, 'That the native people were to be treated well and justly.'

On landing at Sydney town, the passengers travelled to their arranged employment on stations around Canberra, in the high country of Delegate, and McDonalds and MacLeans to the Hunter River area.

The new arrivals were duly cared for in the Immigration Barracks, to await the contact with their employers, or to gain employment on one of the 'stations', families being in great demand to replace the cheap, but less acceptable service of those who were termed 'Government men', ticket of leave men.

DUNTROON STATION – Campbells from Argyll.

Dugald and family members took passage on the "British King" without listing any employer in Australia. This may well be because the factor in Moidart was a Campbell and on arrival they set out for Canberra to obtained engagement to work on a sheep run on 'Duntroon Station' owned by R. Campbell.

Robert Campbell (1769-1846), born in Scotland was the younger son of the Laird of Ashfield in Argyllshire and became the first Merchant in Sydney to build a private wharf on the west of Sydney Cove. He married Sophia Palmer, sister of John Palmer the Commissary General, in 1801.

The Government commandeered his trading ship, the 'Sydney,' in 1806 to transport food supplies from India and the ship was wrecked. After many years of legal action he finally succeeded in 1825 to win a grant of 4000 acres and 1000 pounds worth of government sheep as compensation for the loss of his ship.

This was the start of his Duntroon (' Pialligo') station holdings to 34000 acres.

Robert Campbell lived in Sydney and in 1833 had the original homestead built. He named it 'Duntroon' after Castle Duntrune in Scotland across Loch Crinan in Argyll. Robert extended the homestead in 1862 with an additional two story building .
He owned property at Hawkesbury River, Canterbury, Sydney, Limestone Plains and Monaro.

'Duntroon' homestead built in 1833 is on the left, the two story building was completed in 1862.
His third son Charles managed the property from 1835 and Charles married the daughter of George Palmer in 1837.
Robert Campbell would not employ convicts nor 'ticket of leave' men but preferred free Highlanders for their trustworthiness and industry.

On finalising employment overseeing an out-station of 'Duntroon,' Dugald McDonald and family moved out to Canterbury, preliminary to being forwarded to the interior in the South.

Dugald procured two bushels of wheat for seed purpose, from the Government granary, which was supplied from India, at a cost of £5 pound per bushel delivered up country."

Samuel Shumack, in his book, '"Tales and Legends of Canberra Pioneers," writes of the trip from Sydney to Duntroon :-

"The first night they camped at Mc Donaldtown, where there was a hotel, store and 12 houses.

They saw their first bullock team, 8 gaunt bullocks, chained in yokes, pulling a great loaded wagon, one woman with a long whip drove them, with much shouting and cursing.

A camp was established where water was available [when they could] so that some days they might travel 7 miles, and at other times be forced to travel 21 miles to reach water.

When the Razorback was reached, they had to divide the load, that was on the cart, and make two trips to the top.

What a sight when the Canberra plains stretched before them."

The trek for Samuel Shumack's people would have been the same for Dugald and his family, or maybe a bit drier due to the drought.

David's account continues : -

" In due and uneventful time they arrived at what was considered the far interior, and were located on a sheep station some miles from the nearest habitation. Every sheep station de-pastured two flocks of sheep, and was supplied with three rations, each of which consisted of one pack of wheat, 10 lbs. of meat, 1/4 lb. of tea, and 2 lbs. of refined sugar.

The family on an out-station of two flocks of sheep had the general wages of £50 [pound] per annum.

This was a period of hard times on the land. There had been drought for the past three years the severity of which had not before been experienced, not so much rain came from the heavens as could wet one's shirt.

Lake George, by tradition of the aborigines, never known to have been dry for so long, was a sun baked clay bottom, and the Murrumbidgee though fed from innumerable springs of the Australian Alps, stopped running and consisted of isolated waterholes, with numbers of codfish stranded and rotting, in between.

It was rare to see a green blade of grass, but there being no overstocking in past years, and owing to the extent of land available, the stock survived better than the desolate appearance would lead one to expect.

In every drought that has occurred since that year David writes, that I have experienced, none of those dry seasons though quite serious, were equal in severity to that one which happily was breaking up in late 1839."

Dugald and his family had grazed sheep and cattle in Scotland, so were well versed in the care of flocks and in the building of yards for them, so the erection of temporary 'hurdles' to hold and protect the flock at night was no problem. The difference in Australia was the vastness of the plains and the amount of land available on which to graze the stock. This being said, small cairns of stones were used to mark the bounderies where there was no recognisable landmark.

Having to fend for themselves was not new, for during the harsh winter months in their homeland, they stored, prepared and cooked barley and oats for their main food source.

Now isolated in the Australian bush, in summer, after a full day's work, each day they would take the measure of wheat to the steel mill, fixed to a tree stump, and grind and sift the wheat twice.

"This wheat grinding was pretty hard work, and particularly disagreeable after the dreary, hot and dusty outing with the sheep.

'Bunging the Mill', as the operation of grinding was vulgarly called, was not in much favour, and 'to bung the mill', sift the flour, mix the damper, and prepare the ashes for its reception, so that a successful and edible damper resulted, were processes that required strength, skill and patience, only won by the hut-keeper over time."   ref.ido.

The 'grain mill'

The main difference for them in this new land was the absence of kin and the support of the clan.
There was nobody to turn to if trouble came, and come it did!

"Bushranging and robberies were very common in those days, and the newcomer came in for the full share of animated aversion from the jealous convicts, and our family did not escape scathless.
We were not long on the holding before we were 'stuck up' by armed men from the adjacent station, and plundered of everything we possessed.

The Police recovered some of the things which my father was requested to identify, but he, considering that to do so would jeopardise our lives, refused.

Shortly after this we found a note one morning under our door, which, in effect stated that as we were humane and did not wish to send unfortunate devils to hell on earth, [the penal colony on Norfolk Island].
That the remainder of the things would be found at a certain place near at hand.
We searched, and sure enough, the bulk of our things were restored to us in good order, and we ever afterwards retained the sympathy of that class."   ref: 'In Days of Old.'

Another happening in the lonely bush would be the sudden call by a group of aborigines, who would demand "baccy, some meat!"
To refuse would be to court spearing of self and stock.   ref.sh.

"In the latter part of 1839, and in the beginning of 1840, the heavens gave out an abundance of rain, and floods were common; and although there came comparative plenty as a result, things were at a great price.

Wheat 20 to 25 shillings a bushel, potatoes £8 to £10 [pound] per ton, good sized bullocks were from £12 upwards, hacks and stock horses from £50 to £60.
These prices were not wholly due to seasonal problems, but Port Phillip and Adelaide required stock and produce of every description to replenish those new settlements, and the boom in prosperity continued for some years."

THE CLAN GATHERS - A Clan Lifestyle in Australia.

Undoubtedly Dugald had examined various options for their future, and discussed these with other family members and he would have explored the surrounding country for suitable land on which they could 'squat.'
Settlement around Nimmitybelle seemingly took place about the late 1830's and early 1840's.

Farquhar McKenzie wrote in his Journal of 1837 :-
"June 6- Went into Nimithybell where I had dispatched the dray the previous day, got some bark and planks and bespoke 100 hurdles from Joe Cooper, at whose house I passed the night pretty comfortable, at all events, much more so than I should have done in the forest, where I lost my way and wandered till about 8 p.m. the night was very cold and the native dogs howled most dreadfully ~~~~~~~~~ "
McKenzie had a party of an overseer called William Bell, and eight of Mr. Murchison's assigned servants, they of course are all convicts, but with one or two exceptions seemed very good men.   ref: p. 106,'Cooma Country.'

In his book 'Old Pioneering Days in the Sunny South,' Charles McAlister writes that in 1843 he travelled to Bombala from Taralga to deliver a load of goods, by bullock dray, from Sydney.
He continues, "We went through a sheep station [now Nimmitybelle) belonging to the McDonalds of 'Square Range' [relatives of the Grant's Flat McDonalds]."

Ranald McDonald and his family were from Moidart and also sailed on the 'British King' and by 1840 had settled in the Rhyanna District at Grant's Flat.
Charles McAlister would know these families well, and some years later, his brother Thomas married Ann McDonald, daughter of Donald and Catherine.

The following 'Pasturage Licences' show Dugald as running stock in 1843:-
1844 'Pasturage Licences' for persons to Depasture stock beyond the limits of location, for the year ending July 1st.,1844.
. Maneroo   : Dugald McDonald.
1845
. Nimithy Bell : Dugald McDonald.
. Mohawk   : William Bowman.

"In the year of 1846, from the careful savings of our family, and in combination with two other large families from the same place in the old country, we bought the goodwill of a moderate squatting station, where in common, for a number of years, we depastured our herds of cattle, and grew enough from the soil for our own wants.

We were of the same class and of the same religion, lived as neighbours in the old country, and were relatives".   ref.ido.

Dugald held Pasturage Licences for 1843-44, 45 and 46.
The first Land Commissioner's inspection reports :-
Report on the Square Range Run, Feb.27, 1846-
Dugald McDonald; 11 residents, 2 slab huts, 1 stockyard, 10 acres wheat, 9 acres oats, 377 cattle, 21 horses, approximately 5 miles by 2 miles, open forest, 4 miles from the nearest adjacent station.

The 11 residents would be Dugald, wife Margaret and family, with their daughter Marcella, husband Donald and children in the second hut.
To raise or trade that amount of stock from 1843 and to feed and care for a family of adults and children would require a minimum of breeding stock of 50 cows in calf and 5 horses in foal in 1843.

David gave prices of £12 minimum for a bullock and £50 upwards for a stock horse in 1840; therefore the cost to initially stock the property would be about £750; to reduce this to £600 for stock gained when shepherding was still a large sum of money in those days.

The land was in Dugald's name and it was only his family listed as living on this property, therefore most of the money to buy stock would have come from Scotland.

Report on the Square Range Run, January 27, 1847 :-
Dugald McDonald; 18 residents, 3 slab huts,[the third hut might have been for daugter Christina and Alexander], 1 stockyard, 12 acres wheat, 5 acres oats, 387 cattle, 20 horses, dairy butter 200 per year, thinly wooded, 5 miles by 2 miles.
This indicates 3 family groups.

The Report of September 27, 1847, shows further expansion :-
Dugald McDonald; 23 residents, 4 slab huts, 1 stockyard, 18 acres wheat, 2 acres oats, 1 acre barley, 3 acres potatoes, 445 cattle, 26 horses, nil butter, 5 miles by 3 miles.   4 family groups.

The census of 1848 states :-   all free, no bonded workers.

The land on the Monaro, in the Nimitybelle district, was similar country to that of the Highlands of Scotland, and in winter just as cold.

Wool bales from Yass on Bullock wagon, skins drying in foreground –
Alex' McDonald, Carrier at Spring Valley.

McDonalds on Square Range late 1880s

Hay stack making on 'Square Range' Nimmitybelle,1900s,
by sons of James James & Mary Josephine McDonald.

Daniel Alex' McDonald, Logging Contractor, in
North Queensland, 1930.

Angus Alex' McDonald,
1926, at his Printing
business, in Cairns,
North Queensland.

The following amusing ballad is importantly historical regarding the humour of those times and the climate on the Manaro .

Extacts from, **"The Coachman's Yarn" telling of the winter of 1883.**

Now this 'ere 'appened in Eighty three,
The coldest winter ever we see;
Strewth, it was cold as could be; Out 'ere on Manaro.
It froze the blankets, it froze the fleas,
It froze the sap in the blinkin' trees,
It made a grindstone out of cheese; Right 'ere in Manaro.
Why, even the air got froze that tight
You'd 'ear the awfullest sound at night
When things was put on a fire or light; out 'ere on Manaro.

For the sounds was froze!
At Haydon's Bog a cove 'e cross-cut a big black log,
An' carted 'er 'ome, an' on the fire 'e put,
As soon as the log begins to thaw
They 'ears the sound of a cross-cut saw
A thawin' out; yes, his name was Law;
Old hands them Laws on the Manaro.

David continues his narrative:-

"Each family lived separate as in a village, and the work to be done was light, there being so many of us to do it.
It was a pleasant life in contrast to the isolated monotony of shepherding, the occupation we had left.
We had all our wants supplied at small trouble and were fairly happy, and our community ought to have been a success.

Dugald was the acknowledged head of the community, and no complaint of his actions in that capacity was heard, but he was not invested with absolute power, the enforcing of which would reasonably be called as tyranny, and so what he could not help, he sensibly left alone.

Thus ended a contract which promised to be so prosperous until spoiled by the mental constitution of man, and ended as I am sure all such will ever end."   ref: In Days of Old.

Over the years I have spoken to descendants of these families and it became clear that a couple of the families had not taken up 'runs' after they broke up and so were not a part of the 'Squatter' class, and to them fell the more basic and labour intensive tasks, eg. the hand washing of the sheep which was so fatiguing from the toil, water and cold. That sad experience was retold with some resentment, over the generations.

On 9-3-1847, by Order in Council as notified in the Government gazette 112, published on 30/9/1848, 147 persons named in the Gazette had demanded leases of the Runs on Crown Lands.
Dugald was number 99 for the Nimmitybelle run of 8000 acres to carry 700 head of cattle.

The town and different 'runs' had variations of spelling of the local name:
The Town = Nimoitehool and Nimotehool, later Nimmitybelle, and finally Nimmitabel.
Thus the name may be spelt differently in the same paragraph in relating to different periods.
RUNS =

Dugald McDonald,	No.99	Nimitybelle run, 8000 acres.
Wm. Scott,	No.121	Nimity Bell run, 8000 acres.
John Stanton,	No.124	Nimithybale run, 4000 acres.
Hugh O'Hara,	No.104	Nimitybelle run, 8000 acres.

The name 'Nimmitybelle' means 'place where many waters start or divide.'
Daniel Lucy   No.85   Umeralla run, 8000 acres, 300 cattle,   1600 sheep.

Original slab hut on Square Range Station 1843.

The first dwellings built by Dugald and the other MacDonald families were made from local timber with hand cross cut saws, adzes and axes.

The walls were of timber slabs set in a check in the top and bottom plates; the roof was of bark held by branches; the hearth and basic cooking equipment was similar to that in Scotland; when the family became established on Square Range they built multi roomed dwellings of stone and mortar walls with a shingle roof.

The house yards were of stone walls; some of these dwellings are still standing today, although the yards have collapsed into mounds of stones.

David continues: "By 1854 the times had changed and there was a Depression due to the overspending and careless extravagance from the top prices in recent years.

Wages were reduced and swagmen travelled the 'track' in hundreds."

In 1856 Dugald made full payment of £161/10/- for land on Square Range, which was undoubtedly the future 'Glenfinnan,' and in 1857, £172/- for property off McDonald Creek.

The family of Dugald would have worked on the Station, as a family exercise, but were able to travel and explore for their own interests, or to prospect for gold.

From a family record: "When Bishop Polding rode into Nimmitabel, the McDonald Clan with their Chieftain [Dugald], piped him into the area. They were all dressed in kilts."

From local newspaper articles we are aware that Dugald enjoyed having a race horse and entering his horse for the local races, eg. the first Annual Subscription Race meeting was held in 1857, where Dugald's horse Shamrock ran a close second to Burke's Harkaway in the Squatter's Purse for £12 ; it was run over one and a half mile.

David's story continues, "our family remained on the station until after the death of the old people some many years afterwards, when little by little we scattered far and wide."

The affluence of the graziers and the discovery of gold at Major's Creek and Nerrigundah, [120 and 70 km's from Nimmitabel respectively], encouraged locals in the Jingera mountains near Braidwood, to take up the dangerous, high life of Bushrangers.

One such gang consisted of: Tom, James and John Clarke, known as the 'Jingera Mob' and later as the 'Clarke Gang' who learned their 'trade' from their father an assigned convict who was sent to Braidwood in 1827.

This gang robbed miners at their lonely camps, bailed-up Mail Coaches and travellers, they 'duffed' race horses for their mounts to ensure they could outrace the Police Troopers.

They were so active and violent, carrying out a robbery or shootings almost daily.

Sketch of Hold-up at Oxley Creek, 1867. 𝓜𝓜𝓬𝓓

There were 150 active Police officers and Backtrackers' in the Braidwood area in the early 1860s.

A reward of £5000 was offered for their capture.

About the same time in the southern state of Victoria, the infamous bushranger Ned Kelly was arrested for assault and as the suspected off-sider for bushranger Harry Power.

Kelly continued his escalating outlaw career of robbery and murder with his gang robbing National Bank branches, and holding customers hostage.

Reporters had a newsfeast when Kelly manufactured armour from ploughshares and used this against Police.

He was wounded and captured at a shootout with police in 1880 at the Glenrowan Inn. His armour left his arms and legs exposed.

Kelly forges his armour-

THE HIGHLAND GAMES – Scotland and Australia:

The folk from the Western Highlands may have been scattered in this wide land of Australia, but their culture was part of their life and they gathered for annual major events such as the Caledonian Games in Castlemaine, Victoria.

The artist captures the movement and excitement of the crowd and events of "The Games" in 1861.

Government House Games Brisbane Queensland 1994.
The author has a toss.

The Highland Games in the western highland village of Arisaig in 2014.

Official entry to the Opening of The Games.
Finlaggan Puisivant and the Toisaech of Finlaggan of Clan Donald lead the March.

APPENDIX: Official records of the lifestyle of the Tenant and Crofter.
TESTAMENTS - of 1686.
ref: from the original Notes of Colin MacDonald, Ontario.]
(1) TESTAMENT DATIVE of 27th. September 1686.
Testament Dative of Finnual Nein Dugald Vc Iain Vc Ruary in Inshrory, in
the parish of Oilanfinan who died in July 1684, given up by Donald McEwin,
her husband, in the name of Ewen Mc Dugald Vc Iain Vc Rory, [Roderick],
Executor Dative, goods pertaining to the deceased: fifteen great cows, £200; three year olds £27; two year olds £12; two stirks £6; horses and mares £33/6/8; two bolls of meal £10/13/4d; utensils etc.£18/13/4d.
no
debts owing to the deceased; debts owed by the deceased : rent and teinds
£15; servants fees £26/8d; funeral expenses £6/13/4d; [Cautioner not named.]
Testament Dative and inventory of the daughter of Dugald Vc Iain Vc Ruary in Inshrory given up by her husband Donald McEwin in the name of John son of Dougald g.son of John g.g.son of Roderick

- fifteen great cows, £200;
- three year olds £27;
- two year olds £12;
- two stirks £6;   cow with milk
- horses and mares £33/6/8;
- two bolls of meal £10/13/4d;   1 boll=4 firlotts, each of 5 pecks.
- utensils etc.£18/13/4d.-
- rent and teinds £15;
- servants fees £26/8d;
- funeral expenses £6/13/4d.

From the patronymics used in 1684 there were certain families related to Ewen living on adjacent farms at the head of Glen Moidart.

Testament Dative of 27th September 1686 :-
(2) Testament Dative and inventory of Euin Mc Dugald Vc Innes in Ulgary, who died November 1684, given up by his son Lauchlin Mc Ewen Vc Dugald as Executive Dative. Goods belonging to the deceased and Margaret McDonald his relict, John Mc Ewen Vc Dugald in Ulgary became cautioner.

[MacDonald family of, Lachlan son of Ewen grandson of Dugald great grandson of Angus in Ulgary]. Historian Tearlach MacFarlane in Glenfinnan accepts that the record of the name Angus must refer to Angus X Clanranald.

INCHRORY/ INSHRORY – 78 years later there is still family here:
1764, September 11th, by document made at Ardnafueran, Arisaig, Ranald MacDonald, Younger of Clanranald, lets by Tack the half mark land of Inchrory to:-

Ewen MacDonald	3	cliticks.
John MacDonald	3	"
John Corbet, Wright in Moidart.	3	"

For a term of six years from the previous Whitsunday.
Of the three tenants, John Corbet alone signs as the others could not write. Ewen MacDonald and John MacDonald pay 37 ½ marks Scots each, yearly, and John Corbet 25 marks Scots yearly.
A few years previously, in 1761, at an estate valuation, Ewen and John MacDonald said that each had possessed ¼ part of the croft for the fourteen years past. (1747).

This may have been the first Corbet[34] to come to Moidart, and from all accounts he is the man who, ten or twenty years later on, submitted an estimate for the rebuilding of Kinlochmoidart House.   [Ref.39:The original notes of Colin MacDonald, Ontario].

Added to the Testament evidence is the Privy Council records of 1602 relating to the Siol Dhugail Ruadh,[seed of the line of Dugal the Red], in and about Inverlair:-   Dowgall Mc Rory,
                Alister Mc Dougall Mc Rory,
                Dowgall Oig, his brother,
                Johne Mc Dowgall Vc Rory.
Tradition has members of Siol Dugal Ruadh settling in Glenforslan and Ulgary with relatives, after 1665. [ref: original notes of Colin MacDonald, Ontario.]

As an exercise, we can construct the following lines from these Testaments **(1)** to **(4)** and their records:-

```
                                    Rory [Roderick]
        |                         _____|_____
(2) Angus X.                      |         |         |
        |                         |         |         |
        |                    Dowgall/Dugald  Iain   Dowgall Oig
        |                         |         |         |
     Dugald                    Iain/John  Dugald
        |                         |         |
Ewen = Marg McDonald         (4)  John    (1) Ewen [Ewen Mc Dugald
d.1684, Ulgary.              d.1678,Glenforslan.  |   Vc Ean Vc Rory]
        |                         |         |
    ____|_____          Dugald   Mary
    |      |      |
Lachlan John  (1) Donald  =  married  =  (1) dau. Dugald VcIain, Vc
                                              Ruary
d.1698/                                   |      d. 1684 in Inshrory
=(3)Mary Nin Ian Vc Donell Vic Vurchie.   Ewen Mc Donald VcEwen
    |spouse of Lachlan McDonald in Ulgary.  |
 ___|_____                Ewan Sr. b. Abt.1710
 |      |      |      |                     |
John Donald Dugald Anna          Ewan Jr. [b.abt.1747] = Margaret
                                 abt. 1784.                |

                             Margaret abt. 1785, of Innes a` Chulun
                             = Dugald McDonald, son of john 15R
```

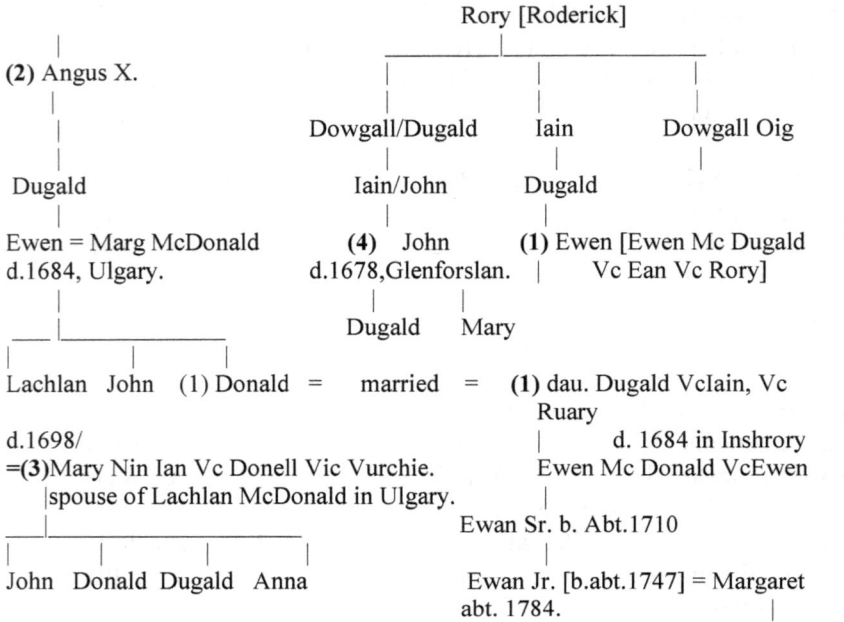

FURTHER related supporting TESTAMENTS:

(3) Dec 3rd, 1700 Inventory of Mary nin Ian vic Donell vic Vurchie (spouse of Lachlan McDonald in Ulgary) who died in August 1698, given up by the said Lauchlan on behalf of John, Donald, Dugald and Anna, children:–

(4) Sept 22, 1686 Testament dative and inventory of John MacEan VcDugald in Glenforslan, who died in June 1678, given up by John McKinnas VcDonald Roy on behalf of Dugald and Mary, children of the defunct:–
"Nyne great cowes, price £13,6s,8d, inde £120; Item, two year olds, price, £12; Item thrie stirks, price £9; Item, two cows and ane halfesworth of sheep and goat (i.e. sheep and goat to the value of two and a half cows), inde, £33,6s,4d; Item, sowen of small oats, ane boll, encrease quehereof in thre bolls, price, £6; Item, the utencillis and domicillis of the house, estimat to £7, 6s, 8d Total, £194,6s,8d; Debts owing by the defunct:–rent £140; teinds, 33s,4d; public dues, 37s, 6d; servants fees, £8; "allowed of funerals", £6,13s,4d; Total £58, 4s, 2d; John MacDonald, son of Donald Gorme, became cautioner.
[Inventory of John son of John g.son of Dugald given up by John son of Angus g.son of red haired Donald on behalf of Dugald and Mary]

Order of naming :-

1. the eldest son named after the paternal grandfather.
2. the second son named after the maternal grandfather.
3. the third son named after the father.
4. the eldest daughter after the maternal grand mother.
5. the second daughter after the paternal grandmother.
6. the third daughter named after the mother.

JACOBITE & JACOBINS.

Some people, when reading of the Jacobites, confuse them with three totally different groups.

(1)   Jacobite : A partisan or adherent of James II after he abdicated the These Jacobites were Protestant, Episcopalian, Roman Catholic etc, whose common thread was their commitment to the royal house of Scotland, the Stewarts.

They were Scottish Nationalists who cared more for the independence of Scotland than for reward and riches from the English.

(2) Jacobin : A Black or Dominican Friar, so called from those friars having first established themselves in Paris in the Rue St. Jacques, or St. James Street.

(3) Jacobin : A member of a club of violent republicans in France during the revolution of 1789, who held their meetings in a monastery of the Jacobin monks, in which measures were concerted to direct the proceedings of the National Assembly.

BIBLIOGRAPHY references:

. Manuscripts Nat. Library Scotland. — MSNLS
. Scottish Bards - ref: K.N. Macdonald, 1900 –Oban Times. — SB
. A Concise History of Scotland - Fitzroy Maclean,1970. — CHS
. "Historical Account of Settlements of Scottish Highlanders in America"
J. P. MacLean, PH. D., LM GSG. -1900 — HASSH
.History of the Highlands and Gaelic Scotland, Dugald Mitchell MD.1900
— HH&GS
. A History of Scotland - Rosalind Mitchison. — rm
. A History of the Scottish Highlands, Highland Clans and Highland Regiments,
vols I & II. – John S.Keltie. FSA Scot. Pub. Thomas C. Jack1885. hsh &
— HSH&HR
. Barbour, John, 'The Bruce', translated, A. A. M. Duncan, 1964.
. 'BANNOCKBURN' by the Historian Peter Reese. — pr
. Massacre, The Story of Glencoe – M. Linkletter. — ml
. The British Army a concise history – Jock Haswell,
1975 Thames & Hudson. — BA aCH
. The Road to Appin - D. Macdonell Macdonald.
. Notes of Colin MacDonald, Ontario. — c
. The Clan Donald, vols.1,2 & 3. — TCD
. Macdonald of the Isles – A.M.W. Stirling. — ams
. Official Parish Records and certificates. — opr
. War Office Records. — wor
. Moidart rentals. — mr
. Kinloch Moidart rentals. — kr
. Moidart or among the Clanranalds – Charles Macdonald. — mac
. A History of the 15th(East Yorkshire)Regiment,
1685 1914 by Robert J. Jones. — H15
. In Days of Old by David McDonald, courtesy of Jim Turnbul. — ido
. Mitchell Library Newspaper articles. — np
. Antiquarian Notes - Charles Fraser Mackintosh. — ant
. An Autobiography, or Tales and Legends of Canberra Pioneers by
Samuel Shumack, 1850 1940. — sh
. Scottish Record Office Edinburgh. — sro
. The War of American Independence 1775/83, by Stephen Conway. — sc
. The Highland Scots of North Carolina, by Duane Meyer. — Dm
— THSNC
. Fair is the Place – two Clanranald families in Judique Cape Breton. — FITP
. Scottish Culture = Dr.Isobel F. Grant. — IG
. Botany Bay Mirages - by Alan Frost
. The Long Farewell - by Don Charlwood
. Caledonia Australis - by Don Watson.
. Ancient Landmarks - by Mary Albertus Bain O.P. — AL

Author's Profile :-

Malcolm Cameron McDonald, Esq., OAM., O.St.J., FPA.
Born in Cairns, Queensland, Australia.

Educated at the Cairns High and Technical College, participating in the sports of Foot running and member of the 1st Rugby League Team.
Played Hockey to 'A' grade standard, successful in Minor and Major Premierships.
Later took up the amateur sport of Motorcycle Scramble racing for a couple of years.
Served in the RAAF in 10 (Operational) Squadron as an Armament Fitter for National Service Course 5, 1952-3 and listed on the RAAF Reserve.

An Officer with the Queensland Ambulance Service from 1959, serving throughout the State and in the Central Queensland Aerial Ambulance, fully operational to Coronary Care; retired in 1993 as Assistant Commissioner, Queensland Ambulance Service, Region 5, Metropolitan.

- Commissioner of Clan Donald Queensland, 1992.
- Granted personal Arms by the Lord Lyon King of Arms, Scotland in 1992.
- Founder Member, Fellow, Past President of The Institute of Ambulance Officers (Aust.).
- Fellow and Life Member of the Australian College of Ambulance Professionals.
- Officer of the most Venerable Order of the Hospital of St. John of Jerusalem.
- Medal of the Order of Australia for " Service to the Community especially the Ambulance, Fire and State Emergency Services, 1992."

PUBLICATIONS:
Professional: 'Papers and Presentations 1975-1992' - on subjects of Pre-hospital Emergency Care, techniques and procedures.
Historical narratives: "Trust Me, I'm an Ambulance Officer" (1993) - on a brief history of the first 100 years of the Queensland Ambulance Transport Brigade and the experiences of an Ambulance Officer.
Hobbies : Bonsai plants; Oil painting - landscapes.

INDEX:

Poems:

EPILOGUE.

This narrative has resulted from some enjoyable early visits to
Scotland and research at the Clan Donald Centre Skye, now the
Museum of the Isles, ably assisted by Archivist Maggie Macdonald.

The magnificent records in New Register House Edinburgh was a trip
back in time with historical manuscripts from centuries past and a
venue of cotton gloves and hush allowing uninterrupted study.

Of course what sort of research on the western Highlands would it
without visits to
Tearlach and Isobel
MacFarlane at
Glenfinnan House
where one would
listen to the history of
the region as told by
a traditional Bard and
then enlivened by
Tearlach in the
Drawing room at
Glenfinnan House
playing a reel on the
violin or bringing the

time period to life with a piobaireachd (pibroch) on his pipes with the
painting of the 'Raising of the standard at Glenfinnan' in the
background.

It was he who discovered the ruins of our ancestors dwelling of 'Innes
a` Chulun' in Moidart and led me to it in 1996 – what an experience to
stand where ones ancestors had stood centuries ago.

I trust you have enjoyed this narrative and gained an appreciation of
the, (at times), hazzardous life of the folk of the Western Highlands
during that period in history.

Leis gach deagh dhurachd.

www.ingramcontent.com/pod-product-compliance
Lightning Source LLC
Chambersburg PA
CBHW060739050426
42449CB00008B/1271